"**H**EY, JOHN," PLEADED THE TERRIFIED LOUIE DI BONO. "I wanna tell you, like a brother, I told this guy when we were driving, I said: 'You know, I love John, he's a good man. He's honest, he's straight as an arrow. I owe him so much—to make money for this man that you have no idea!'" In the dispute over the money, Di Bono maintained that he had paid his debt. If he could prove it he thought he would be off the hook.

But Di Bono had failed to recognize that for the Gambino Family it was no longer a question of money. It was a matter of honor. In October 1990, a policeman stumbled over a bullet-riddled corpse in the basement parking lot of the World Trade Center. It had been Louie Di Bono's last place of work.

THE
WAR
AGAINST
THE
MAFIA

Tim Shawcross

HarperPaperbacks
A Division of HarperCollinsPublishers

HarperPaperbacks *A Division of* HarperCollins*Publishers*
10 East 53rd Street, New York, N.Y. 10022

A hardcover edition of this book was published in Great Britain in 1994 by Mainstream Publishing Company (Edinburgh) Ltd.

First HarperPaperbacks printing: January 1995

Printed in the United States of America

HarperPaperbacks and colophon are trademarks of HarperCollins*Publishers*

10 9 8 7 6 5 4 3 2 1

Contents

Preface

THE SHOW TRIAL

"**THIS IS NOT A MEDIA EVENT. THIS IS NOT A MOVIE. IT'S** not about movie stars. This is not a stage for oratory. This is a trial in an American courtroom, a trial in which your decision will be based on the evidence that came from that witness stand, from the tape recordings, the other physical exhibits, and on that alone. It's not nearly as exciting as the other stuff."

With these words John Gleeson, the young Assistant U.S. Attorney from the Eastern District of New York, summed up the Government's case against the gangster who had risen to become the most notorious public enemy since Al Capone.

For three months at the beginning of 1992, an American jury and the world's media observed a trial which easily outdid the sensationalism of any Hollywood script. To those who followed the trial, the procession of witnesses, video surveillance and audiotapes which documented the rise and fall of John Gotti, the head of the Gambino Family, was far more gripping than any feature film. This was life imitating art imitating life complete with stars, supporting cast and high drama.

John Gotti's notoriety had reached extraordinary heights through a combination of his own flamboyant image and the Government's failure to secure a conviction in three separate trials. Then, just six months before the trial began, one of Gotti's codefendants struck a deal with the Government. Now the "Teflon Don" would be betrayed by the Mafia's highest-ranking traitor and one of his closest friends.

Six hours of secretly recorded audiotapes would catalogue the daily business of the modern American Mafia. A world of money, mayhem and murder. For a public exposed to the mob through an endless diet of Hollywood movies, the real thing would show that beyond the fiction of *The Godfather* existed an organization driven by violence and greed. The Mafia was alive and well and like many a successful American company its corporate headquarters were in Manhattan.

As the prosecution was quick to point out in their summing up, all the jury had to do was listen to the tapes: "Out of his own mouth, John Gotti told you that he has people in his crime Family who control the docks, who control garbage hauling, who control the construction industry, who control virtually the entire concrete industry in New York City. He shared control of the illegal business of skimming unpaid—unpaid to the Government—taxes from oil and gas. They control the garment center.

"Murder plays a central role in the business of this enterprise. It is the way in which discipline was maintained. It's the way in which power was obtained. It was the way to deal with people who have the audacity to speak to the Government about the enterprise. It was the way to deal with people who have the audacity to be someone who John Gotti thinks might be a rat some day. Murder is the heart and soul of this enterprise."

On Thursday, April 2, 1992, after 48 hours of deliberations, the jury returned a guilty verdict against John Gotti. A stake had been driven through "the heart and soul" of the American Mafia.

Acknowledgments

THIS BOOK EXAMINES THAT "HEART AND SOUL." USING tapes that American law enforcement agencies have painstakingly acquired over the last decade, it is now possible to present a frighteningly real portrait of the Mafia in modern America. It is a world far removed from the lives of ordinary people, yet one which affects virtually every single business in New York City. It is an organization which conducts its operations in seedy social clubs and fancy restaurants; an enterprise that is underwritten by violence, intimidation, torture and murder; a world inhabited by men who live by a strict code and yet flout all the normal rules of decency and morality which sustain the rule of law. It is a world of naked ambition, unrivalled greed, fierce loyalties and deadly betrayals; a secret society populated by men of immense power and charisma supported by killers, thieves and drug dealers.

It is also a world which has undermined its own power through a combination of treachery and overreaching arrogance. At its height the Mafia's power constituted a direct threat to the authority of the American Government. Its tentacles reached into the heart of the political establishment and it would take an unprecedented effort by the forces of law and order to reduce their power. This book documents that effort and draws on research carried out in the last five years in New York, Washington, Palermo, Rome, Zurich, Lugano and Rio de Janeiro.

It includes the personal testimony of the two highest-ranking informers ever to have betrayed the Sicilian Mafia and who have detailed the connections between the Italian and American Mafia that center on the heroin trade. High-ranking American Mafiosi, currently sheltered from Mafia hit teams by the Witness Protection Program, have also been interviewed for the book. The U.S. Attorneys who spearheaded the drive against the Mafia in the last decade were interviewed, as were the FBI agents and supervisors who worked the cases which formed the basis for the series of successful prosecutions which culminated in the conviction of John Gotti in April 1992.

There are many people who cannot be named who have contributed to this book. This is a list of some of those who can: Rudolph Giuliani, former U.S. Attorney, Southern District of New York, Richard Martin, Judge Louis Freeh (Director of the FBI and former Assistant U.S. Attorney, Southern District of New York) and also at SDNY—Walter Mack, Arron Marcue, John Savarese and Dennison Young; Ronald Goldstock, Director, Organized Crime Task Force, New York State, Joe Coffey, Richard Tennien, Jim Stroh, Fred Rayano, also at OCTF; Mike Fahy, U.S. Customs Service; Tom Sheer, former FBI Director, New York; Andris Kurins, former FBI agent, New York; Frank Storey, FBI: Dan Russo, Jo Valiquette, FBI Public Affairs; Tony Petrucci, Mario Alessa, John Huber, Frank Panessa, Kevin Gallagher and Con Docherty, Drug Enforcement Administration; Edward McDonald, former head of Organized Crime Strike Force, Brooklyn; Bobby Hernandez, former detective NYPD.

Very special thanks for friendship as well as assistance go to: Frederick Martens, Director, Pennsylvania Crime Commission, whose patience and professionalism provided invaluable support in New York, Palm Springs and Los Angeles; Ernest Volkmann, who along with coauthor John Cummings has written some of the most gripping accounts of modern crime and the Mafia in recent history; Marnie Inskip, the New York producer of the television series who gave tremendous support and encouragement along the way and who provided organizational skills that were second to none; John Miller, NBC correspondent, whose beat in New York City encompasses the reporting of "The Mob" and whose scoops stand out as a landmark in television crime reporting; Charles Rose, Assistant U.S. Attorney in the Eastern District of New York, a fine prosecutor who provided fascinating detail from past cases and great company at Elaine's! Also in New York, I would like to thank Daphne Pinkerson for her generous help on the television front and Marc Levin of Blowback Productions who made a successful documentary which became an invaluable database.

In Italy, I express special gratitude to former Investigating Magistrate Giovanni Falcone whose tremendous personal integrity and success against the Mafia had earmarked him as their most serious enemy. Although he always downplayed his role in Sicily it was widely recognized that Falcone was the one man who posed the greatest threat to the Mafia. As such he was singled out for the highest praise by the law enforcement community on both sides of the Atlantic.

Falcone's courageous and uncompromising stand against the forces of corruption earned him many enemies. Following several failed assassination attempts, the Mafia finally succeeded in exacting their revenge on Falcone by planting a 1000-pound explosive device in an underground road tunnel en route to Palermo airport on May 23, 1992. Giovanni Falcone, his young wife and his bodyguard were blown to pieces. It was a terrifying display of both the power and the callousness of the Mafia. There were dark rumors of inside intelligence and high-level collusion. It was not the first time that a servant of the State was gunned down in the line of duty while fighting the Mafia.

Thankfully, Falcone's death seems to have precipitated a long overdue clean-up of the organic corruption which has eaten into the core of the body politic of the Italian State.

A debt of gratitude is also owed to Falcone's colleague, Paolo Borsallino, another courageous Examining Magistrate in Sicily who also paid the ultimate price for his dedication and integrity.

In 1993, the political corruption endemic to Italian society finally began to unravel. It was a belated recognition of the campaign waged by Falcone and Borsallino. Yet the political fallout which has touched the highest in the land is a devastating indictment of the post-war Italian Government. The reverberations of the links between the Mafia and Italy's top political leaders will continue way beyond the scope of this book. At the very least it will have tainted an entire generation of Italy's post-war leaders. At the time of writing it was threatening to destabilize Italian political life to such an extent as to make the country almost ungovernable.

The achievement of any book pales into insignificance compared to the ultimate sacrifice paid by men such as Giovanni Falcone and Paolo Borsallino. It was their investigations which caused the political scandals of 1993 which began to unfold the full story of the complicity between the Italian Government and the Mafia.

The fact that the reputations and political careers of the highest in the land now lie in tatters is vindication of the tenacious investigations of Sicily's Examining Magistrates. The exposure of the political links between Rome and the Sicilian Mafia has drastically altered the landscape of Italian politics and in the long term has severely weakened the historic hold that the Mafia was able to exert on Italian society. The timing of the arrests of Mafia leaders such as Salvatore Riina and Benedetto Santapaola, the latter discovered in bed with his wife at a remote Sicilian farmhouse in the spring of 1993, bore testimony to the fact that the Mafia's "most wanted" had been protected by highly placed political sources. As their protectors found themselves under investigation so too did their political influence begin to wane and their ability to prevent the arrests of their Sicilian Mafia contacts vanish.

Recent events in Italy where endemic corruption has threatened an entire Government are a salutary lesson for the United States. Apart from cultural differences, the Mafia in the U.S. was fast approaching the heights of its power through the early Eighties. If American law enforcement had not decided to launch their onslaught when they did it is not inconceivable that the Mafia's influence would have ultimately developed along the same political lines as Italy. Past revelations of Mafia influence and contacts with U.S. intelligence agencies and even Presidents demonstrate that Mafia power can never be underestimated.

In Rome, I express gratitude to Giovanni de Gennaro and Antonio de Luca from Criminalpol; in London to Margaret Gilmour, former colleague at Thames Television, for her interviewing skills; at BBC Television, Christopher Olgiati for a supportive presence in both London and Florida; at London Weekend Television, Daniela Newman for logistics, schedules, research and support for the documentaries in the U.S. and the U.K., and Simon Shaps, Controller of Factual Programs at LWT, for launching and supporting the proposal to the ITV Network and helping to focus a wealth of material into a major documentary series; Stuart Prebble at the Network Centre for commissioning the series for ITV; Peter George, director of photography in New York, and Maggie Knox for editing skills in the U.K.; Phil Heath for graphic design at XTV; Charles Walker, at Peters, Fraser and Dunlop, for realism, pessimism and optimism at the appropriate moments; Christabel and Peter for manuscript support. I would also like to thank Martin Short and Thames Methuen for permission to reproduce material from *Crime Inc.*

Love and gratitude go to my wife Marion, who put up with my absences and did so much to allow me the time and space which such projects demand; to John and Gisela for help that made all of the above possible; and last but not least Alexander and Edward, who patiently allowed the computer to be used as something other than a games machine. I hope that one day they will read this and find that it was a worthwhile sacrifice.

TIM SHAWCROSS
January 1, 1994

1

THE GAMBLER

JOHN GOTTI WAS A COMPULSIVE GAMBLER.

As the most powerful Mafia gangster in America he was one of the few people who could afford to be. Although he prided himself on meeting his losses, few bookies could resort to the time-honored, strong-arm methods to recover their bets. But with "Johnnie Boy" it was a matter of honor. Out on the street his credibility would plummet if he reneged on his debts.

Gotti's losses in one week were more than most people could earn in a lifetime. With that sort of gambling habit, it was hardly surprising that John Gotti had an ambition from an early age to strive for the ultimate position in the hierarchy of the American Mafia. It offered job security, steady employment, respect, a company car, a loyal staff, untold wealth and instant celebrity. Few other jobs could provide the piles of ready cash that Gotti needed. The annual turnover of the organization that he headed—the Gambino Family—ran to hundreds of millions of dollars, most of it conveniently packaged in anonymous brown envelopes stacked with hundreds of dollar bills, none of it ever declared or filed to the Internal Revenue Service. Nevertheless, it all had to be accounted for down to the last nickel and dime for the benefit of the Chairman of the Board: Mr. John Gotti.

By the beginning of the 1980s the Gambino Family had become the largest of the five American Mafia Families. In terms of corporate success, the Gambinos were a model of red-blooded capitalism. They controlled the lion's share of the illicit millions generated by the traditional rackets of organized crime. Their ill-gotten gains came from narcotics, prostitution, hijacking, illegal gambling, waste disposal, the labor unions and the construction industry.

For half a century the five New York Mafia Families had tightened their grip on the city. Now it was paying what amounted to a "tax" on a whole host of legal services ranging from hotels and restaurants through to building sites.

The ultimate cost was borne by the long-suffering citizens of New York City. The residents of "Big Apple" enjoyed one of the highest costs of living in the world, a privilege which was earned in no small part due to the efficiency of the mob and their unparalleled expertise in the art of extortion.

Many of America's most prestigious companies have their corporate headquarters in New York City. The Gambino Family were no exception. Their head office is located at Number 247 Mulberry Street. In outward appearance the Ravenite Social Club is a far cry from the chromium-plated steel and glass skyscrapers of corporate America. It is a small and seedy private social club in the heart of the restaurant district of Manhattan's Little Italy. In the cramped front room with its cheap but functional tables and chairs and small bar, a wide selection of Italian-American "businessmen" congregate throughout the day and into the small hours of the night to meet old friends, make new acquaintances, discuss business deals, initiate new contracts and settle old scores. The Ravenite's clientèle range from adolescent streetwise kids with diamond earrings, gold chains and Giorgio Armani suits to elderly and wizened old men in ill-fitting suits and fedora hats.

Every week on a Wednesday night the narrow street is jammed with double-parked limousines. Mercedes Benz, Audi sports coupés, Ferraris, Corvettes and the latest model BMWs vie for attention all round the block. Dark-suited men disappear quickly through the door of the Mulberry Street headquarters while leather-jacketed wiseguys loiter on the streets, shooting glances down the sidewalk, sizing up curious passers-by who may be agents or undercover cops trying to monitor the weekly ritual of the comings and goings in a vain attempt to construct a who's who of the Gambino Family.

Once inside the welcoming door of the Ravenite Club, mobsters, whose demeanor and bearing on the street are 100 per cent dedicated to striking an attitude that exudes fear and violence among fellow gangsters and members of the public, adopt a mask of patience and deference as they silently queue for the privilege of catching the eye of their boss and shaking the hand of the man to whom they have to offer loyalty, respect and, above all, a large envelope stuffed full of cash.

Old and young alike, the soldiers and capos of the Gambino Family know all too well that the man whose attention they seek to capture can signal in the space of one look, gratitude, contempt or death. With the exception of those closest to the head of the Gambino Family, none of the wiseguys nervously waiting to hand over their weekly token of respect to the King of Little Italy can ever know how they are going to be received by the man to whom they owe their position. As in any kingdom, those who serve within the court derive their legitimacy and authority from the king they serve. Without his authority they have no power; without their power the king has no authority. Both are in desperate need of each other, neither can afford to acknowledge it but the first to deny it risks instant dismissal from the inner court, exile and death. It is a medieval power struggle which can work in both directions. Once a kingdom is bereft of the support of its courtiers, the power of the throne is in serious jeopardy and may be toppled at any moment.

It is a lesson of history that John Gotti was all too aware of; after all, his ascendancy to the throne had only been made possible by the overthrow of the reigning monarch. John Gotti was no fool. What he had done to others, others could do to him. Loyalty, friendship, shifting alliances, power-brokering and betrayal were the common currency of the world that was presided over within the confines of the Ravenite Club. The dollar-saturated envelopes were useful and welcome tokens but woe betide those who placed too much trust in the smiling faces that proffered the fattest envelopes.

Payments could vary from a modest offering of a few crumpled hundred-dollar bills to the crisp luxury of new bills running into the thousands. His loyal and devoted underboss, the psychopathic fitness freak, Sammy "The Bull" Gravano, regularly deposited $100,000 every week with his boss.

Each payment was a cut from a different illegal racket, the combined weekly take from a "crew" of working wiseguys under the direction of a "capodecina"—literally "the head of ten." The Gambino captains collect a share of their crew's rackets and pass it on to the head of the Family.

Gotti's day was spent commuting between his modest suburban home in Howard Beach, Queens, his old Ozone Park hangout, the even less salubrious Bergen Hunt and Fish Club, and his Manhattan headquarters at the Ravenite.

Joe Coffey was watching the Ravenite from an unmarked car; not that it made much difference—the mobsters and residents of Mulberry Street had a sixth sense for unwanted visitors, especially cops, agents, undercover men, the IRS and the FBI. In this case Gotti's own contacts within the law enforcement community had tipped him off about the impending arrest. Coffey spotted Gotti immediately by the mobster's carefully coiffured gray hair, sharp double-breasted $3,000 suit, heavily jowled face and the playful smile with its aura of power, self-satisfaction and an overbearing arrogance.

As a veteran detective with New York State's Organized Crime Task Force, it was Joe Coffey's job to know the hangouts, cars, confidants and identities of New York City's top mobsters. In the past, the city's top Mafiosi had jealously guarded their privacy and carefully cultivated their anonymity. John Gotti had changed all that. John Gotti enjoyed his celebrity status to the full—strutting around Manhattan with a style and swagger that had more in common with one of the joke villains of the Gotham City of *Batman* movies than the self-effacing style of his predecessors.

It seemed as if John Gotti was more relentlessly pursued by the media than by the forces of law and order. Every week his defiant features stared out at the readers of the New York tabloids, his face had graced the front cover of *Time* magazine and he was extensively photographed, filmed, taped and written about whenever he appeared in court. Celebrity status had given Gotti a sense of invincibility, further fed by an extraordinary run of luck which had enabled him to fend off a succession of prosecutions.

A coded message squawked over the car radio. It was the signal for Coffey and his fellow agents from the Organized Crime Task Force to move in.

As Joe Coffey got out of his car he couldn't help looking forward to puncturing the gangster's almighty ego by arresting him in the street and on his own territory. The six-foot-three-inch detective came up behind the broad-backed Mafioso and tapped him on the shoulder of his elegant suit jacket. "Hey, John, how ya doing? You're under arrest!"

The detective then took great pleasure in unceremoniously pushing the King of Little Italy flat against the plate glass window of a shop-front, forcing his hands behind him and his feet apart as if he were a common criminal arrested in a street bust.

Gotti knew what it was all about and went through the motions with the resigned indifference of a motorist picking up a parking ticket.

Coffey began to pat him down, carrying out the customary search for a hidden weapon. To his surprise, Coffey felt something heavy and metallic around the mobster's waistline. It felt like a gun. Normally, gangsters of Gotti's stature don't carry pieces, precisely to avoid the inconvenience of a charge for carrying an unlicensed weapon. Drivers and bodyguards are usually armed to protect their boss but only rarely will the boss himself be armed on the streets.

Joe Coffey swore at the startled gangster and asked him if he had a gun on him. Gotti grunted a profanity. Coffey searched some more. The "gun" turned out to be a massive designer belt buckle. Gotti smirked at the detective's discomfort and casually sauntered back to the radio car to be driven down to the local precinct where he would be charged.

As Coffey escorted him up the steps of the station house, where the "boss of bosses" would undergo the further humiliation of being formally charged and fingerprinted, Gotti turned to the lawman and said with a smile: "I'll give you three to one odds that I beat this!"

It would have been beneath the detective's dignity to have taken a bet with a man he regarded as the ultimate "lowlife"—immense though his power was. Coffey turned him down. In Joe Coffey's book the wiseguys were all lowlife. The only exceptions he made were for those who might be cooperating; not that it made any difference to the fact they were still the lowest of the low—but in order to keep them turning in their buddies, Coffey was prepared to at least treat them as human beings.

For John Gotti, he had nothing but contempt and a pair of handcuffs. "Some people say he's a borderline moron," says Coffey. "I go one step further, he's a moron. He's got the IQ of an ice cube. He's a ruthless killer and a thug."

But Gotti's spell of good fortune was to remain unbroken—for the time being. When the case came to court the jury acquitted him. John Gotti walked down the steps of the Brooklyn courthouse into the outside street raising his fists in the air with the triumphant demeanor of a conquering hero.

To the cheering masses waiting for him outside that was more or less what he was. His smiling right-hand man and gofer, "Jackie the Nose," shepherded him through the milling crowd and into the back of a waiting limousine. Flashlights popped and TV crews fell over themselves in an attempt to get a shot of New York City's hottest celebrity. The charge of shooting John O'Connor, the carpenters' union official, was quickly forgotten and for a while would join the long list of unpunished crimes that John Gotti had under his belt.

With the distraction of the court case out of the way,

Gotti could now give his undivided attention to his Family, in particular the gambling operations run by the Gambino Family. Five Families ran New York City along territorial lines. Although there were no strict geographical boundaries where the jurisdiction of one Family ended and another began, the Families were highly proprietorial about any operation which fell under their control. Whether directly run by one of their capos or soldiers or franchised out to an associate, it was important that people knew who they were dealing with. The ability of a drug-dealer, loan-shark or pimp to be able to say, "I'm with the Gambinos," was almost priceless. The dealer would be unlikely to have his stash ripped off, the loan shark would find the recalcitrant debtor falling over himself to keep up with his payments and the pimp would be blessed with a stable of prostitutes who would happily work all hours of the day and night.

The power of the mob should not be underestimated. It is not so much the power derived from the staggering size of organized crime's annual turnover, a figure almost impossible to calculate but which can be safely assumed to run into billions of dollars. Such figures are popular with politicians, bureaucrats and law enforcement officials on fund-raising missions but bear little relation to the ultimate source of Mafia power. The power and influence of the Mafia culture begins and ends on the street. It is power that cannot be measured by outward appearance, size of bank account, length of limousine or number of bodyguards. Power in the Mafia is all about "respect." Although John Gotti is the most notorious of recent mobsters, his style and demeanor were in marked contrast to the old school of Mafia bosses. The founding father of his Family, and the alleged model for *The Godfather* movies, was Carlo Gambino, a small, stooped, narrow-shouldered old man with an immense hooklike nose, who, contrary to his appearance, could wield more power and respect with the gesture of one raised hand than an entire stretch limo full of Mafia thugs.

The unspoken power of the mob is expressed by the ritual of the Mafia introduction. If you are a fellow member of the mob and we are in the presence of another Mafioso, I would introduce you as "A friend of ours." If, however, you are not in the Mafia you are merely "A friend of mine." It is for that "connection," and all the kudos, power and prestige that it brings, that young men live and die on the streets of New York.

And that is just to become a "made" guy. Some gangsters, thieves, and hustlers literally devote their entire lives to try and become members. They know that a wiseguy will always command respect and that their earning power can be vastly increased.

While there is inevitable rivalry and treachery between the New York Families, there is far greater resentment if they are threatened by outsiders. Wiseguys display the same territorial imperative as any wild animal carving out its own space in a commercial jungle. The higher up the Mafia hierarchy, the more protective the Mafioso will be about his image as a "Man of Respect." The head of a Family can be severely weakened when he is no longer accorded the respect that is due; without that respect, he can no longer count on the loyalty of his minions. That was precisely what had happened to Paul Castellano, Gotti's predecessor and the boss who had been murdered to make way for the heir apparent.

John Gotti knew the value of respect. In his own words, he ruled that no one should be allowed to "challenge the Administration." His security depended entirely on maintaining respect and instilling its necessity into those beneath him, and above all into the hearts and minds of those who might in one careless moment contemplate challenging him.

When Gotti discovered that a Greek rival called "Spiro" was running a gambling operation in direct competition to a card game under the protection of the Gambinos, he knew he had to put an immediate stop to it. "It's the first time we've heard this guy's name in a fuckin' year. First time in a fucking year . . . and you've got a game," complained Gotti to the Gambino soldier who had reported the problem to him. "We got a game for years there. That's ours—about 20 years. We got a game for 20 years. Is that fuckin' Greek's name Spiro?"

"That's right," replied the wiseguy who ran their card game.

"You tell this punk," ordered the boss, "that I, ME, JOHN GOTTI . . ." Gotti's voice swelled with uncontrolled fury as the full realization of the insult dawned on him.

"I'm meeting him tonight," interrupted the Mafioso.

Gotti ignored him and carried on, imagining that he was personally confronting the unfortunate Spiro. ". . . will sever your motherfucking head off! You cocksucker! You're nobody there!"

Gotti was warming to his theme. He wanted the "punk" to realize that although the threat was being conveyed by one of his soldiers, it still carried the full weight of the head of the Gambino Family. Lack of respect for one of his men was a direct affront to the head of the Family.

For the benefit of the messenger, Gotti rehearsed the exact manner in which the threat should be delivered. "Listen to me, tell him. Tell him, 'Listen, you know better. HE'LL SEVER YOUR MOTHERFUCKING HEAD OFF! You know better than to open a game there!' Now who does he answer to?"

Spiro's eventual response is unknown. Men had been killed by Gotti for far less. But it wasn't Spiro who lived to tell the tale of the mobster's threat. The Godfather's conversation was being recorded by a secret FBI microphone that on January 18, 1990 was faithfully recording the mobster's every word.

One week later Gotti was in the second-floor apartment at the Ravenite. Rented from an 80-year-old Mafia widow, the club provided Gotti with the silence and privacy required for the secretive strategy sessions of the Gambino Family. Ever alert to the possibility of a bug in the downstairs Ravenite, or even, God forbid, being overheard by an informer, a "rat," Gotti reserved his really private conversations for the second floor. He knew he was safe in the apartment.

Sitting with Gotti were the two next highest ranking

members of the Gambino Family, Frank "Frankie Loc" Locascio, his underboss, and Salvatore "Sammy the Bull" Gravano, his trusted friend and consigliere. Gotti had brought his acolytes upstairs to discuss a matter of the greatest sensitivity, the forthcoming trial of a member of the Family for heroin trafficking. The defendant was Johnny Gambino, a cousin of the Family's founding father, Carlo, and a key figure in the New York heroin business.

The drugs came from Sicily—"over there," where the Gambino family had sources of relatives by marriage and by blood, many of whom were deeply implicated in the transatlantic heroin trade. The dealer who had acted as the "liaison" between New York and Sicily was in trouble. Word had reached Gotti that two of the Sicilians had "turned." They were negotiating a deal with the New York prosecutor. In return for a lighter sentence they had agreed to become Government witnesses. In Mafia-speak they were "rats" and in the Mafia world, rodents had to be exterminated.

In hushed tones, Gotti broke the bad news to his friends. "I heard this guy that's 'ratting' is a 'friend' from over there. He was the 'mixologist,' " explained the Godfather—the person responsible for turning morphine base into heroin at one of the Sicilians' secret refineries. A "friend" meant that he was a member of the Mafia. "He's a 'friend.' They just turned another guy, another friend ratted. Two friends of ours, from over there. An old-timer and the guy about our age, like he's 47 . . . and an old-timer. They're bringing the both of them over here. And they got depositions and tapes. They got a video surveillance caught with a 'minchia' over here in the corner . . ."

"Minchia" was slang for a close friend. Another Gambino member had been captured on a video surveillance in Little Italy, whose network of small bars and cafes was often used to set up deals.

Sammy "The Bull" Gravano echoed his boss's displeasure. The Gambino Family's Sicilian connection had let the Family down. "Some fucking thing in Italy," complained Gravano in a low growl. "Your people . . . Italian people.

That's gonna come out. They going . . . 'Friends' are in
Italy; and here, back and forth . . ."

"Ya know, ya know what we gotta do . . ." interrupted
Gotti.

The Mafia vocabulary is so riddled with code, slang and
semi-Italian phrases that much of the time mobsters don't
even need to communicate verbally at all. In this instance
everyone sitting round the table knew exactly what Gotti
meant. The penalty for "ratting" was a mandatory death
sentence. The oath of loyalty, "May I burn like this piece of
paper . . ." was the first commandment of the initiation
ceremony both in Italy and America.

At best the vocabulary of the Mafia is obtuse, partly
because of the increasing wariness of intrusive hidden microphones, but also because the culture is surrounded by
all the trappings of a secret society. Ancient rituals, rules,
formalities and initiation rites, some of them stretching
back to the ways of medieval Sicily, survive somewhat incongruously in the midst of modern day life in the center of
Manhattan. One commonly used phrase from the Mafia vocabulary is "to whack" or "whack out." The literal translation is murder.

"The liaison guy's getting whacked because . . ."

Sammy "The Bull" coughed.

"That don't belong to us," continued the man who had
just uttered the death sentence. "That's their fucking crew.
And he's gotta get whacked! Because he's getting the same,
for the same reason that 'Jelly Belly's' getting it. You wanna
challenge the Administration, well we will meet the challenge. And you're going, you motherfucker!"

The Sicilians weren't the only rats. Another member of
the rodent population had been spotted even closer to
home. Gaetano "Corky" Vastola, a soldier from the
DeCalvacante Family of New Jersey, was under suspicion.
The New Jersey mob had extensive dealings with the
Gambinos and Vastola was currently facing a long prison
sentence for narcotics trafficking. Gotti was worried that
"Corky" might "uncork" himself to the wrong ears. It presented another awkward problem for the Administration.

Gotti summoned John D'Amato, underboss of the

DeCalvacante Family and the immediate boss of Corky Vastola, to a sit-down at the Ravenite apartment. The purpose of the meeting was to bring the DeCalvacante Family on-side. Mob protocol dictated that the Gambinos should seek the consent of the DeCalvacantes for the murder. An unlicensed hit could provoke a mob war.

"If you think the guy's a rat, or he's weak, you're jeopardizing a whole 'Borgata,' a whole Cosa Nostra, for this guy," explained the head of the Gambino Family. "Minchia!" continued Gotti. "If I know a guy's weak and I let him go running around the street, get you locked up, I'm a fucking rat, too!"

In the case of both the Sicilian "liaison man" and Corky Vastola, John Gotti was confronting what was becoming an increasing problem for the mob. The crackdown by the Reagan administration in the war against drugs had not only given the FBI joint jurisdiction over narcotics cases, it had also resulted in much lengthier sentencing for anyone caught in drug trafficking. Where previously ten to 15 year sentences had been handed out—which could be served within three to five years after parole and remission for good behavior—dealers and traffickers were now getting 20 to 40 years without parole. It amounted to a life sentence, and almost overnight the number of Mafiosi willing to cut a deal and become informers or Government witnesses doubled. It was a serious threat to the integrity and loyalty that in the past had been the Mafia's secret weapon in fending off the attempts of law enforcement to destroy the organization. It was one of the reasons that Gotti's predecessor as head of the Gambino Family, Paul Castellano, had forbidden Family members from dealings in drugs on pain of death.

Now, Gotti's problem was that there was a flood of cases like Corky Vastola. The only way to solve the problem was to get rid of informers as soon as possible in the hope that sufficient examples would act as a deterrent. In reality, from the Mafia's point of view it merely exacerbated the problems. Now the wiseguys had to confront the prospect of a lifetime in jail and the possibility that they might be suspected of becoming a "rat" even if they had no intention of cutting a deal. In Gotti's book, it was far better to err on the side of caution. He couldn't be sure that Vastola was an informer—but one thing he could be sure of was that dead men tell no tales. In addition Gotti had come across Vastola in prison in the early Seventies. Although in on separate offenses, they had both been doing time together and Gotti had not been impressed by what he saw.

"I was in the can with him," recalled Gotti. "Well, you asking me how he does 'time'?"

D'Amato wasn't but Gotti was going to answer anyway.

"The worst I ever saw in my life," lamented "Johnny Boy," who took great pride in his ability to shrug off a jail sentence. Gotti continued to browbeat D'Amato with tales of Vastola's weakness in prison. "I wasn't made to be a rat on anybody. Didn't he tell you how I treated him in jail?"

"Yeah," said D'Amato.

"How I treated him in jail?" repeated Gotti, driving the point home.

It was an essential ingredient of Mafia machismo to serve your time without fear or complaint. A prison sentence was a minor inconvenience, a calculated interruption of a life devoted to crime and an occupational hazard of being a Mafioso. The Mafia had no time for wimps who could not "do" their time like a man. As the ultimate exponent of Mafia machismo, Gotti attached the same importance to a prison sentence as most people would to a parking fine. Above all, whatever an individual felt inwardly about being incarcerated in some hellhole of an American prison, outwardly he had to display complete indifference to the humiliation and discomfort that the system was designed to inflict.

"Don't worry about us going to jail. Me number one," Gotti had once boasted to a friend. "I like jail better than the streets!"

The camaraderie between Mafiosi while in prison was another part of the culture. At the height of their power, the mob ran the jails. Warders would pay due deference and corrupt guards would trade privileges inside in exchange for favors and cash on the outside. The higher up the Mafia hierarchy the better the treatment you could expect—from warders and inmates alike. Prison was also one of the few places that Mafia gangsters felt free enough to talk openly to each other. There was little danger of hidden FBI microphones or police surveillance. Some gangsters, with access to pay phones and other privileges bought from corrupt guards, even kept control of their criminal empires from within the very institutions designed to destroy them. With time on their hands fellow Mafiosi had endless days to plot, conspire and exchange personal confidences with each other in a way that they might never have done on the outside.

That was Corky's mistake. Vastola assumed the rising star of the Gambino Family was a friend, a fellow Mafioso in whom he could safely confide. It never occurred to Corky that any admission of weakness might be carefully filed away for future reference by the man whose ambitions depended on knowing as much as possible about all his potential friends and enemies. John Gotti may not be a great intellectual (although he was reported to have a very high IQ), but he has an excellent memory.

"He used to tell me: 'you know when I'm near you I feel like I'm sucking on my mother's tit,' " recalled the Godfather with an air of palpable distaste. " 'That's how comfortable I feel.' Those are the words. Definitely used that kind of language . . . Minchia!" Even as he recalled Corky's conversation, John Gotti felt a wave of revulsion pass over him. To his mind there was something extremely distasteful about a Mafioso displaying such emotions. Worse, there was a serious problem with a man who would actually admit to them. Gotti's world was a macho universe where men didn't speak their feelings and women knew their place.

"My mother," exclaimed Gotti with an air of moral indignation, "I can't even use those, that word with my mother. 'I'm gonna fuckin' '. . . in the same vein, you know what I mean?"

Coming from a man whose conversation was peppered with more four-lettered expletives and obscenities in the space of an hour than most people utter in the course of a year, even in New York City, this was rich indeed.

"Ahhh," replied the somewhat nonplussed underboss of Corky's New Jersey Family.

"Well," mused the Mafia boss, positively rejoicing in his newfound moral fervor. "I don't know if he's a rat now. Is he gonna be a rat someday . . . ?" The question was rhetorical but considering this was a matter of life and death there was only one answer. "Yeah," breathed Gotti.

D'Amato listened and finally spoke up. He wasn't about to contradict him. "Yeah," agreed Corky's boss. "That's the way I feel about him. That's the way I feel about him."

Gaetano "Corky" Vastola was running out of friends. If he lived to make any in the future, he would have to remember not to confide in any of them.

Corky's erstwhile colleagues turned their attention to the protocol of who else they might need to communicate with. Gotti advised D'Amato to keep quiet. "You know why?" he demanded. "We're not, when we're doing this, we gonna, we're gonna be part of—God forbid—a mass conspiracy, and . . . it's got no right to be taking place. The object is that this guy gotta get hurt. You came here. Whoever it is, they coming to you, and that's it! You know what I'm saying? If we cut it, we'll do it, and that's the end of it. Ya know? It's not, not a thing ya gotta ask ya to."

"That's the way I am," agreed D'Amato, anxious to humor the man who dealt out death sentences with as much concern as most people choose a meal from a menu.

Gotti knew he was right and who was going to tell him if he wasn't? "That's why," explained Gotti, "that's why I tell him, John, in the future we gotta do all the things like this and we'll never hear these motherfucking tapes again."

The head of the Gambino Family was referring to the tapes which were slowly leading to more and more cases against the Mafia. Ironically, even as he was speaking he was completely unaware that their conversation was being taped.

The bug in the Ravenite apartment posed a silent threat which far outweighed any damage, real or imagined, that Gaetano "Corky" Vastola could ever inflict. Indeed the Ravenite bugs were only a small part, although the most important, in an ever expanding network of secret microphones concealed in mob haunts throughout New York City. While John Gotti was dispensing summary justice to Mafia rats, he was damning himself with his own words. John Gotti was providing far more effective evidence for the FBI and the prosecuting attorneys of the Eastern District of New York than they could ever have dreamt of acquiring from some "rat" within the Mafia. There was supreme irony in the fact that John Gotti was "ratting" on himself and didn't even know it.

For the most part this gold mine of intelligence came from hidden microphones planted during clandestine operations within the city's secret citadels of crime. It was aided by informers on the street and by physical surveillance. John Gotti's movements were tracked from the moment he got up in the morning to the moment he went to bed at night. As a creature of habit it had been relatively easy to discover how and where he spent his working days. Now, there were very few places that Gotti could go without either being followed or secretly recorded or both.

While well aware of the risks of the secret microphones, somehow the mobsters could never conceive that their habitual meeting places could be bugged. They took reasonable precautions and even hired experts to sweep their houses and clubs. On occasion, when they had to discuss something particularly incriminating, such as a murder, they would go on a "walk-talk," a walk around the block or on the streets which was virtually the only guarantee against being overheard. But Gotti and his fellow mobsters were soon lulled into a false sense of security. It seemed impossible to believe that the FBI could have bugs everywhere—besides, in the middle of winter it was much too cold to go on a "walk-talk" every time they needed to discuss something.

The result was that night and day in secret locations scattered throughout Manhattan, agents in apartment blocks, basements and unmarked surveillance vans were crouched over tape recorders spooling in the collective wisdom of the New York Mafia. From jokes, threats and curses through to murder contracts it was all being recorded on the Mafia tapes.

━━ 2 ━━
INITIATION RITES

As 1991 DREW TO A CLOSE, NEW YORK CITY WAS basking in some unusually warm weather. The bright sun bathed the mean streets of Brooklyn with an unseasonal light. The main avenues were embroidered with Christmas lights. The cross streets were bordered by detached wooden-fronted houses and in small front gardens stone and plastic effigies of the Nativity, illuminated by fairy lights, fought a silent contest for best decorated porch. Mock baroque blue and white statues of the Blessed Virgin Mary smiled sweetly at the more secular red-hatted replicas of Father Christmas. Black-hatted white plastic snowmen gazed blankly through the fences at the slow-moving traffic.

In the Italian-American neighborhoods of Brooklyn and Queens, Christmas festivity was always taken seriously. It was a heady mixture of commerce and religion and the time of year to celebrate the two most important rituals in the Catholic calendar: Church and Family. But for some people living in the New York suburbs Christmas 1991 was not a time to celebrate anything. It was a time to be forgotten, if they could live long enough to remember. For members of the Colombo Family it was a time of rising tension on the streets and diminishing life expectancy at home.

There was a Mafia war on the city streets.

A fortnight before Christmas a loyal and devoted husband was carefully arranging the Christmas lights on his balcony patio when two men driving past in a van unleashed a hail of bullets from high-powered automatic weapons. The Colombo soldier was killed instantly.

Within minutes local TV news crews converged on the scene—one correspondent even arrived before the police. That night's show broadcast moving pictures of the grieving widow dressed in black sobbing over her husband's corpse which was covered by a white sheet stained with blood. It was one of five mob murders that dominated the headlines in the final fortnight before Christmas.

The body count was rising and by the New Year of 1992 mob "rub-outs" had become almost mundane. To the frightened citizens of New York City, and the innocent victims who got in the way, it was, as Charles Hynes, Brooklyn District Attorney, reluctantly admitted, like "a shoot-out in the Wild West."

Then, as suddenly as the violence had erupted, it subsided. The power struggle for control of the Colombo Family petered out. Law enforcement officials were puzzled: there was no clear victor but a truce was declared and the killing stopped.

The Christmas of 1991 was a bad time for another infamous Mafia institution—the Gambino Family. John Gotti was spending the day before Christmas nursing a heavy cold in the dismal concrete surroundings of the Manhattan Correctional Center. He passed the time weightlifting, reading books and poring over sheafs of documents in preparation for his trial, scheduled to begin in the middle of January.

According to his closest friend, Lou Kasman, a young millionaire from the garment center, Gotti was limbering up for his trial, confident that justice would once more vindicate the "Teflon Don"; so-called because in the past three court cases the prosecutors had inexplicably failed to make any of their charges stick.

John Gotti, his defense lawyers and friends had tremendous faith in the American jury system. It had served them extremely well in the past by returning three identical verdicts of "Not Guilty." But as new tapes from the upcoming court case revealed, the previous verdicts had been achieved by bribery and corruption. This time the prosecution would go to extraordinary lengths to protect the 12 good men to keep them "true."

"I'm very close to him," grinned Kasman, leaning back on his black imitation-leather executive armchair. Kasman exudes an aura of bonhomie and injured innocence, partly accounted for by his inherited wealth and partly through his friendship with Manhattan's most notorious mobster. His modest office is in the center of 34th Street in midtown Manhattan. Downstairs a taciturn assistant sits inside a wood and glass booth, checking the movements of cardboard boxes and coathangers being wheeled out on to the sidewalk. It seems an unlikely source of such wealth but the garment trade has many millionaires. On the office floor lie crates of fine Scotch whisky waiting to be dispatched to Kasman's friends and customers. On the office walls there are several silver-framed black and white photographs of his smiling friend, John Gotti—mementoes of happier times, including one picture of Gotti emerging triumphantly from court after yet another acquittal and surrounded by a cheering and jostling throng of supporters, admirers and media followers. Another picture has Gotti sitting next to Kasman, both wearing dinner jackets and black ties—the very image of a wealthy and respectable businessman attending a society function. It is difficult to believe that the same man is reputed to have cut one of his enemies in half with an electric chainsaw while still alive.

"I looked to him as a father, as a parent, someone for guidance, advice, someone to talk to. A friend, a father."

Kasman was on the phone to Gotti almost every day in the run-up to Christmas lending moral support to the Godfather as he prepared for the trial and the media circus that would swing into action in the second week of January. "Hi Gramps!" was the incongruous greeting as Kasman got through to the Correctional Center. Kasman wanted to know if there was anything he could do for his beloved Godfather. He advised Gotti on different medications for his flu and mediated between the various different lawyers battling for the ear of the most famous criminal client in New York City.

In the eyes of Louis Kasman, John Gotti can do no wrong. "John Gotti is a man of great integrity," gushes the effervescent garment trader. "Brilliant, *brilliant* man, avid reader. Man with a high regard for family and friends. Values his friends, values his family, great sense of humor. A man you would enjoy to be around, a man you would enjoy to bring your children around, your family around. A wonderful person!" All the unsavory rumors are the work of jealous rivals and a malicious press. The godfather to Kasman's daughter is the victim of a vicious campaign of character assassination.

While this wonderful person was contemplating his future from the grim surroundings of the Correctional Center, his elder brother, Peter Gotti, inheriting some of the Family good fortune, had recently beaten the rap on a charge of racketeering. The indictment had alleged that Peter Gotti was part of a massive organized crime conspiracy to extort payoffs from the New York City Housing Authority on contracts to replace windows.

The Mafia had a "hook" into the Architectural and Ornamental Ironworkers Union, Local 580, which enabled them to rig the bids on all the public housing window replacement contracts in the City of New York, at first sight an unlikely business scheme for the Mafia. Closer scrutiny revealed the reason for mob interest. Over one ten-year period the Housing Authority ordered over a million new windows at a unit cost of $150—$150 million. It was such good business that every Family in the city eagerly sought a piece of the action. Peter Gotti, or so the Government alleged, had helped them all gain their rightful share.

Peter Gotti doesn't look like a window salesman, or even a millionaire broker of crooked housing contracts. A gray-haired, bespectacled man of medium height who wears anoraks and ill-fitting sweatshirts, Peter Gotti possesses none of the designer-suited panache of his younger brother, but in common with his more infamous relative Peter Gotti has the unmistakable aura of a New York wiseguy, right down to the dangerously exposed belly-button and arrogant stare. Peter Gotti is a "capo" or captain in the Gambino Family, and given the intensity of law enforcement interest in the Gambinos due to his brother's headline-grabbing activities it was something of a miracle that he managed to escape the clutches of the law.

High-profile mobsters like John Gotti never liked to admit it to themselves but they were living on borrowed time. Time borrowed from Uncle Sam and financed by the American taxpayer, the unwitting victims of the lucrative rackets which fueled the coffers of the New York Families. When Gotti ascended to a throne steeped in blood in the New Year of 1986 he took over an organization already reeling from the combined efforts of several Government law enforcement agencies.

By the late 1980s the heads of New York's Mafia Families were in a far more perilous position than their predecessors. The first generation of Mafia bosses had been unassuming and publicity shy—they knew the value of a low profile: that way they would attract less attention from the press and prosecution. John Gotti represented a radical change of style and made the mistake of failing to acknowledge a marked difference in the tactics of the federal agencies in their fight against the Mafia.

Gotti quickly became a media celebrity, partly because of his own hubris and partly because he was an infinitely more colorful character than his predecessors, men like Paul Castellano, the archetypal mob businessman. Gotti hailed from a generation that inherited its traditions from the culture of the American dream, a dream which worshiped fame, notoriety and wealth. The Sicilian traditions of quiet power and authority exercised with stealth and ruthlessness were alien to the Mafiosi of Gotti's generation.

Gotti's high profile marked him down as an immediate target for the FBI and the prosecutors from the U.S. Attorney's offices. A series of highly successful investigations, court cases and convictions had raised the collective morale of the law enforcement community and increased the mass of intelligence on mob operations to a degree where the tactical advantage was firmly on the side of law and order.

Undercover operations in which agents risked their lives to pose as wiseguys and audacious break-ins of mob homes and social clubs had provided an unprecedented amount of information concerning the secret workings of the American Mafia. By day, Mafia bosses were religiously tracked on their daily rounds through the streets of Manhattan. By night, hidden microphones in the clubs and bars they frequented faithfully recorded the power struggles and business deals which were the lifeblood of the Cosa Nostra.

Gotti's predecessor, Paul Castellano, the "boss of bosses," head of the Gambino Family and the most powerful Mafioso in the nation, had suffered the ultimate humiliation of an FBI bug inside his own home. Even the bedrooms of Mafia mistresses had been bugged. Discreet bugs recorded the business talk that frequently followed the bedroom antics of the Mafia dons. The mob haunts of Manhattan were wired for sound. Some tapes even revealed mob bosses complaining about the bugs in places that they *knew* to be safe. One aging Mafia boss who had survived every attempt to prosecute him was devastated to discover that his limousine was bugged. Was nothing sacred? In the war against organized crime nothing was.

When the former head of the Gambino Family was gunned down by a team of hit men in the center of Manhattan en route to his favorite steak house, the finger of suspicion pointed immediately to John Gotti. The investigative teams who had hounded Castellano now had a new target; not that Gotti was unknown to them. Word from the street and intelligence from the tapes had yielded tantalizing glimpses into the feud that had finally been settled in a hail of bullets on December 15, 1985.

Taking over the reins of power in such a brazen manner guaranteed that as far as the U.S. Government was concerned John Gotti became "Public Enemy Number One." For the next six years, from 1985 to 1991, Gotti was the focus of the most intensive investigation ever mounted against one individual by the law enforcement community.

Their efforts were well rewarded. The investigators compiled a graphic and chilling insight into the secret world of John Gotti. They accumulated such an overwhelming body of evidence against Gotti and his closest associates that the FBI were able to entice his most loyal companion into an act of epic betrayal. His former underboss became the most important Government witness ever to have emerged from the Mafia hierarchy. Both he and Gotti were on the tapes, conducting the business of the Gambino Family. They were clearly heard deciding on promotions, arbitrating business disputes, bribing cops, buying jurors and arranging contracts to murder their rivals. Never before had a Mafia boss unwittingly revealed so much about himself and the organization he represented.

It was not a flattering portrait. The picture that emerged from the FBI investigation was in stark contrast to the image Gotti presented to the readers of the *New York Post* and the *Daily News*. Here was a man with a vicious temper and a brutal character who would not lose a moment's sleep after ordering a man's execution for merely forgetting an appointment with his boss. It was easy for the press and public to relate to the flashy gangster with his double-breasted suits and a passion for gambling and expensive restaurants. Not so easy to comprehend a man whose world revolved around threatening to cut people's heads off and terrifying his underlings into submission with a baseball bat.

But in addition to the unprecedented attention from law enforcement, by the late 1980s the Mafia had also become its own worst enemy. Attacked from without, the empire of crime was now beginning to decay from within. For half a century the Mafia's most effective weapon against law enforcement had been the fierce oath of loyalty sworn by its members. No one could even begin to be considered for membership in the Mafia without being personally recommended and vouched for. The candidate had to earn the approval of the senior members of the Family that he wished to join and often serve a lengthy apprenticeship to convince them that he was a worthy candidate, capable of substantial earnings and unswerving loyalty. The screening process was specifically designed to ensure that the intake of new blood would strengthen and renew the organization. A common entry requirement was murder. Once he had qualified and met the approval of the Family, the candidate would then have to undergo the initiation rite, swearing an oath of secrecy and undying loyalty on pain of death. Only then could he earn the honor of becoming a "made" man, a fully fledged "wiseguy." In Italy, such a man would be known as a "Man of Honor," a member of "The Honored Society." In America it was "Cosa Nostra"—"Our Thing."

The ritual oath, like the Mafia itself, originated in Sicily, a country steeped in the shadowy tradition of secret societies. The secret vows of the initiation ceremony were described to me by a former Sicilian Mafioso who reached one of the most important positions within the organization. "The oath went as follows. They put the image of a saint in my hand. While I had this saint in my hand I read the 'commandments'—which were: not to look at other men's women, not to harm my neighbor, not to steal . . . and many others. If I betrayed the Cosa Nostra, the organization that I was entering, I would be burnt like the image I had in my hand. They set fire to it and everything was burnt. If I betrayed the Cosa Nostra, I would come to the same end."

The Sicilian version is replete with religious overtones. It is a sacred vow, swearing loyalty and devotion to a single object while forsaking some of the earthly temptations that might tempt lesser mortals, a vow of priesthood where the false idol to be worshiped was the unholy trinity of power, wealth and corruption. The American version was watered down over the years. As the initiation rite became more secular and less formal so too did it seem to lose some of its power. Where once it would have been unthinkable for those who had taken the oath to contemplate abandoning the faith, in modern-day America it was all too easy. One such heretic is Tommy Del Giorno.

Tommy Del Giorno is a short man of slender build. He has sharp features and dark hair. There is a nasal tinge to his voice but otherwise he looks like an ordinary businessman. Del Giorno is an American Mafioso whose career began on the streets of Philadelphia, where he rose through the ranks with several murders under his belt to attain the rank of "capodecina" or captain: "They have like a ceremony. They'll invite twenty or thirty guys. You go to a place—it could be a club, a house or any place. My thing, it was a house. You go into a house and then you'll go into another room. At the time I got made, eight other guys got made with me, so there was nine of us. There were about twenty-five or thirty made members, they were sitting in another room, and one at a time they'll bring you into the room . . . [they] ask you, 'Do you know everybody in the room?' and you'll say, 'Yeah.' They'll ask you 'Do you know why you're here?' You're supposed to answer 'No.' You're told that, you know, but you know why you're there. Then he said, 'Do you know everybody in this room?' You tell them, 'Yeah.' 'Would you do anything for anybody in this room?' You tell them, 'Yeah.' There was a table, the boss was there, the underboss and the consigliere, in front of them was a knife and a gun, a little drawer with a pin in it and some tissue. Then he says, 'There's a gun and knife there' and he picks out a guy to prick your finger. He usually picks out the guy closest to you, the guy that proposed you, that brought you there. He'll get up and prick your finger and then he'll take a Kleenex, a piece of tissue, and wipe the blood off and then he'll burn the blood and he'll take it and put it in your hand and rub the ashes out and say, 'May I burn like the Saints if I betray my friends.' Then I turned around and went to everybody in the room and shook their hands and kissed everyone of them on the cheek, and came all the way back to him and then I shook his hand and kissed him and then went into the circle and waited for the next guy to come up."

Tommy Del Giorno likes to compare his initiation ceremony to its counterpart in straight society: "It would be an equivalent to some people graduating medical school. It's over, you went through it all—and now I could reap the rewards. The reward is more power, more respect. It's a way of getting respect without working for it. Like, a lot of people, like to be respected, they have to be a great writer or a great architect or a great doctor. All you got—it's simple: all you gotta do is write numbers and be a loan shark and get involved in some kind of shooting. And you become respected. It's not right but that's the way it is!"

For Tommy Del Giorno, loan shark, drug dealer and killer, the act of becoming a "made guy" in the Philadelphia Mafia Family was the logical reward for his ability to earn money for the Family. Above all it was an endorsement of his readiness to kill for the Family. The amount of respect accorded to a Mafia soldier increases in direct proportion to the level of fear he can instill. In Del Giorno's Family fear was at a premium. If Nicodemo "Nicky" Scarfo had not been in the Mafia, he would have almost certainly been declared criminally insane.

A second-generation immigrant from Calabria, Scarfo was fiercely proud of his Italian heritage to the extent of loathing Sicilians. In contrast to his predecessor, Angelo Bruno, dubbed the "Docile Don" for his tendency to arbitrate disputes rather than resorting to murder, Scarfo was a vicious killer. He proudly boasted of his passion for violence and presided over more murders than any of his contemporaries, and that was just within his own Family.

One of Tommy Del Giorno's first tasks as a "captain" was to murder Salvatore Testa, a young Mafia soldier. In the eyes of Nicky Scarfo, Testa had humiliated the Family by canceling his marriage to the underboss's daughter. The contract went to Tommy Del Giorno.

"He embarrassed the underboss's family and the underboss. It's a bad thing to do so close to the wedding. It's understandable in one sense, I mean let's put it this way, I don't know how I'd have reacted if it had been my daughter. I may have wanted the guy killed. But it's up to the father—in this instance, he wanted him killed." Salvatore Testa had unwisely called off the engagement just three weeks before the wedding. The timing was bad—a very expensive firm of caterers had already been hired and all the invitations sent out.

Of course the bride was devastated but far worse within the high society of the Philadelphia Mafia was the public humiliation and the loss of face for Nicky Scarfo.

The bride had already chosen her dress.

The Mafia take their weddings seriously.

The Family honor was at stake.

Salvatore Testa, the reluctant bridegroom, realized he might be in trouble. As a Mafioso he suspected he might well be murdered. His fiancée's tearful grief followed by her raging fury did nothing to allay his fears. Salvatore's prospective mother-in-law was also speechless with rage.

The embarrassment was the worst thing that could have happened—not least because they were a Family with powerful connections within the Cosa Nostra. In fact, when the paranoid Scarfo received a nervous visitor in the shape of Sal Testa, who had come to seek his blessing for the marriage, Scarfo's immediate concern was that the marriage would create a powerful faction that could only threaten his own position.

As soon as he started to have second thoughts Testa returned to see Scarfo, this time to ask his advice and seek his boss's permission to break off the wedding ceremony. Scarfo, secretly relieved, appeared to give his blessing. Testa knew that Scarfo's approval was vital to help dissipate the fury of his prospective in-laws and save his life.

"Break it off," counseled the wily Scarfo. "If you want to—break it off."

Relieved at what appeared to be his head of Family's approval, Testa went ahead and canceled the wedding.

Predictably, Ciancaligni, the father of the bride, lost no time in driving over to see Scarfo. His request was simpler and more straightforward. Ciancaligni merely sought approval for the murder to avenge the honor of his family.

Scarfo listened, shook his head wisely and smiled. The wedding contract canceled, a new contract was born, awarded to the bridegroom's best friend, Tommy Del Giorno.

Their first plan, in true yuppie fashion, was to shoot Testa at the tennis courts where he took lessons. On reflection they rejected the idea, the courts were too public. The next plan was to get him alone. Del Giorno and the other members of the hit-team bombarded the reluctant bridegroom with invitations to breakfast, lunch and dinner. Testa became increasingly bewildered by his newfound popularity. Meals with the "boys" had been a fairly regular occurrence before he had broken off the engagement—but never on this scale. Testa wasn't dumb—he knew something was up. He was always too busy for dinner or any other invitations.

The hit men were beginning to despair. Reluctantly, Del Giorno reported back to Scarfo and told him it was impossible. Nicky Scarfo came up with a plan. They were to contact a wiseguy called Joey, Testa's best friend from school. It was then pointed out to Scarfo that because he was the best friend of the man that they were now proposing to kill, he might be somewhat reluctant to set him up.

In the world of Nicodemo Scarfo personal ties, friendship and loyalty could be brushed aside like a speck of dust on an expensive suit. "Tell him to set him up," ordered Scarfo. "If he won't, tell him we're going to kill him, his father and his brother!"

Tommy Del Giorno relayed the message. The best friend, Joey, agreed to the proposition.

"He said, 'Alright, I'll set him up.' In all fairness to him he really didn't want to do it, but he did it."

Now Salvatore Testa started to accept the dinner invitations, reassured by the presence of his old school friend.

"What we did was to get another made guy who was always in gambling debt and we got Joey [*the school friend*] to tell Sal that this guy owed Joey money and Sal had to settle the beef. They had a store that was being remodeled and the guy was supposed to be over there. So Joey brought him over there and the guy who was supposed to owe him money shot him. We wrapped him up, this was one o'clock in the afternoon. We came back at nine o'clock at night and took him out and drove him over to Jersey and dumped his body."

The moral of the story was that if you were going to marry the boss's daughter you'd better think twice before calling it all off. The atmosphere of terror and intimidation in Nicky Scarfo's Family was unusual even by Mafia standards. Like John Gotti, his fellow gangster in New York City, Scarfo was a throwback to the hoodlum of the Thirties. Both Gotti and Scarfo subscribed to a rule of terror and intimidation to enforce discipline. Where their prede-

cessors had concentrated on consolidating interests in legitimate businesses, their successors were reverting to the
style and tradition of the street gangster.

According to an FBI agent who had targeted the
Gambino Family for many years: "John Gotti took the mob
down to gutter level. He was much more inclined to run the
mob with a hard hand, much more the street activity, the
thuggish type of activity, hurting people, breaking arms and
legs, and even murdering people."

Drugs, gambling, shakedowns and robberies—it didn't
really matter what it was providing the boss got a cut. The
word on the street was that you had to make the "payoff"—pay the tax whether you were dealing drugs or running an illegal card game. But whereas Paul Castellano, the
former head of the Gambino Family, or Angelo Bruno, the
former head of the Bruno Family, prided themselves on
making the transition from street crime to racketeering,
their successors had little time for the old Sicilian traditions.

"Bruno was a racketeer," sniped Nicky Scarfo: "I'm a
gangster!"

A "gangster" ready to kill at the "drop of a hat." When
word reached Nicky Scarfo that a construction contractor
had called him "crazy" he ordered the man's execution.
His underboss dutifully shot and killed the offending businessman. As they were getting rid of the body, Scarfo personally supervised the operation: "Here's what I want you
to do. I want you to tie him up like a cowboy. Tie his hands
behind him, tie his feet behind him, wrap him up in this
blanket."

While his bemused underlings were carrying out his instructions, Scarfo gazed fondly down on the mutilated
corpse, now so tightly wrapped in the carpet that only his
head was showing. "I love this," he murmured, "I love
this."

Though this new ruthlessness worked in the short term,
the psychopathic nature of Nicky Scarfo would inevitably
lead to his own demise. While his unmitigated paranoia
earned him a blind loyalty based on fear it also generated a
degree of contempt and hatred which would ultimately

manifest itself in an orgy of betrayal. Scarfo's reign of terror produced more informers and Government witnesses than any other Family.

So many of the soldiers and capos were being demoted, threatened and actually killed that it soon became impossible for the Family to function as a viable entity. Even men like Tommy Del Giorno, who had sworn loyalty and killed a dozen men to prove their allegiance to Scarfo, began to feel threatened. He realized he was now dealing with a madman.

"For four or five years, every year, we killed a guy that was made, or a captain that was made. This annoyed me, it bothered me, because we were friendly with them and the next two months we were killing them. That was the little thing that was bothering me. Then he [*Nicky Scarfo*] takes a guy, thirty-three years his best friend. All of a sudden he's on the 'out.' Now this guy's an underboss. So he changes him and he takes him down—makes his nephew the underboss. Now he's going to kill this guy someday, I know it because there's no way that he could leave him alone, because he will never forgive him—he'll never forgive him. He has to kill him."

Scarfo's former underboss was saved by an eight-month prison sentence for bribery. When the news reached Scarfo, he was beside himself with rage. He was furious that he had missed an opportunity for murder.

One night after a heavy drinking session, Tommy Del Giorno was summoned to report to his boss. Despite the fact that his "enemy" was in prison, the scheming Scarfo was able to devise an alternative plan.

"Kill his son," ordered Scarfo.

Del Giorno was startled. After all, they were talking about an old family friend. He had known the son since childhood; he could remember playing with the kid when he was a five-year-old toddler. Now he was being asked to murder him in cold blood. Del Giorno wasn't exactly a saint, indeed he was a hardened killer, but even so he found it difficult to summon up any enthusiasm for such a dastardly deed.

Scarfo had also been a lifelong friend of both father and

son. "Kill him and bury him," he ordered as Del Giorno stared at him in a drunken stupor.

The drink must have made him bold because Tommy would never have gone against the mad Scarfo while sober. "Hey, Nicky, that's a stupid idea. We shouldn't be doing this, ya know."

Even as the words spilled out of his mouth, Del Giorno knew he had said the wrong thing. Scarfo fixed him with a thoughtful stare and paused before saying: "Yeah, oh yeah, you're right."

The paranoid Scarfo was playing for time. Tommy's response could mean only one thing: he must have taken sides with the former underboss. Now they were both plotting to kill him.

Del Giorno realized that one drunken slip of the tongue was enough to sign his death warrant. Like his friend, the demoted underboss, Del Giorno was granted a temporary reprieve by receiving a jail sentence. While he was inside, detectives from the State of New Jersey were still investigating the Scarfo Family. They had succeeded in placing a bug in some of the haunts that were frequented by Nicky Scarfo and his associates. Two of the New Jersey detectives made an appointment to see Del Giorno in his cell. They produced a tape recorder and played him a tape. What he heard on the cassette was to change Tommy Del Giorno's life. Two friends, soldiers in the Scarfo Family that Tommy regarded as "closer than brothers," were discussing their plans to murder him.

Although he had realized that standing up to Scarfo had been a bad mistake, the confirmation on the tape sent a shiver of fear right through his body. Del Giorno didn't need any prompting as to who was behind the contract. Reminded that both he and Scarfo were facing multiple murder charges, Del Giorno didn't need much persuading to switch sides. With bitter irony he remembered the oath he had sworn while blood dripped from his finger and he held the burning piece of paper.

Tommy Del Giorno believed he had remained true to the ideal—he had certainly lived by the gun and the dagger. Who was betraying whom?

Del Giorno still feels sick at taking the decision to turn his back on the Cosa Nostra. But today he recognizes that his world had become so riven with hatred and treachery that the question of betrayal of Nicky Scarfo was merely a matter of survival. "Is murder an act of betrayal? Who betrayed first? Was his idea to murder me an act of betrayal? And that's how I justify it. Who betrayed first? Was his idea to murder me an act of betrayal or was that alright and just my cooperating an act of betrayal? Whose betrayal came first and was it a betrayal?"

The Mafia had long been a world governed by terror, deceit and treachery but in the past the intrigues had been concealed from the outside world. The high-grade intelligence that law enforcement agencies were accumulating from the tapes enabled them to turn the treachery to their own advantage. Now at last they had an insight and an entree into a secret society where the psychotic behavior of Mafia killers like Nicky Scarfo could be used to their own advantage.

3
THE CLUB

"Organized crime has so infiltrated legitimate business in New York that every resident of the city has, in one way or another, become a victim of the mob."

Frank Storey, FBI Headquarters, Washington, D.C.

IN THE CASE OF **TOMMY DEL GIORNO**, THE TAPES THAT HE heard inside his prison cell were something of an eye-opener. Even for someone whose whole life had been dedicated to the Cosa Nostra and surviving the murderous machinations of his boss, the scheming antics of his friends came as a total shock. Other tapes were equally revelatory. An FBI squad based in Queens was reeling in hours of self-incriminating dialogue from a Mafia soldier. His conversations were providing the FBI with a trail of evidence that reached right into the headquarters of the New York Mafia: "the Commission."

Ralph Scopo was in the cement business—in a big way. He was the Mafia's man in town, the wiseguy who could fix any deal on any construction site. His leverage was simple: muscle and raw material. The raw material was concrete, the muscle—the mob. At 11:30 in the morning Scopo was due to meet a customer at the Skyway Motel in Queens, New York City. The FBI had been tipped off and had bugged the location. Sal D'Ambrosi was a construction manager who made his living by acting as a middleman between the building companies and the clients who commissioned the construction. Like most people in his line of business, his livelihood depended on contacts in the trade—which was why he needed Ralph Scopo. Sal D'Ambrosi wanted some advice on the finer points of a contract. It was a $200 million deal. D'Ambrosi wanted permission to bid as a general contractor. But as all the bids were fixed by the mob in advance, he needed prior approval. That was where Scopo came in. Without Scopo's say-so, he could kiss the deal goodbye.

"Two hundred million dollars, could I bid it? As a general contractor?"

Scopo thought about it. He wasn't quite sure what D'Ambrosi had in mind. "Two hundred million dollars, as a GC? Sure, why not?"

D'Ambrosi needed confirmation that Scopo would pass on a recommendation further up the line. That meant direct access to the ultimate decision-making body: the Commission. D'Ambrosi knew he couldn't get it in writing, but a nod and a wink from Ralph Scopo was the next best thing. Misunderstandings with the mob were rarely dealt with by referral to Fifth Avenue law firms.

"I could do it?" D'Ambrosi enquired hopefully.

Scopo repeated his question. "As a GC?"

"Yeah."

"You ain't doin' the concrete," declared Scopo.

"Sure I'm doin' the concrete. Why not?" asked D'Ambrosi.

"How much is the concrete?"

"Concrete's gotta be nothin'," said D'Ambrosi.

Scopo wasn't going to let him get away that easily. "How much?"

D'Ambrosi tried to cover his tracks. "What could concrete be, seven, eight, nine . . . ?"

Scopo could see he was trying to bullshit him. "The job's $200 million!"

"Everything's upstairs, everything's above," started D'Ambrosi with a tone of righteous indignation. "All glass, mirror, chromes . . ."

Scopo made some quick calculations in his head. "But if the job's $200 million the concrete's gotta be $12 million."

D'Ambrosi knew the game was up. He was as good as anyone when it came to bullshit, but there were some people who didn't buy it. There were others who, if they found out, could make your life real uncomfortable. Ralph Scopo figured on both counts. "Yeah," sighed D'Ambrosi. "Why can't I do the concrete?"

Scopo spelled it out for him. "You can't do it. Over two million you can't do it. It's under two million, hey me! I tell you go ahead and do it."

D'Ambrosi wasn't going to admit defeat, not yet. "Who do I gotta see? Tell me who I gotta go see?"

Scopo knew it was crazy to even think about it. But like a patient club secretary explaining to the unwanted guest why he was never going to become a member, Scopo wearily spelled it out. "You gotta see every Family. And they're gonna tell you 'no.' So don't even bother."

Sal D'Ambrosi still wasn't going to give up. "If Tommy goes to talk to them?"

Scopo rolled his eyeballs. "They'll tell you no. No matter who talks. I know they'll tell you no. I went through this not once, a hundred times. I can't get it for myself! How could I get it for somebody else?"

D'Ambrosi thought of a different tack. "What'd happen if they give me a million at a time?"

Scopo tells him to forget it. D'Ambrosi knows when he's beaten; he switches the conversation to another job. Another deal. This time it's a development at La Guardia Airport, a new terminal for one of the airlines.

"They're looking to extend Gate One, to make another building out of it. And, uh, I could, we could, I could do it all at once or I could do it in pieces. What would you suggest?"

Scopo lays it on the line. "First of all the job costs you two points."

"Why two points?" asks D'Ambrosi.

"That's what they pay. Anything over two million. All the guys in the Club got so much out, pay two points."

"Uh, huh," says D'Ambrosi.

"So I put two points into the job. You see that's without union, without nothin'. That's what I say, you gotta put it ahead of time."

"Yeah, I know what you're saying," says D'Ambrosi.

"Then you got nothing, that's just for the job," replied Scopo. "Out here I think I could do something for you."

"Should I go to talk to Tommy?" inquired D'Ambrosi.

"Ain't gonna do you no good," explained Scopo patiently. "They're gonna come back to me."

Ralph Scopo was the point man, as he helpfully explained to the listening FBI agents, the chosen representative of the heads of the Families who ran "the Club."

There was scarcely a commodity or service in the city of New York which the mob didn't take a cut of along the way. The Big Apple was rotten to the core. Restaurants, clubs, drugs, gambling, prostitution, Fulton Fish Market, the garment center, loan-sharking, the unions, the docks, the meat market and concrete.

The stranglehold on the construction business had developed naturally from Mafia control of the labor unions. Now it was one of their most lucrative rackets and almost legitimate. Any construction project where the cement supply was worth more than two million dollars—you had to deal with the Mafia. As Ralphie Scopo had reminded D'Ambrosi, "Anything over two million, the guys in the club got so much out, pay two points."

Ralph Scopo was a bull of a man with thickset shoulders, short neck and a broad back; a physique which spoke of years of hard toil in the construction yard, heavy drinking in the dock-front bars and murderous brawls on the street. Not a man to be reckoned with lightly—but despite his powerful appearance Ralph Scopo would rarely have to resort to physical violence. His power was derived from the highest levels of organized crime in America: the Commission. Scopo's other title was President of the Concrete Workers' District Council in New York City. As an expression of their gratitude for his devotion to duty his fellow workers had awarded him an annual salary of $104,000 and a few little extras amounting to another $200,000 a year—plus the Cadillac.

Anyone driving through the streets of Manhattan could admire the gleaming skyscrapers which soared ever higher. But few who appreciated the architecture also realized that they were staring at expensive symbols of the deep roots of

Mafia power in Manhattan. Whether it was a brand new hotel like the gleaming chrome and glass Marriot Hotel Marquis, the Times Square showcase of the Marriot Hotels group, or a terminal building for Delta airlines out at La Guardia Airport, there were rich rewards on every multi-million dollar contract in New York City for Scopo, his union cronies and the Mafia Families.

By the 1980s it was such an accepted practice that no one even balked at the prospect of having to pay their dues. It was like an official tax. If somebody from out of town did not know the score, then the general contractor in charge of the project would tip them off. The innocent party would be sent down to talk to Ralph Scopo. If there were ever any problems, Ralph would invite his reluctant guest out for a meal. The wiseguys sitting around the table in the Little Italy restaurant wouldn't have to say much. Mafia control of construction was institutionalized.

In order to break their grip, the FBI would have to adopt a concerted approach that would dismantle the hierarchy that regulated the extortion and imprison the corrupt union officials whose complicity made the whole thing possible. U.S. Attorney Giuliani had the idea that the RICO law could be used against an entire union in the same way that it could be developed against a Mafia Family.

All they needed was the evidence. Some of the tapes from the FBI's electronic eavesdropping enabled them to confront mobsters and their associates with such detailed knowledge of their criminal activities that it left them open-mouthed. Tommy Del Giorno had been shocked to hear the voices of his friends plotting his death. In other cases, the tapes provided such overwhelming evidence that the Mafi-oso was presented with a *fait accompli:* "Cooperate or face a lengthy prison sentence. It's up to you." After letting the wiseguy stew for a while, the FBI would offer the easy way out: "Work for us and we'll see what we can do for you." It usually worked. The degree of cooperation varied as did the quality of the intelligence but at best it provided law enforcement with a unique opportunity. The ultimate goal was to get an informant out on the street wearing a wire. In reality it amounted to the informant wearing a miniature tape recorder strapped under a shirt, usually on his back, with a tiny microphone hidden in a jacket sleeve or behind a lapel. A more sophisticated version existed in a combined microphone-transmitter. It was not always as reliable because the range was limited and the power pack was almost as bulky as the recorder. Nevertheless, a "live wire" was one of the most valuable assets in the battle against organized crime.

The FBI team investigating the Mafia's wholesale extortion of the New York concrete industry had acquired just such an informer. They were able to "run" their informer in much the same way as an espionage controller handled an agent inside enemy territory. Encounters and conversations could be directed to supplying the evidence that the agents needed for a successful prosecution. The supervising agent in charge of the investigation could even confer with assistant U.S. Attorneys from Giuliani's office to develop a strategy which would work in court.

While it made life easier for the prosecutors, it put enormous pressure on the informant. All the time he was wearing the wire he ran the risk of being found out. If caught in the act, he was liable to be killed on the spot. When his treachery was later revealed, as it would inevitably be in court, a murder contract and automatic death sentence would be the reward from the mob.

To protect their informants, the FBI could offer them a new identity and relocation to another part of the country. The Witness Protection Program had a very good record but not everyone was prepared for the total upheaval it involved.

By 1983 the FBI had succeeded in turning a top executive in the New York City construction industry. His position brought him into close contact with a figure that the FBI had in their sights for many years: Ralph Scopo, the "administrator" of the mob's multimillion-dollar building rackets. Scopo was not only a union president; he was also a fully made member of the Colombo Family. The investigation of Scopo would provide critical evidence for a RICO conviction. Ralph Scopo reported directly to the Commission and what was that if not a "Racketeering Influence

and Corrupt Organization"? Scopo was a big fish alright
and it would require a large net to catch him.

Scopo had been under surveillance for months. The FBI
knew all his favorite haunts, knowledge which had helped
them to plant the bug in the Skyway Motel. But Scopo
conducted most of his business deals in parking lots. How
the hell could you bug that? You could aim a directional
parabolic mike through the windshield but that was tricky
and unless you were close and had an uninterrupted line of
sight the sound quality was unreliable. It was just possible
to put a bug in the car but it would be extremely difficult
and would require weeks of planning. There was the risk of
being caught in the act or of the bug being discovered later.
Either way it could jeopardize the whole case.

That was where Stanley Sternchos came in. He could
wear the wire.

Queens municipal parking lot is a multistory car park. A
drab and shapeless building of fluted gray concrete, it concealed a bland American shopping center with piped mu-
zak and a fake Mexican restaurant. In good traffic it's ten
minutes drive from the center of Manhattan; normally it
takes an hour. Fortunately the FBI had an office in Queens.
Ralph Scopo had decided that the municipal parking lot
was the perfect meeting place.

Some of the techniques used by FBI surveillance teams
are the best in the world, rarely disclosed to the public, but
acquired over the years and handed down. Unlike other law
enforcement agencies the FBI has dedicated teams of men
and women who do nothing except surveillance. Scopo
thought the Queens parking lot provided him with perfect
cover. It also provided the FBI with the perfect opportunity.

Driving unobtrusive looking cars and adopting the cover
of innocent shoppers and pedestrians were two of the com-
monest tricks of FBI surveillance teams. Beat-up vans covered in graffiti driven by ponytailed hippies might attract
the attention of a passing traffic cop but would rarely be
suspected by a wiseguy. The modern Mafioso tended to
have a fatally flawed stereotype image of a cop or agent as a
man in a uniform, raincoat and hat or a three-piece suit.

For the FBI there were few better locations than a shopping center and a car park. Indeed, they were often used in training exercises. The agents could melt into the background as itinerant shoppers, disappear into a store, sit at an open cafe, and who was going to notice a car in a car park? But for Scopo it worked in reverse. He suspected everybody. Constantly looking over his shoulder, Scopo would always check out every car in his rearview mirror and because he used the route so frequently, he spotted anything unusual in an instant.

The agents, fully conscious of Scopo's persistent paranoia, took equally elaborate precautions. They often aborted an entire surveillance operation rather than run the risk of being noticed by their target. Being spotted by the subject you were trailing was the worst thing that could happen to an agent on surveillance duty—it was known as getting "burned."

At 8:55 A.M. on a cold, gray winter morning Ralph Scopo eased his black Cadillac round the corner of 59th Street and 92nd Avenue in Elmhurst, Queens, and took a right turn into the entrance of the municipal parking lot. Pausing momentarily to collect his ticket, he drove past a row of cars before finding a space.

Five minutes later another car drew up and parked alongside Scopo's Cadillac. The man inside was wearing a dark suit. Stanley Sternchos was the president of one of New York's largest construction companies. But his power and prestige counted for nothing without the say-so of the mob. He had joined the Club and was still paying the price. But now the debt had been called in.

When the FBI had cottoned on to the secret arrangements between New York's major construction companies and Ralph Scopo's wide-shouldered and thick-necked friends, they had lost little time in applying pressure to the weakest link in the chain—Stanley Sternchos. Now the businessman was risking his life and family to get enough evidence to put Ralphie Scopo behind bars for the rest of his life. The president of the New York City construction company had a miniature Uher tape recorder strapped to his back. Stanley Sternchos was wired.

The company president climbed out of his car and went over to the Cadillac. He eased himself into the passenger seat alongside the 224-pound frame of Ralph Scopo. Ralph favored wide-check shirts with the collar folded outside his suit jacket. It gave him a smart appearance while paying lip service to his position as the champion of the blue-collar workers in the construction trade.

"How ya doin'?" said Sternchos.

"What happened?" grunted Scopo, wasting no time with pleasantries. "You got any jobs?"

The businessman breathed a mental sigh of relief. It was easy with Scopo: all he wanted to talk about was business. And business as usual was money, and the more he brought in for the Colombo Family and the Club, the better for everyone. "It's a job on 44th Street—alright? For Manchurian and there's only one other bidder."

Scopo thought for a moment. "S&A?" he asked.

Sternchos nodded in agreement.

It could be a problem—"Fat Tony." Tony Salerno, the oldest and fattest Mafioso in Manhattan who bore an uncanny resemblance to The Joker in *Batman,* had a share in S&A. Unlike The Joker he didn't have much of a sense of humor. The initials stood for Salerno and Associates. As the head of the Genovese Family, Fat Tony presided over a powerful empire. Along with Paul Castellano, the aging Godfather of the Gambino Family, the two Mafiosi were the elder statesmen of organized crime. A fat squat little man, Fat Tony had a round face with a bulbous nose and bulging cheeks, two small darting eyes and a mouth permanently clamped in a snarl around a fat cigar. A brown Homburg covered his balding head and as his legs were weakening from old age he was often seen wielding a walking stick, shuffling down the sidewalk clutching it as if it was an offensive weapon. Old he might be but there was nothing weak about Fat Tony Salerno. His organization even had the grudging respect of the law enforcement community. Wiseguys from the Genovese Family were compared to graduates of Harvard Business School. More sophisticated, better informed and richer. "The Ivy Leaguers of organized crime," quipped one veteran agent.

Salerno and Associates may not have been in the *Fortune* Five Hundred but it was not a company to mess with. In addition it was the Commission that controlled all the companies involved in the concrete tenders and, as head of the Genovese Family, Salerno was on the Commission. Fat Tony was a key player all the way round and his membership in the Club meant there was little room for honest competition.

Sternchos, prompted by the FBI, was seeing if an exception could be made to the rule. Sternchos had thought it through. They had to be careful. "There's a three and a half million dollar price in there—right? I'm gonna take the job for two million eight ninety. They're gonna go back to S&A and tell S&A that they can't do the job because his price is too high. The building is not gonna go ahead. So they'll see if he is then gonna go down in his price—which he's not going to. At that point, they're gonna give me the job."

Scopo liked the idea. It was clean and simple. He knew the rules. If you wanted a contract you had to play by them and you had to pay off the wiseguys. You had to pay them respect and you had to pay them dollars—there was no argument. The problem with this deal was that S&A had been "allocated" the job a year ago. Scopo had no particular brief for Fat Tony, who after all was the head of another Family and in many ways a rival, but he was the administrator of a system. There were rules and standards to uphold.

"That's when we have a problem," said Scopo. "That job was given to him about a year ago. Eight months ago. Fuck him, we'll fight it out. The only thing I'm afraid of is, uh, if it comes to a point where, you know, this guy could have got the job for three million and a half, because of Technical, it's two eight, now they're gonna hold us responsible for the difference if we don't do the job. That's the only thing I'm worried about. It becomes a lot of money. That's the big problem."

Sternchos gently suggested bringing in the other Club members. "Well, let me ask you something. I mean a lot, uh, in the sense of winning, probably depends on, you know, a few levels above you. I know that . . ."

Scopo was quick to cut him off. "No."

"No?"

"No," he repeated. "It's rules and regulations and that's it. That's it. Regardless of what level you are, you gotta follow those rules and regulations."

Later on the two men were joined in the Cadillac by Richard Forcino, an associate of Sternchos who was managing various different construction deals. The deal on 44th Street involved 175,000 square feet. Although Sternchos was preparing to put in a lower bid, it looked as if Fat Tony's company could pull rank.

"So what would end up happening?" inquired the businessman. "We would end up finishing the job, or we'd have to give them a certain amount of money. Is that what would happen?"

"No," said Scopo unhelpfully.

"Or we'd just be told to get off the job?"

"No. If you're told to get off the job and he [S&A] has to take the job for your two eight, they're gonna look for the difference between two eight and three five from you because they're gonna say they had the job for three five until you interfered with it. If you don't do the job, or you don't do what you're doin', do they get it for three five?"

What Scopo was getting at was that S&A would have to lower their tender by $700,000 to match Sternchos's quote and win the contract. If they were forced to do that they would be looking to make up the shortfall by squeezing Sternchos's company for the difference.

The mob ensured that bids were agreed in advance to avoid the danger of a competitive tendering process; in this instance market forces had reasserted themselves—but at a price. The alternative was for Sternchos to withdraw his bid, thus leaving the field clear to S&A. "Yeah," admitted the businessman, "the guy's gonna have no choice but to give it to them for three five."

Sternchos's companion, Richard Forcino, was loath to give away the contract. It would mean a loss of face, plus they had put in a very low bid on another building contract in Whitehall Street on which they risked losing money. They needed the 44th Street job to balance the books. Forcino laid it on the line for Scopo. "How the hell do you say, ah, 'We can't do the job now. We add this thing, I checked, I rechecked my figures and I can't do the job for that price.' I'm gonna look like a fuckin' asshole with the Manchurians, with the Millsteins, with the fuckin' Goodsteins, Kalikows, all the main guys, the fuckin' multi-millionaires. We can't do a job. I tell you. It's a shame. Stan, how about the Whitehall Street? The profit . . ."

"How much is Whitehall?" asked Scopo.

Forcino continued trying to work out if they could still make a profit by juggling the two contracts. "You say the profit on this is four hundred, but that compensates for the Whitehall Street. That's a low number you gave."

"Whitehall Street, I was fuckin' around with the numbers on Whitehall Street," replied his partner.

"I know that. So it's not . . ."

"We wanted to do a job . . ."

". . . it's not really four hundred thousand."

"So I had, you know, I had two million plus extras. It ended up to be two million six, okay?"

"Whitehall?" asked Scopo, not sure which deal they were now arguing about.

"Yeah," confirmed Sternchos.

"So that's what I'm sayin' now," added Forcino. "When you said four hundred thousand on this 44th Street job, it's not true. That covers the money on the Whitehall Street that you went very low on. So really, maybe it's what? Two hundred fifty thousand profit, if we did get it? That's, that's shit. We never had a job that we made, you know, now, I mean we make nothin'. We make fuckin' one hundred fifty, two hundred thousand and when the job is over, the rough part of it, then when you finish it up, you're lucky to make a hundred. And then by the time you collect your fuckin' money, which we still ain't collected . . . I don't know, I don't know how the fuck we do it!"

Stanley Sternchos was weighing up the options. "So you think there's a good possibility that they won't tell us just to get off the job?"

Ralph Scopo knew the answer to that one. "If they would tell you just get off the job, in other words, if we lose the beef and they say, 'Get off the job,' that's the end of it.

No problem. I woulda said, I would advise you, 'Go ahead, we got nothin' to lose.' "

"Yeah," said Sternchos, not entirely convinced.

"But if they tell you to get off the job and it's too late, where his price had to go down to the three fifty, I know there's gonna be a squawk about the money. They're gonna say here's a job where they were ready to get three and a half and only because of this beef, they had to do it for two eight. That's six hundred, seven hundred thousand difference."

"Hmm," Forcino corrected him, "six hundred and ten."

"Well, whatever . . ." said Scopo.

"Six hundred and ten," repeated Forcino. "A lot of fuckin' bread!"

"That's where I'm worried," agreed Scopo. "I'm not worried about losin' the beef and comin' to tell you: 'Hey, hey don't do the job.' It's the money part. You know, you know the old story, you hurt the guy in the pocket and that, that's where it really hurts him."

"Sure," agreed Forcino.

Sternchos hadn't given up yet. "Should I, you know, open this whole thing up to Manchurian?"

Manchurian was the lead company on the contract and would be paying the bill for the concrete.

"No, you can't," replied Scopo.

"You can't—he's a fuckin' nut," warned Forcino.

Scopo wasn't that easily intimidated. "They're all big."

"He's scared," said Sternchos, "He's scared of his own shadow."

"They're all big," repeated Scopo, unimpressed. "What do they do?"

"Well, they're not gonna do nothin', but you can't, you can't . . ."

It was no good telling someone like Ralph Scopo what he could or couldn't do. The shadowy power invested in his stocky frame was not something to be lightly challenged. While the businessmen in their boardrooms might feel emboldened to challenge the power of the Mafia, in the cold light of day they didn't stand a chance. As the companies had found to their cost, it was easier to go along with the system. The Mafia too had been quick to learn, it was to their advantage to become the system.

"They're all big," replied Scopo wearily, referring to the major construction corporations. "Let me tell you somethin'. These fuckin' guys got more to hide than what the Club has to hide!"

"No he's not giving it to us. He's not givin' it to us. He's the guy that called up, uh, Nick and told him that, uh, they were talking about giving me Whitehall Street and was it okay. Of course Nick said, 'Sure.' It wasn't his job."

"He don't care," said Scopo.

"So I mean he's scared of his shadow. He was at lunch yesterday . . ."

Scopo interrupted. "Who, Nick?"

". . . and he was saying, 'Is this gonna hurt me on my big job, up at 69th Street? Is it gonna hurt me here? Is this guy gonna . . . ?'"

"So, he's leery about giving it to you."

"'. . . crucify me or something like that?'" said Sternchos. "He's leery about it, sure, that's why he asked to go, that's why he asked to go, that's why he set up this whole scenario of going back to Nick. He thinks Nick's his . . ."

"The Godfather," interjected Forcino helpfully.

"He's the Godfather," said Sternchos, "Okay? You know . . ."

"That's good," grunted Scopo. "Let them all think that. So, speak now or forever hold your peace, Mr. Sternchos," said Scopo, eager to wrap up the deal on 44th Street. It was a case of either put up or shut up.

"Six hundred thousand?" said Sternchos. "What do I do? I don't have the $600,000. I don't have it."

Forcino was trying to think of a way out of the impasse. "Well, do you think a stupid thing to say to the guy is, 'Look, we'll do it for two million nine, okay? Or two million eight ninety,' whatever the fuck it is, 'two million nine, okay, we're gonna try and do it. If we get told we cannot do it, okay, that's it, you gotta go to the other guy and you give him the fuckin' money, three million five.' And that's it. He knows there's, uh, an operation goin' on, he knows . . ."

Scopo knew the answers. "He won't give it to you."

"Whaddya mean?" said Forcino, "He won't give us the . . ."

Scopo cut him off. "If he tells you that, he'll say, 'What am I lookin' for trouble?' Give it to the guy . . ."

"Give it to the other one?" asked Forcino.

Scopo gave him the answer that he would have given. "'I was gonna give it to him anyway,' that's really, his mind, that's how his mind will work. You can't tell a man that."

"That's right," said Forcino, realizing the logic of Scopo's argument. Whatever the sums involved, because of the nature of the people they were dealing with, it was not realistic to expect to have the power to tell them where to get off. Still less cancel a contract worth more than three million dollars. "Why should I have the fuckin' troubles?" concurred Forcino.

It was trouble they could do without. The rules and regulations ensured that everyone got their fair share from an unfair system. It was mob capitalism. The purest form. A license to make money and a license to eliminate the competition by threats, intimidation and ultimately violence. The Club was nothing more than a crude variation of capitalism. The cartel operating in the construction business worked on exactly the same price-fixing principles of monopoly supply that had been used in other areas of the American economy—notably the airlines and the oil companies. In both cases, secret agreements had been struck to eliminate the possibility of outside competition—so why shouldn't the Mafia do likewise? In common with any powerful commercial sector, they realized the value of a captive market. First, they could guarantee they would get the contracts and second, they could dictate the price for their services in the sure knowledge that there would be no other competitors. By controlling the supply of concrete, the raw material, the five Families had a stranglehold over the entire business. Without concrete there were no skyscrapers, without the mob there were no laborers, without laborers there was no building.

With the ability to stop work on any site in Manhattan

and incur huge and costly delays on multimillion dollar projects, the Mafia, through their representative, Ralph Scopo, were capable of wielding immense power. Total control of the means of supply allowed them to dictate the terms of any contract. Whether it was heroin or concrete the same rules applied. The Families were doing no more than supplying public demand. Monopoly supply allowed them to extract a price from the public which bore little relation to the normal mechanisms of a free market economy. The mob had learned the lessons of the American Dream and had turned it into a nightmare.

The first generation Mafiosi were justifiably proud of their achievement. Like other immigrant groups, they had arrived, established themselves and carved out a niche in the commercial jungle of the American economy. It was not surprising that many now saw themselves as legitimate businessmen. They wanted to be liked and they liked to be wanted.

Just as it became the fashion for American tycoons to write their biographies of management success, so it became acceptable for first generation Mafia Godfathers to describe in glowing terms their economic struggle for survival—reflecting as it did the identical virtues of independence, raw ambition, naked greed and ultimate success. Ironically, this perception of the Mafia ethic, as something worthy of respect, merely strengthened the resolve of those who had already embarked on an unprecedented crackdown on the leaders of organized crime in America. It was a myth which enraged another Italian-American: the United States Attorney for the Southern District of Manhattan, a district which gave Rudy Giuliani jurisdiction over the headquarters of the American Mafia.

Joe Bonanno sought to perpetuate the myth in his 1983 biography, *A Man of Honor.* The title alone was enough to enrage Giuliani who was furious that a respectable New York publisher should bring out a book written by a vicious killer masquerading as a Sicilian gentleman.

For his part, Bonanno saw no reason to hide the peculiar practices of the "Honored Society." In his mind they glorified the same virtues which had long been worshiped in

America: hard work, survival and wealth—the driving force of the immigrant ethic in the New World. As "A Man of Respect" who had reached the pinnacle of his profession, Bonanno saw nothing wrong in writing down the rules and regulations of the "Honored Society." To Bonanno, the book was in the same genre as the best-selling autobiographies of America's modern pioneer capitalists.

The U.S. Attorney's office in the Southern District of Manhattan took a different view.

Ken Caruso, a young Assistant U.S. Attorney, recalls going into his boss's office to find him hunched over a document making intense notes. Caruso looked closer and noticed it was not a legal tome—Giuliani was wading through Bonanno's book scoring passages with a red marker.

"Looks like an interesting book—what are you doing?" asked a puzzled Caruso.

"If he can write about it, we can prosecute him for it," replied Giuliani, hardly looking up from the offending volume. The U.S. Attorney, driven by political ambition and a fierce moral fervor that was equally outraged by corruption in Wall Street and the crimes of the Mafia, was true to his word. There was poetic justice in using the book as part of the crusade against organized crime.

For anyone who has seen *The Untouchables* Rudy Giuliani looks the part: thin, ascetic face, long aquiline nose and close-cropped black hair that Eliot Ness would have been proud of. In manner and appearance there is something of the Jesuit about Giuliani, which is no coincidence as he once seriously contemplated the priesthood. In an interview with the author, he elaborated on his code of conduct.

"I did not represent and would not have represented organized crime people and drug people, basically just because of my own feelings about them and attitudes. Although I agree wholeheartedly that they are entitled to a defense and they should get the best defense that they can buy, I just couldn't find within my own set of ethics and rules the ability to say I'm going to represent organized criminals and drug dealers for profit. I would have felt that I was selling some of myself if I got paid huge sums of money for representing them. I guess maybe at the core I've always had a very strong feeling about what they do. I find criminals organizing to commit crimes considerably more offensive than individual criminals, because they can do many more dangerous things and they can bully and intimidate people. And the line between organized crime groups and terrorism is a very, very thin one. You can see with the Mafia in Italy how they've crossed that line and actually from the point of view of the loan-shark victim or the businessman whose business they've moved in on, or the poor immigrant who is being preyed on by an immigrant organized crime, like the Mafia used to be and some of these oriental groups are today, they might as well be in the clutches of the PLO or a terrorist group because they have no rights anymore. If they don't do what is in the interests of the organized crime bully that wants them to do something, they're going to get beaten, or their families are going to be hurt, or they're going to be killed or their business is going to be taken away.

"I think for a long time in the United States, in the Thirties, Forties, part of the Fifties, we didn't recognize the peril of organized crime. We didn't see it as a national priority—that we had to crush this emerging organization that was getting more and more powerful over the decades. And, in essence, we gave them immunity from aggressive federal investigation and prosecution and they took advantage of that and grew from a street organization to a somewhat better organized group to a corporate kind of enterprise. And that didn't happen magically and it didn't happen by mystical forces that we can't figure out, analyze and do something about. It happened because we let them do it, we ignored them, and we had people in federal government going around saying organized crime didn't exist."

The myth of the nonexistent Mafia reached a climax in the early Seventies. An Italian-American civil rights movement was shrewdly exploited by leading lights of the New York Mafia. Joe Colombo, the head of the Colombo Family, was one of the organizers. Ironically, he was gunned down near Central Park while addressing a crowd several thousand strong about civil rights.

"An awful lot of decent, innocent people were taken in by all that," recalls Giuliani, himself an Italian-American. "And politicians were intimidated by it. You had John Mitchell putting out a memo in the Justice Department in the Seventies saying you couldn't use the word 'Mafia,' directly related to Joe Colombo's efforts to ban the use of the word Mafia. That's incredible."

It was.

But little more incredible than the Director of the FBI, J. Edgar Hoover's point-blank refusal to acknowledge the existence of a nationwide criminal conspiracy. He would readily dismiss reports of the "Mafia." Hoover was much more excited by the worldwide threat of Communism and the ability of his beloved "G-men" to shoot it out with Public Enemy Number One. Too many public enemies might shatter the image. Fortunately, Hoover's successors in the mid-1980s harbored no such illusions. They fully supported Giuliani's crusade and were eager to clamber aboard. Much of the success was due to the FBI, but other agencies were also involved in the war against organized crime.

The New York State Organized Crime Task Force, or OCTF for short, was not as glamorous or as well known as its more celebrated counterpart with its mammoth headquarters in Washington, D.C., and field offices all over the country. Based out in White Plains, Westchester County, the OCTF was housed in a 19th-century post office building. Much of its equipment was ramshackle, its organization underfunded and its resources wholly inadequate to take on the might of the New York Mafia. But the Task Force had some of the sharpest brains in the business and some of the best technicians and agents ever to have joined the war against the mob. This little known agency was on the verge of one of the most successful coups ever against organized crime.

The impotence of the ordinary citizen in the face of the might of organized crime was an affront to the notion of a civilized society. What made it worse was that it had become widely accepted in many quarters of the law enforcement community and amongst the general public. A combination of ignorance and fear had led to an atmosphere of inertia which had induced apathy. As the wiseguys became an increasingly accepted part of the social fabric so did it become correspondingly more difficult to eradicate them.

To a large extent the Hollywood myth of the gangster as hero had become reality—though who is copying whom gets confusing. John Gotti, when head of New York City's Gambino Family and head of the Commission, was regularly fêted on the pages of the city's tabloid press—a real-life "Godfather" with designer suits, dark limousines and game-show host hairstyle.

The popular myth of the outsider, personified by the gangster as outlaw, has powerful roots in the folklore of modern America. The Wild West and the rip-roaring days of prohibition provided plenty of role models from Billy the Kid to Al Capone. The world of the 20th-century wiseguy is one of pump-action shotguns, tortured, mutilated corpses and drugs which leave havoc, devastation and misery in their wake. Yet almost without exception the aspiring mobster sees himself as the rightful heir to a romantic tradition where men with double-breasted suits and diamond rings hand out rolls of $20 bills to poverty-stricken neighborhood kids and hat-check girls while escorting beautiful women in evening dress to exotic nightclubs. The reality is different but it is the image which matters and it was one that the public and press alike are happy to share in. They are both willing accomplices in a total illusion. According to his best friend, John Gotti was getting over a thousand letters a week when he was waiting to go to trial in 1992!

The myth is nostalgia for a world that never really existed in the first place which is probably why it exerts such a powerful hold over the public imagination. Hoods like Gotti have every reason for perpetuating the image; prosecutors like Giuliani had an equally vested interest in destroying it.

"Government can't promise society a solution to the problem of crime. But it can and should be able to promise them a solution to the problem of organized groups that get together and operate" as Robert Kennedy said in the Fifties, "as an enemy within. As a Government, we should be able to crush organizations like that, people have the right to expect that of Government."

Part of the reason for Giuliani's driving conviction against organized crime, and one shared by a multitude of law enforcement agencies which took part in the crackdown against the mob in New York City, was the realization of missed opportunities in the past. Too many more missed opportunities held the all too real prospect of the Mafia becoming so powerful that it would become invincible. The hydra-headed monster that had become the Mafia in the United States only existed because it had been allowed to grow almost uninterrupted, partly because of outright corruption but mainly because of bureaucratic inertia. To Giuliani, that was far more dangerous.

4

THE CAR THAT TALKED

IT WAS ONE OF THOSE NIGHTS THAT NEW YORKERS DREAD. Gusting winds whipped across the city and torrential rain was pouring down. Most New Yorkers returning home that night took a yellow cab if they could find one or braved the overcrowded and steaming subway to get home. But there was one group of workers for whom the night's foul weather was a godsend. The driving wind and rain guaranteed that no one would stay outside for long.

For the Task Force agents sitting patiently inside their unmarked cars, it was ideal weather for the operation that they had been planning for six months. Their audacious mission was to put a concealed microphone inside the car used by one of the most powerful Mafia bosses in Manhattan.

In contrast to many of his colleagues, Tony "Ducks" Corallo, head of the Lucchese Family, had a certain amount of taste. His car for one. It was a black British Jaguar XJ6 with a walnut fascia and leather upholstery. Unlike the more vulgar stretch limousines and high performance German sedans, the Jaguar represented old money, style and understated power. Tony Corallo spent a lot of time in the car. It was the best way to do business. Corallo's business interests were spread around New York State, from Suffolk

County and Long Island through to downtown Manhattan. On some occasions Tony "Ducks" would be driven around all day and still have unfinished business.

Like any successful executive, Corallo had a driver. Salvatore Avellino was in his early forties and was a trusted companion of Corallo. He looked after the Jaguar and although only a soldier he ranked number three in the hierarchy of the Lucchese Family. It was accepted practice in the Mafia to have as one's driver one of your most trusted associates, particularly as knowledge of the boss's movements and whereabouts was closely guarded information, intelligence that would be dearly sought by enemies and law enforcement agencies alike. Having the ear of the boss was good for promotion prospects and guaranteed any mobster a great deal of respect from other members of the Family. Avellino was a business associate, driver, fixer, bodyguard and gangster.

His boss, Tony Corallo, prided himself on his personal security. It was one of the reasons he liked the car—inside he felt safe. It was one of the few places he could talk openly. And even if some agent did get lucky and followed them—so what? They could always shake them off. Tony "Ducks" Corallo thought he could spot a cop a mile away. It was a fatal misjudgment.

In the months they had spent in preparation, the agents from New York State's Organized Crime Task Force had realized that Avellino's routine was perfect for the operation they planned. He dutifully collected his boss every morning and spent the day and often the night driving the foul-mouthed Corallo around the city. His regular haunts were in Brooklyn, Queens and Manhattan. It was Avellino's job to drive his boss to an endless series of meetings and "sit-downs" in restaurants, seedy diners and mob social clubs.

Corallo's business interests ranged from the John F. Kennedy airport, where the Lucchese Family had a long-standing involvement in the import-export business through to 35th Street in the center of town, the heart of the garment district. Construction, shake-downs, loan-sharking, illegal gambling, hijacking, restaurants and garbage collection were just a few of the businesses that Corallo had to supervise on his daily rounds. There were countless others that the agents suspected he was attending to but without sitting in on the meetings or gaining a high-level informant, they could only guess what these might be.

Unlike his friend Fat Tony Salerno, Corallo never stayed put in one place for very long. While Salerno would hold court in the Palma Boys Social Club for hours on end, Corallo tended to avoid the clubs and bars that were Lucchese Family hangouts. It meant that placing a bug in a strategic location was out of the question.

It was a problem that the OCTF had pondered for a long time. Ronald Goldstock, the Director of the Organized Crime Task Force, had considered a number of options and dismissed them all. The Task Force was receiving intelligence from bugs in other locations about the Lucchese Family but it didn't add up to much. Evidence from other sources suggested that Tony Corallo was quietly consolidating his interests. Even more frustrating was Corallo's ability to maintain a remarkably low profile while constantly increasing his power and authority within the secret realms of the Mafia.

When the idea of putting a bug in the Jaguar was first raised nobody thought it could be done but Goldstock thought it was worth a try. Some of the Task Force detectives thought Goldstock was losing his touch.

Tall, thin and balding with a dry sense of humor, Ronald Goldstock looks and sounds more like a university lecturer than a law enforcement executive. In fact he was a familiar face on the lecture circuit of organized crime conferences and well known for lecturing his audience on the finer points of the hierarchical structure of organized crime in America. He liked to compare the structure and power of the five Families and the Commission to the United Nations.

But crazy though it seemed, there was an impeccable logic to Goldstock's notion. Maybe it wasn't off the wall. After all the car was where Tony "Ducks" spent most of his time and did most of his talking. The more the OCTF thought about it the more attractive the proposition began to appear. Even the ultracautious Corallo would never suspect that his car was bugged. The only problem was how and where.

On the night of March 18, 1983, the Private Sanitation Industry Association of Nassau-Suffolk Counties held its fourth annual dinner dance in the elegant surroundings of the Huntington Town House on Jericho Turnpike. A mock Victorian building with a red brick and white wood façade, the town house was particularly proud of its spiral staircase enclosed by a semicircular, two-story window frame. The Huntington Town House specialized in hosting dinner dances and business conventions for local citizens. It was conveniently situated off the main road and offered ample car parking facilities in its own grounds with valet parking. The annual festivities of the Garbage Association was the perfect opportunity. The Lucchese Family had extensive interests in garbage disposal and Salvatore Avellino was scheduled to attend the ceremony as a guest of honor.

Dick Tennien, a veteran OCTF agent, was keeping a lookout for the Jaguar; luckily there weren't too many of them around. Working with him was Jim Stroh, a technician whose job was to break into mob hangouts and install microphones. It was a hazardous line of business and Stroh had had a few close shaves but so far had never been caught in the act. He hoped tonight wouldn't break his run of luck.

Until the Jaguar was safely parked there was little they could do except wait, watch and listen. Their van was parked on the approach road which ran parallel to the Huntington Town House car park. The two agents peered through the rain at the Huntington entrance, mentally rehearsing the procedure they had been practicing for the last few months. They watched guests arriving and being ushered into reception. Outside, Town House valets stood by ready to park the cars, a security jeep driving behind them to ferry the attendant back to the entrance to pick up the next car. The guests could be seen as they climbed up a spiral staircase leading to the first floor where the reception was being held. Long Island politicians, top union representatives, carters, local businessmen, public officials and mobsters were disgorged from their cars and limousines and could be seen sipping their cocktails and nibbling on their hors d'oeuvres. Tennien and Stroh watched intently as the black Jaguar XJ6 pulled up at the entrance, its heavy tires swishing through the rivers of rain running across the tarmac. They breathed a sigh of relief as they saw Mr. and Mrs. Salvatore Avellino step out under the umbrella of the attendant before disappearing into the welcoming warmth.

The only sound discernible apart from the noise of the driving rain was the faint crackle of a small, handheld walkie-talkie. There were three unmarked backup cars parked within a quarter of a mile. It was their job to keep the parking lot and the Town House under constant surveillance. Tennien and Stroh had spent hours practicing their mission on an identical Jaguar inside a State police garage to prepare themselves for tonight's operation.

It had been just over a week since they had learned of Avellino's plans to make a guest appearance at tonight's reception. It looked to be the best chance that they were going to get. Once they had heard of the location, Tennien and Stroh had made several visits to memorize the layout of the Town House and its parking lot. The golden opportunity lay in the knowledge that while Mr. and Mrs. Avellino were inside paying their respects to senior officials of the carting industry, their car would be left unattended outside.

From their position the agents could observe the spot where the Jaguar was parked—all they then had to do was to avoid the Town House security patrols that circled the parking lot. Torrential rain and gale-force winds would give them cover and help deter any security guard from walking round the parking lot. Even before the Avellinos arrived, the OCTF agents noticed that the security detail preferred to stay by the entrance or just inside the hallway.

But there was an unexpected problem. Dick Tennien and Jim Stroh had noticed the presence of several other cars. Some were on the outside road while others were on the parking lot itself. There were people sitting inside who were clearly keeping a watch on the arriving guests. Using the walkie-talkie a message was sent to Fred Rayano, who was in charge of the operation. Rayano carefully approached each car to find out who they were, praying that none of them were connected to Avellino.

To Rayano's intense relief, it turned out that the vehicles belonged to rival law enforcement agencies: the FBI, the local Suffolk County police and even agents from the Federal Probation Service. The Organized Crime Task Force had deliberately not informed any other law enforcement agency of their plan for fear of a leak. Equally they knew that tonight's gathering was likely to attract attention from other agencies. Rayano went up to the vehicles, quickly identified himself and explained their plans. He pleaded with his colleagues not to jeopardize their operation. To their credit, any interagency rivalry was put aside for the evening and they agreed to back off. Rayano relayed the news on the radio handset to a relieved Tennien and Stroh.

By now most of the guests had arrived, their cars had been parked and the reception was in full swing. The agents waited for the next security patrol, a cursory drive round the parking lot by one of the Town House guards.

The guard drove his jeep down to the parking lot. Then, to their alarm, they saw the man stop and get out right alongside where the Jaguar was parked. Perhaps he had been dispatched by Avellino to watch over the car for the evening. It had always been a possibility that the Jaguar wouldn't be left unattended, in which case they could kiss the whole operation goodbye.

The guard made his way to another car near the Jaguar. It was his own—he was just fetching something out of it. The agents breathed a collective sigh of relief, realizing that if they'd launched their mission just a few minutes earlier they would have been caught red-handed. The guard got back in his jeep. They watched him return to the entrance where he jumped out and opted for the warmth of the lobby.

This was the moment they'd been waiting for. The surveillance van drove slowly down the road past the Huntington Town House and stopped parallel with the fence that cordoned off the parking lot. Dick Tennien and Jim Stroh took a deep breath, leapt out of the van and expertly scaled the iron post fence surrounding the property. Dressed in dark clothes and carrying a tool kit bag which contained the microphone and the instruments needed to fit it, they ran half-crouched into the wind and rain towards the black XJ6. The Jaguar was parked four rows in from the section nearest the fence and was surrounded by other cars that brought the visiting dignitaries to that night's Garbage Association festivities. The valet parking facility meant that the car doors were unlocked with the keys left in the ignition for easy access later on when the function had finished. Stroh silently opened the Jaguar door and crouched down in the front while Dick Tennien moved into the backseat. Stroh's hand reached instinctively for the catch recessed into the front door which triggered the front interior light. Stroh passed his tool kit to Tennien in the back, who then handed over the screwdrivers and pliers that his colleague would need. In addition, Dick Tennien carried a pocket flashlight and his radio handset to communicate their progress to the backup cars. He knew they could only use it sparingly for fear of any intercepts by passing police cars or even a passing Mafioso tuned into the right frequency.

In their rehearsals, Jim Stroh had worked out that the best place for the microphone was behind the dashboard. It was the least obtrusive position and by being placed in the center of the car would be ideally situated to pick up the conversations of both the driver and his passenger, Salvatore Avellino and Tony Corallo. It was also the best position to minimize external interference from within the car and to provide the strongest transmission to the relay vehicle which would have to trail the Jaguar to pick up the radio signal from the microphone transmitter. But to get it in place, Jim Stroh had to remove the leather padding which was secured to the top of the dashboard.

The mechanics of the operation had been helpfully explained to them by a cooperative Jaguar dealer in Manhattan. They had approached him on the pretext that they had to strip search a car which was carrying drugs. The cooperative car dealer had shown them how to loosen two screws at each end of the dashboard next to the driver's and passenger's door. The only problem was that in order to access the screws they had to open each door in turn. While Stroh was doing this, Tennien had to make sure that he held the door light switch down so as not to turn on the overhead light which might fatally illuminate his colleague in the front. If Avellino wandered out and caught them, the whole operation would have to be aborted. Even though they had obtained Court authority for placing the hidden mike, Avellino would have been perfectly within his rights to challenge the two men whom he could claim he mistook for car thieves. Suppose he was carrying a gun? It was a train of thought the Task Force agents didn't like to follow. They ran similar risks of being detected by the Huntington's own security patrols. The only thing to do was to get in and out as quickly and as unobtrusively as possible.

Fred Rayano in the backup car was getting anxious. He picked up his walkie-talkie. "Are you done yet?"

Stroh looked at his partner and ignored the interruption. Their best time in their practice sessions had been 20 minutes. But that had been inside a warm and dry police garage. Outside in the cold and the dark and getting soaking wet it was a different story.

Deftly unscrewing the cover, Jim Stroh lifted the padded section of the front dashboard and rested it on his lap. He then leaned forward, shining a small torch with his left hand, and unscrewed the map light from the center panel. Stroh pulled the map light socket out and, using a small piece of chewing gum, stuck the microphone with its miniature transmitter in the recess.

The rain was still coming down in torrents, beating against the roof of the car and blustering through the side doors when Stroh held them open to unscrew the dash. Still, that was something they could worry about later. Stroh checked the three wires. One came from the bug, another was wired to the 12-volt connection while the third was a ground wire. Then they informed Fred Rayano that the operation was finished. Tennien and Stroh waited for what seemed like an eternity before word came back from the control van that they were receiving them loud and clear—not from the walkie-talkie but from the bug they had just installed. It worked!

Just then a security patrol jeep came squelching past

through puddles of water. The agents ducked low. The jeep drove round the parking lot and doubled back to the reception area.

Jim Stroh carefully replaced the leather-padded dashboard, while both he and Tennien looked the car over to ensure they had not dropped any wire clippings or anything else that might tip off Avellino or Corallo that someone had got inside. They then carefully wiped the rain off the leather upholstery with paper towels. Water had been blown in by the wind every time they had opened one of the doors to remove the dashboard cover. Fortunately for them, the car had been immaculately maintained, and there was no telltale dust which might have left a line or a smear from their frantic wiping.

Tennien and Stroh silently closed the car's doors, checked that there were no security patrols in the vicinity, and as swiftly and silently as they had arrived they ran bent against the rain and wind until they reached the fence which they jumped.

Within seconds they were back inside the control van, a safe and dry haven crammed with electronic surveillance equipment, a mobile tracking device, cell-net telephone, broadcast-quality recording equipment and, most important of all, a low-frequency transmitter which would ultimately relay the words of a real-life Godfather to a jury in Manhattan. The most sophisticated electronics technology of the 20th century would give one of the Mafia's most powerful bosses the unrivaled license to hang himself with his own words.

The operation had taken an agonizing 45 minutes. Eventually Tony Corallo would go down for more than a hundred years. Not bad for one night's work—it was even worth getting soaked to the skin.

Tony "Ducks" Corallo didn't look like a Godfather. He looked more like a grandfather. Corallo was in his seventies, running to fat and had failing eyesight. He was an old man with gray hair and black-framed spectacles who favored loose fitting and comfortable cardigans rather than a

formal business suit. Appearances, as always, were decep-
tive. On the inside Corallo was a foul-mouthed, vicious and
aging Mafioso, as capable of murder and violence as any
street hood. It was just that his elevated position in the
Mafia hierarchy meant that he no longer had to dirty his
hands by performing such tasks himself. As head of the
Lucchese Family and with a seat on the Commission, such
activities were beneath his dignity.

If the car bug worked it could provide the agents with a
ringside seat at the inner council of the New York Mafia.
But much to their frustration the agents had to wait almost
a week to test its effectiveness. The agents had been driving
past Avellino's house and garage every morning to see if
they could pick anything up and although the bug was
working they hadn't yet received any conversations. "They
tested it with a small portable receiver," recalls Stroh.
"They were still getting a signal but they didn't get any
conversations." Then, one morning, the agents followed
Avellino in the Jaguar to Tony Corallo's mansion estate.

The size of the bug meant that a surveillance car had to
stay within a certain radius of the Jaguar. The microphone
inside the Jaguar's map socket was attached to a low-
powered, one-watt transmitter. The success of the system
involved picking up the broadcast signal and then boosting
it so it could be received by the van following at a greater
distance where it could be recorded. "The whole device
worked off the 12-volt system of the vehicle. The one-watt
transmitter was sufficient for intercepting the conversation
inside the vehicle, depending upon the locality you're in—
maybe up to a quarter of a mile or as close as maybe a car
length depending on where you are at the time. We were
able to use a repeater device located in a surveillance vehicle and by picking up the one-watt signal we were able to
boost it up to perhaps one or four watts which gave us a
wider range of intercepts and of course that was done to
avoid being seen. Most of the time sitting in the van and
during the first several weeks of the surveillance, the major-
ity of the intercepting, we were able to see the vehicle from
the van and the people in it kept talking. Although we used
the repeater vehicle, it wasn't used that extensively. We

were unable to use it, for instance, in certain sections of Long Island because it had a possibility of being picked up by local police bands."

To keep track of Corallo and Avellino, the Task Force sometimes needed as many as six vehicles. Even so there were several occasions when they would lose their quarry. The procedure would then be to use a radio tracking system which could home in on the transmitter signal and pinpoint the Jaguar's position. As the surveillance stretched from weeks into months, Tennien and Stroh's familiarity with the Godfather's routine enabled them to make pretty good guesses as to where he might be going but there were inevitable occasions when they would lose the car.

"Usually by having listened to the conversations we had a general idea where the vehicle was going to go and what I would do was try to send a car on an alternate route, perhaps a quicker route, to wait and let us know if in fact the vehicle did go that way. Of course what we would have to do is put all our marbles in one basket because we would be depending on those cars going to those locations and if he didn't go there then of course it would be impossible to find him again. That happened on rare occasions—we lost them. But by and large there were very few days we actually lost them for any period of time."

There were times, especially driving through the gridlocked traffic jams of New York City, when Tennien and Stroh lost sight of the Jaguar. One problem was the British car was very low on the ground whereas the van they were driving was quite high. Sometimes they just couldn't see the Jaguar in front of them. Toll booths were another problem. The lines were inevitably long and if the van was too many cars behind they stood a good chance of losing their prey at the other end of the tunnel. On one occasion going through the midtown tunnel into Manhattan, the agents were stuck behind a large truck with the other surveillance cars backed up behind them. Unless they acted quickly, they would lose Corallo. At the last moment the van changed lanes to jump the queue, risking the oncoming traffic and screeched to a halt in front of a startled toll booth operator. Before he could call the cops the agents

quickly flashed their ID at the attendant and drove dangerously fast through the tunnel hoping they would catch up in
time to work out which route the Jaguar would take at the
other end. They just made it in time.

There were several hair-raising car chases when the van
would suddenly mount the sidewalk or turn down a narrow
one-way street traveling at high speed in the wrong direction and avoiding the trucks parked on each side by centi-
meters.

They knew that Corallo would sometimes suspect that
he was being followed but they also knew they could over-
hear him voicing his suspicions. Their tracking equipment
meant they could always drop back if he was getting too
suspicious and by frequently changing the other backup
cars there would be little danger of either Avellino or
Corallo becoming familiar with their tail.

Day in and day out, sometimes working 18-hour days,
which would begin at seven in the morning with Avellino
picking up his boss from his home and which might end in
a restaurant or a social club in Manhattan in the small
hours, the Task Force team developed something like a
sixth sense for knowing how far they could go before risking getting "burned."

In one conversation they picked up from the Jaguar,
Corallo and Avellino boasted of their skill in spotting the
cars that would follow them. "They described vehicles that
they had seen driving down the streets they live on, that
perhaps were surveillance vehicles. They would imagine
seeing vehicles during the time we did the surveillance—
but they weren't us! When they described them they were
no one that was in the surveillance. As a matter of fact on
one particular day, when I think we had four vehicles for
about eight hours following them around, Mr. Avellino
made a comment to Mr. Corallo that if they have followed
us today they are geniuses. And we had been with them all
day with four vehicles!"

Today Tony "Ducks" Corallo was angry. The object of
his annoyance was an article that he had read in the *New
York Times*. The paper had run a piece on organized crime
and the five New York Families.

Corallo grunted and cursed the press—he had been particularly incensed by the fact that the reporter had correctly identified the names and titles of the top members of the Lucchese Family, including Salvatore "Tom Mix" Santoro, his underboss. Although it was fairly common knowledge in law enforcement circles and among informed journalists, Corallo liked to think it was secret. He asked Avellino if he had read the offending article. Avellino, it turned out, was not a *New York Times* reader. He asked his boss what was in it.

Tony "Ducks" Corallo told him. "Castellano, the junk business, that we're in the junk business and all that shit. Like Tom was the underboss, the consigliere is the other guy and all that shit. I hope we didn't make a fuck up. I hope there's nobody that we took in the last shot. Fuck 'em—they know what they got."

Corallo's business had to be kept underground and when it emerged into the light of day through the press, Corallo knew it could generate increased police activity. He wasn't called "Ducks" for nothing; he had earned his nickname by bobbing and weaving out of trouble, frequently "ducking" subpoenas. Part of the strategy for his success was his realization of the value of secrecy and his avoidance of "cocksuckers" who might bring on the heat, attract surveillance, or worse, the press.

"I like to be by myself," confided Corallo. "Misery loves company, a lot of cocksuckers—they bring them to you. I know, I remember when they brought them to Paulie, him and a few others. The guy says, 'Why did you bring me?' He says, 'They follow, they follow, so what?' When they went in the club, you hear? They went in the club then they called up the patrol wagon and picked everybody up. Tony the Sheik and somebody else who worked with him in Brooklyn says, 'So what, they followed us, but we only come to this club.' They goin' in the club alright. They called up the patrol wagon to pick everybody up."

"Pay 'em off!" grunted Avellino from behind the wheel.

Corallo was not convinced that bribing the cops was the answer. "That's what you contend with, a lot of fucking waste. Today is wasted. Now I couldn't be any fucking plainer than I was with some of these guys, 'cause I don't want nobody fuckin' around with anybody fucking with junk. They gotta be killed. That's all. Fuck this shit. They look forwards over here to us. What do they think they do? Christ sakes!''

Avellino thought for a moment. "Sure this is the whole fuckin' problem—the junk. They don't care about the gambling and all that other bullshit. They never did. It's the money . . ."

"It's just the fucking junk," agreed his boss.

Avellino continued his train of thought. In fact, there was a lot of truth behind what he was saying. Drugs had brought a lot more heat down on the mob, not least because in 1982 the FBI had been given jurisdiction over narcotics. "That's where all the appropriation of the money is though . . ." said Avellino.

"We're not involved," added Corallo.

"I know, but the only way they could get money and keep their jobs going is they need the appropriations from the Government and the only way they can get the appropriation is on junk. They can't get appropriations on gambling and all this other shit. Big money is what I'm talking about: millions and billions. You heard D'Amato [the New York Senator] the other day: 'We gotta put more prosecutors on, we gotta put more of this on,' you know. Only he didn't say, 'To eliminate organized crime.' He says, 'To eliminate organized crime in the NARCOTICS business, in the HEROIN business.' He didn't say nothin' about in gambling and unions. He just says, 'Narcotics.' That's where they appropriate all of these millions.''

Corallo was still thinking about his last remark. "You think they know we're not in it?"

"Right," said Avellino, trying to reassure his boss.

Corallo was relieved. For once he wanted to believe in the powers of law and order. "They know who's in it."

"They know," agreed Avellino.

Corallo began to warm to his subject. "Now, of course, you cannot be in the narcotics business and put it on your fucking stomach. You can't hide it. You gotta be exposed to it, you gotta, you gotta go out on the street, you gotta sell it.

You can't be in the junk business without goin' in the fuckin' streets and selling this cocksucking shit. We should kill them. We should have some examples. Alright? Alright. We should make some examples. See other people ain't like us. They talk a lot, you see. That's like an informer to me, see? They think they know what they're doing when they go and talk to lawyers and stuff. Say we'll kill the first cocksucker. You know we'll kill 'em. We'll kill anybody with us, anybody comes near us, you know, we'll kill 'em. Don't worry, that gets to their fucking ears. See." Whether Corallo was referring to a bullet in the head or the message getting through is unclear.

Avellino wanted to know more about the *New York Times* report. "In the paper the other day, they tried to link you into the junk too?"

"They say everybody's in the junk business," grunted Corallo. "Castellano—us."

"But they mentioned the names, huh?" asked Avellino.

"Yeah, yeah. The Family, the Family, our Family. Tom. Tom's the underboss . . . and believe me, I really stood out of everybody's joint and every place that they've ever seen. They coulda tossed a coin and just they had to be told not to be seen with me. They never seen me, you know?"

Avellino was keen to reinforce his boss's false sense of security. "Oh no? You know, usually they don't mention you."

"No, because I stay clear of all these things. I don't go to half of these places where all these guys hang out."

"This is new information?" asked Avellino, referring to the article.

"No, they had this type of information before," said Corallo dismissively.

"Yeah, yeah, they had you but they . . ."

"But they always left me out," interrupted Corallo.

"Yeah, right. Right! Right!" agreed Avellino, foolishly seeking to reassure his boss that he maintained some kind of invisibility just because he wasn't mentioned in every newspaper article that appeared about the mob.

"Because they don't see me downtown," boasted Tony "Ducks," letting slip what he believed to be the success of his low profile in the Mafia. "They don't see me too much now, they don't see me goin' and comin', goin' and comin'."

"And they're never mentioning Tom as the underboss either," surmised Avellino wrongly.

His boss corrected him. "Yeah, they got it."

Sal Avellino weighed up the implications. "See now they got it solid—for them to give the three top guys, they got it solid. Prior to this they never used to say Tom Mix, never would say him, they never would say Chris."

"Tom, Tom Santoro, ah, what's his name . . ." Corallo was having difficulty remembering exactly who was in his own Family.

"Chris?" suggested Avellino.

"Chris," murmured Tony "Ducks."

"The Family, the Family, the Family . . ."

Later on Avellino read the article and mentioned it again to his boss. "It said in that article, it says about Tony 'Ducks,' about how he controls the garment center; he controls the waste disposal business."

"Yeah, sure, didn't you know that?" joked Corallo.

". . . and the construction," continued Avellino.

"Yeah, but didn't you know that?" laughed Corallo.

" 'Course I know that," said Avellino, taking him seriously. "I know it because I'm with you, but not everybody else knows."

"Yeah, well they ain't supposed to know," quipped Corallo.

Avellino laughed at his boss's joke.

"I got the worst two: the garbage and ah . . ." The absentminded Mafia boss had temporarily forgotten exactly what he did control.

Avellino was quick to remind him. "You got the garbage, the garment center, unions and construction."

"Even construction," mused Corallo.

"And of course junk and everything else, you know. But see the article went on to say about the taking over of legitimate business."

Corallo was still amused. "I ain't got time to sleep at night, right?"

5

THE JUNK MEN

CORALLO'S ANGER AT THE "COCKSUCKERS" WHO DEALT
drugs was not based on any moral conviction about
the dangers of the trade. His sense of outrage was
motivated by his instinct for survival. His threat to murder
"anybody with us," any member of his own Family who
was dealing "junk," was meant to deter any of his soldiers
from being tempted by the quick and easy profits of the
heroin trade.

Tony "Ducks" Corallo and the other aging members of
the New York Commission had watched aghast as the
Reagan administration had declared war on drugs and
given the FBI jurisdiction over narcotics cases, in addition
to the Drug Enforcement Administration. It was bringing
additional heat on the New York Families. DEA and FBI
agents had discovered that the center of the network for the
Sicilian Mafia's heroin trade was a Family within a Family
in the heart of New York City.

In the early 1980s over a billion dollars of heroin was
crossing the Atlantic courtesy of the Sicilian Mafia. The
money, distribution and financial arrangements were all
centered in Manhattan. Whatever scruples the New York
bosses had about dealing in dope were patently not shared
by their cousins from Sicily. The economics of the heroin

trade outweighed any other considerations. The Sicilians were buying morphine base from Turkey for an average price of $7,000—depending on the size of the order. Using their own laboratories in Sicily, which could be set up in a public housing estate in the slums of Palermo, or in a converted garage in a luxury seaside villa, the Families could refine their own heroin. One kilo of 90 percent pure heroin would be worth $50,000 in Italy. In New York, the wholesale price for the same kilo was $200,000. The Sicilians were exporting to New York shipments of heroin which could weigh anything from a few kilos to over a hundred. One transaction could yield $20 million. The profit margin was in the region of 2,000 percent.

Tommaso Buscetta, known as "The Godfather of Two Worlds" for his dealings in South America and Italy, described how prevalent drug trafficking had become when he emerged from an Italian jail in 1979: "After I returned to Palermo, I noticed that all the members of the Cosa Nostra were incredibly well off and Stefano Bontate told me that it was because of the drug trafficking. He agreed with me in thinking that the drug trade would lead to the collapse of the Cosa Nostra. He said that in the beginning it had been Nunzio La Mattina's idea. They had begun to abandon tobacco smuggling around 1978, either because of the increased risks due to greater pressure from the police or because of internal arguments which had often caused important deals to fall through. As a smuggler, La Mattina had access to the sources of production and supply of the raw material for heroin production—he wanted to try his luck and succeeded in convincing the more prominent members of the Cosa Nostra."

La Mattina's luck ran out when he ran off with a suitcase containing more than a million dollars and was murdered.

Buscetta's friend, Stefano Bontate, known as "The Falcon," was not far off in his prediction about the effects of the trade on the Mafia. The huge profits from heroin intensified rivalry between different Families and led to a bloody war between the Corleonesi and the old guard of the Sicilian Mafia headed by "Men of Honor" like Bontate and

Buscetta. Stefano Bontate was cut down in a hail of bullets from a Kalashnikov on his 40th birthday as he was heading for his country estate outside Palermo. Buscetta escaped to Brazil where he watched powerless as the Family he had left behind in Sicily was decimated by the ruthless executioners of the Corleonesi. His moment of revenge came after his arrest and a failed suicide attempt when he became the highest ranking member of the Sicilian Mafia to betray the sacred oath of "Omerta"—the vow of silence before the threat of death.

Buscetta was flown to Italy where he was debriefed by Giovanni Falcone, the courageous Sicilian magistrate who was tragically murdered in a massive car bomb explosion in the summer of 1992. Buscetta provided an unprecedented breakdown of the organization of the Sicilian Mafia. He gave prosecutors from both Italy and America priceless information on the drug trade between the two countries. Eventually, realizing that they would never be able to protect him in Italy, they flew Buscetta to the United States in a military aircraft under tight security and amidst the utmost secrecy. On arrival he was driven at high speed to a secret U.S. Army base where he stayed until he could be moved to a safe house where he was protected by armed DEA bodyguards.

One of the most important confirmations that Buscetta was able to make for the U.S. authorities regarding their investigations was the interlocking nature of the Sicilian and American Mafia. It was a business relationship, complicated by intricate Family ties of blood, and it amounted to a secret Mafia Family in the heart of Manhattan. Most of its members dressed modestly, had respectable white-collar jobs, spoke broken English, if at all, and in less than a decade had dealt in more than a billion dollars of high-grade heroin. When the FBI discovered their existence they called them the Sicilian faction of the Bonanno Family. The wiseguys in New York were more dismissive—they called them "spics."

It was the Sicilians in New York who were supplying most of the drugs that Tony "Ducks" Corallo was so incensed about. Although both he and Paul Castellano, head of the Gambino Family, had strictly forbidden their Family members from dealing in narcotics, the temptation was too much for many Mafiosi. Corallo and Avellino were both correct when they had complained about the appropriations from the Government because of drugs. There was a certain amount of public tolerance for the accepted vices that the Mafia supplied, such as gambling and prostitution. But drugs were a different matter.

The whole issue threatened a civil war within the ranks of the New York mob. The Bonanno Family was ostracized by Corallo and Castellano. The head of the Bonanno Family found himself frozen out at important Commission meetings. While the Lucchese, Gambino, Genovese and Colombo Families were striving to consolidate their legitimate businesses, it was being jeopardized by the Bonannos.

Joe Bonanno had a lot to answer for. First of all his autobiography had enraged Giuliani, prompting him to redouble his efforts to bring Bonanno to justice, then the rump of his Family was threatening to bring down the full might of the forces of law and order because of their drug trafficking. For the current mob leaders the final straw was when the retired Godfather appeared on CBS Television's *60 Minutes* program boasting about his life in the Mafia to Mike Wallace.

With his aversion and loathing for all forms of press and publicity Corallo could not for the life of him understand why Bonanno would appear on prime-time television. Apart from anything else, the law of Omerta prohibited anyone speaking up about Cosa Nostra on pain of death.

Speaking in an almost incomprehensible Sicilian-American accent, old Joe Bonanno was shooting his mouth off by lamenting the passing of a golden era and praising the Family tradition of Italians such as himself. Despite the odd question from Mike Wallace about the violence and murder which had characterized such a way of life, the old man emerged virtually unscathed.

Driving through the center of the city, the surveillance team from the New York Organized Crime Task Force listened with amusement as the hierarchy of the Lucchese

Family discussed last night's TV. In the car was Lucchese underboss Salvatore "Tom Mix" Santoro and Sal Avellino.

"I was shocked," claimed Avellino. "What is he tryin' to prove? That he's a Man of Honor? He actually admitted that he has a Family, that he was the boss of a Family!"

"Right, right," agreed Santoro.

"Even though he says, 'This was my Family, I was like the Father,'" recalled Corallo's chauffeur.

"He's trying to get away from the image of a gangster," said Santoro.

Avellino agreed.

"He's trying to go back to, ah, like in Italy. See, when he says, 'My father taught me.'"

"Yeah."

"His father was a friend of ours in Italy," continued Santoro. "See, 'cause the town he come from when he came here. He's full of shit, 'cause I know he was a phony. Like he says he ain't never been in narcotics, he's full of shit. He was makin' piles of money, ah, what's his name was in the junk business."

"They were in the junk business and they were partners like with him," added Avellino. "Now there's gonna be a part two."

"Yeah?" replied Santoro.

Avellino remembered the end of the broadcast: "Mike Wallace says, 'We'll continue about his kidnapping.'"

"This cocksucker," said Santoro contemptuously. "What's he gonna make, this cocksucker? You know how much money he's gonna make now, his book?"

"Is it out already?" inquired Avellino. "I knew that they were writing it."

"Yeah, it's coming out, it's coming out. Because he's quoting from the book."

"Mike Wallace's questions were from the book," recalled Avellino. "About killing people."

"Right, right," said Santoro. "Now right, now what's gonna happen? Hollywood is gonna come along . . ."

"And make a movie . . ." continued Avellino.

"Make a movie and this guy's gonna be like the technical director. Forget about it, this cocksucker will make a fortune," said the Lucchese underboss with a mixture of envy and disapproval.

"This will be like, ah, now they'll say: 'We have the original Godfather,'" said Avellino. "We really have a Godfather now!"

What intrigued the investigators and angered his former mob colleagues even more was that Joe Bonanno had actually mentioned "the Commission." The Mafia liked to think this was a closely kept secret—although it was more or less an open book to the law enforcement community, its deliberations were closed. Ever since the raid on Appalachin in 1957, when different crime bosses from around the United States were surprised at their annual convention by a police raid and forced to make an undignified exit into surrounding fields and woods, the police had fairly accurate intelligence on the Mafia's secret government. But for their part it was still regarded as one of their most sacred and secret institutions. Just as the boardroom of any major corporation would regard the meeting of their top executives as highly confidential, so did the Commission. Yet here was a former head of a Family and Commission member actually writing about it.

"The Commission was not an integral part of my tradition," wrote Bonanno. "No such agency existed in Sicily. The Commission was an American adaptation. First of all, we had to establish procedures. For example, who would open our meetings? Who would call us to order? Who would be in charge of contacting everyone else for a meeting? If an out-of-town Father visited New York, who would he contact in order to get in touch with the Commission?

"We selected Vincent Mangano to chair our meetings. Joe Profaci became a sort of secretary for the Commission. I don't know what you would call Mangano. Maybe 'chairman' or 'speaker of the house.' He continued in this role until the early 1950s, when he disappeared and was presumed dead. Then I replaced him.

"On substantive issues, we agreed that no Family and no Father should interfere with the affairs of another Family, but that the Commission, as an agent of harmony, could arbitrate disputes brought before it. The Commission would have influence but no direct executive power. It had respect only insofar as its individual members had respect. More than anything else, the Commission was a forum.

"Modes of power are everywhere the same. In my world there were some Fathers I liked and some I detested. But I had to try and work with all of them. Also, some of these Fathers were more powerful than others, and these men, like myself leaders of powerful Families, were entitled to sit on the Commission. By participating in these diplomatic conventions, Families did not give up their independence; they were free to do what they wanted. The Commission could only exert influence."

Bonanno omitted to mention the sort of influence that the Family Fathers could exert. It ranged from breaking someone's legs through to a cold-blooded killing—the aging capos of the Mafia Families in America had the power of life and death. To be "made" as a member of a Family required at least one "hit" from an aspiring soldier and there was no shortage of recruits. In the mid-Eighties the main New York Families had so many willing recruits that they had to close their books on new membership. Family associates and up-and-coming wiseguys had to exercise patience along with their macho displays of violence. Although Bonanno conveniently skipped over the more unsavory aspects of the "Family tradition" he clearly sketched in the power structure of the modern Mafia complete with soldiers and captains and consiglieres, who acted as the right-hand men to the Family bosses.

When Avellino and Santoro heard Joe Bonanno talk about it to Mike Wallace on network television, they were aghast. Bonanno had been telling Wallace that the Commission could not tell a Family what to do.

"So that means he was even saying that about a Commission?" asked Avellino incredulously.

"Yeah," replied Santoro.

"He was admitting that there was a Commission?"

"He did," confirmed Santoro.

"Yeah," said Avellino.

"He says, you see, the Commission that first started, Charlie Lucky . . ." said Santoro, referring to Lucky

Luciano who had originally proposed the Commission in the Thirties. "And, ah, five bosses of New York."

"Right, Joe Profaci," said Avellino, mentioning one of them.

"Yeah, that was the original Commission," said Santoro.

"Right," said Avellino.

"Then they took in Chicago," recalled Santoro. "Then they took in, you know, they were making 'em all . . . He don't call it La Cosa Nostra, he don't call it a Mafia, I don't know in the book."

"Maybe in the book, but ah, on the TV he didn't call it, he just said: 'I'm a Father of a Family,' " said Avellino.

"Is that a fact?" asked Santoro.

" 'With total obedience,' " Avellino continued, quoting from memory, "like a Father is supposed to have."

"Right, right, right," remembered Santoro, "See what they told him: 'Did you shake anybody down?' 'No.' And then they told him, 'Well, how'd you get involved in these businesses?' He says, 'Because people think, I was a well-known man, a well-respected man, people come to me, and tell me if I wanna go in business with them.' " It was *The Godfather* movie version of the mob and one that was liked and accepted by the Mafia itself.

"He's 78 years old," murmured Avellino. "He looks in good shape for 78."

"Yeah, he's in good shape," agreed Santoro. "Yeah, you know, he ain't doing nothin' no more. He retired in Arizona for the last ten years or some 20 years, he's in Arizona."

"Now he's gonna give out, now it seems that he's gonna tell about the kidnapping and all of that," said Avellino, foretelling part two of the interview. He was referring to a curious episode in Mafia history in the autumn of 1964 when Bonanno mysteriously vanished. There was a dispute on the Commission. Bonanno had threatened to kill Carlo Gambino and Tommy "Brown" Lucchese, the founding father of the Lucchese Family. Joe Colombo, then a rising capo in the Profaci Family, heard about Bonanno's plans. Colombo worshiped Carlo Gambino and promptly tipped him off about the plot. It was at this point that Joe Bonanno disappeared—only to reappear a few weeks later, claiming that he had been kidnapped. Most insiders believed that he had faked his own disappearance to avoid being shot by Gambino, biding his time to negotiate his survival, which he presumably succeeded in doing as he was still alive for the CBS interview. Gambino was so grateful to Colombo for saving his life that he made sure that he succeeded Profaci to head the Family which today bears his name. Carlo Gambino also loaned him a million dollars to put to work on the street as capital for loan sharks.

"He kidnapped himself," confirmed Santoro sitting in the Jaguar. "He's gonna say the mob; he ain't gonna admit to that. He never did admit to it, that he was saying Joe Colombo was full of shit. Joe Colombo was the one that brought the story back and they rewarded him. They made him the boss."

"They made him the boss," said Avellino in agreement about the reasons for the promotion of Joe Colombo.

The second part of the *60 Minutes* interview with Bonanno was due to be shown the following week. Amongst the audience looking forward to it were several Mafia bosses, including Tony Corallo. On a later journey Avellino asked the head of the Lucchese Family what he thought of the TV show.

"He's been squawking for years, the cocksucker," said Corallo.

"So what is he going to tell them about this kidnapping when he disappeared now? He's going to tell them the story that . . ." asked Avellino.

"What kidnapping?" asked Corallo.

"When he ran away," replied Avellino.

"He ran away, that phony cocksucker! What kidnapping?" said Corallo, his voice full of contempt.

"That's what I mean," explained Avellino.

"He's got to make that legitimate. He's got to make it a kidnapping," said Corallo. "I wonder if he's gonna say on the windup that when they got together that they wanted to kill Gambino, Tommy Brown."

"He said that was a lie," explained Avellino, "they asked him that on the TV. He says, 'Lie, lie.'"

"What do you mean, they knew that?" asked a surprised Corallo, once again astonished that what he had believed to be a Mafia secret could possibly be known.

"Yeah, they asked him that, in his book. That's when he said about the Commission. They said, 'Isn't it so that you wanted to kill Lucchese and Gambino . . .'"

Corallo couldn't believe it. "How could they know that?"

". . . and Magliocco," Avellino continued, "they mentioned Joe Magliocco." (Magliocco was the boss of the Profaci Family before Colombo took over.)

"Well, how do they know that?" asked a bemused Corallo.

"Mike Wallace asked him the question. And he says, 'A lie, a lie. I never wanted to do that. I never said I was going to do that.'"

"How could it be in the book unless he puts it there?" asked Corallo.

"He put it in the book," explained Avellino. "He put in the book that he was accused of trying to mastermind the killing of Lucchese and Joe Colombo. And then, he says, isn't it true that Joe Colombo went and told this here story. OK. And he says, 'This is the story that was told but it's a lie. I never planned to kill Lucchese and Gambino.' And he mentioned Profaci and Joe Magliocco."

"Magliocco . . ." repeated Corallo, who was old enough to have lived through this rich period of Mafia history which had been almost Roman in its rivalry, strife, civil wars and plots.

"Magliocco, okay?" continued Avellino. "He said that. It was a lie, lie, never happened."

"But he must have known Magliocco, don't you think?"

"Yeah, yeah," agreed Avellino, "and then that's when the guy said to him, 'Well, about the Commission?' And he says, 'The Commission has got nothing to do with the Father of the Family. He operates the Family however he wants.'"

Tony "Ducks" Corallo, the head of the Lucchese Family, couldn't come to terms with it at all. A Commission member himself, it was unthinkable. You weren't even supposed to talk about Commission business with soldiers from your own Family. "He said that? You know that guy what he says there? They could call him in and lock you up and under this Act over here." Corallo certainly knew his law. It was precisely what Giuliani was intending—the Commission was the ultimate "Continuing Criminal Enterprise."

"This RICO act," added Avellino helpfully. "He admitted that he was in charge of a Family. He says, 'But I was like a Father in the Family.' "

"Yeah, but he mentions people, right?" inquired Corallo.

"Yeah. Oh yeah . . ." answered Avellino.

"Now they could call him in," continued Corallo, playing the part of a mob lawyer. "They could ask you a question if he mentioned your name. And, they call you in, and you'll deny it and they call him. See? They call him as a witness. What are you going to do then?"

Avellino thought about it. "Well, so far, everybody that he mentioned on TV was dead."

Corallo seemed to be reassured. "The rest he's going to say he don't know nothing about the rest; he wasn't involved in it for 20 years or 15 years. You know what I mean?"

"Um hmm," grunted Avellino.

"He probably gonna say, 'I wasn't involved for 15, 20 years, I don't know nothing that went on.' So he'll talk about all the dead ones. You understand? He'll talk about all the dead people. You know when, uh, Fat Tony told them, what did he tell those FBI's? What did he tell those FBI's? When they said that guy belongs to them, he's an FBI?"

Avellino recalled the incident for his boss. Apparently Tony Salerno had discovered that an undercover FBI agent had infiltrated the Genovese Family. "He says, 'You know. Mob guys don't kill agents.' "

Corallo's mind was back on Bonanno's television appearance. "They shouldn't have even let him be there." Whether Corallo was criticizing the CBS decision in allowing him to appear or the failure of the Commission to permanently silence him is unclear. Given Corallo's temperament the latter is the most likely.

Avellino remembered that another part of the program had featured an archive clip from a U.S. Senate hearing on organized crime. "They asked Frank Costello on the TV, 'Do you consider yourself an American citizen?' He said, 'I pay my taxes, don't I?' And they were showing excerpts of different people; see when they come to him, he says, 'I pay my taxes.'"

Bonanno probably had paid some taxes but as the wily Tony Corallo was quick to point out, going public like that meant Joe Bonanno could be issued with a subpoena and questioned as a material witness. Sure enough, shortly before the Commission trial, prosecutors from Giuliani's office issued the old man with a subpoena. The U.S. attorney savored the poetic justice in forcing the elderly capo to be interrogated as the result of his autobiography. The book, with its euphemisms of honor that disguised a life of murder and violence and written by a hand steeped in blood, had infuriated Giuliani. Tony Corallo's prediction came true.

"We questioned him for three and a half hours and he answered questions," recalls Giuliani. "I can't tell you the answers that he gave or the questions that were asked because it is still under seal. Then after we indicted, that was prior to the Commission indictment, we then made a motion to take his deposition for trial. He resisted that. We had a long hearing on whether he was healthy enough to testify because he claimed he was too sick to testify. The judge ruled that he was healthy enough to testify in a hospital-like setting. He refused and he's now sitting in prison."

Joe Bonanno's vanity in writing his memoirs was rewarded in the professional interest taken by the federal prosecutors from Giuliani's office. Although they were deprived of their reluctant star witness in court, they were able to cite chapters from his book at the Commission trial. In total Bonanno had devoted 62 pages to the subject of the Commission. Although some of the descriptions vaguely referred to "The Family" and "Fatherhood," his accounts of the power structures were accurate enough to be cited as evidence.

In addition to his book, Bonanno had left another legacy to the New York Family which bore his name. For over a decade the Bonanno Family had been split by internal rivalries which frequently spilled out into open bloodshed on the streets of Little Italy. Joe Bonanno and his fearsome underboss, Carmine Galante, were the principal architects of the heroin trade between Sicily and America which was now reaching epidemic proportions. International smuggling networks had been established at a secret meeting between Bonanno and the heads of the Sicilian Mafia in the elegant surroundings of Palermo's Hotel des Palme in the autumn of 1957.

The key to the traffic was Bonanno's connections through Canada. There, the Cotroni Family maintained close links with the New York–based Bonanno Family. Carmine Galante made frequent trips across the border and heroin was smuggled back to New York concealed inside secret compartments built into luxury American cars.

Galante was a "stone killer," a Mafia term for a man who displayed no emotion at the act of murder. Galante was small, bald-headed, fat and immensely tough. Rarely parted from a smoking cigar end, he had earned the nickname "Lillo"—"Little Cigar." Galante had always been an ambitious and determined gangster and proved a useful foil and enforcer to his tall and rather patrician boss. True to Mafia tradition, Carmine Galante's reputation was enhanced by a spell inside Lewisburg Federal Penitentiary. There he earned the respect of prisoners and warders alike. He also served time in the maximum security "G-Block" which housed the most notorious Mafia prisoners and where Galante was known as "the *capo di tutti capi* of Mafia row." A fellow inmate was Vincent Teresa, a New England Mafioso who later joined the Witness Protection Program.

This is what he had to say about Galante: "[He's] a stone killer. I think he took care of at least 80 hits himself . . . In or out of prison, Lillo is Mr. Big and anyone who thinks differently doesn't know what makes the mob tick.

He ought to be out of jail soon, and if he is, the New York mobs are in for real trouble. He hated Vito Genovese while he was alive. To him, Genovese was a pimp, two-faced, a man you could never trust. 'When I get out,' he used to say bitterly, 'I'll make Carlo Gambino shit in the middle of Times Square!' "

Fortunately, by the time he was paroled in 1978, Carlo Gambino had passed away peacefully in his sleep. Gambino, a small man with an enormous nose and even greater power, had established the Gambino Family as the largest in New York. He was fond of complaining that there were so many soldiers in his Family that he didn't know who was in and who was out! After his death the leadership mantle passed to Paul Castellano, a tall thickset man, also with a large hawklike nose. Castellano had sensibly married the boss's daughter and thus automatically obtained old man Gambino's blessing. "Big Paulie," as he was known to his friends, claimed to be a successful businessman in the chicken business.

Despite the death of Carlo Gambino, Carmine Galante still nursed a hatred for the other Families—not least because he confessed that they were an obstacle to his ambition to head the Commission. First, Galante needed to consolidate his position as self-appointed leader of the Bonanno Family. The nominal leader was Phil "Rusty" Rastelli who had become leader in 1973. When Galante got out, Rusty was serving a short prison sentence. To Lillo it looked like the perfect opportunity to make his bid for the leadership—and not just for the Bonanno Family.

In many ways it was a move reminiscent of Joe Bonanno's earlier move against the Commission which had ended in ignominious failure. In this respect, history didn't quite repeat itself. Carmine Galante had been just a little too boastful about his intentions. "There was no doubt in my mind that Lillo planned to take over the New York mobs when he got out," wrote Teresa in his autobiography. "He's got the enforcers, an army of them, to make it stick. He's been off the street for years, but he's still got tremendous influence and respect."

Teresa was convinced that Lillo had been planning his takeover bid well in advance from the inside: "Lillo's brought in an army of men because he wants guys he can depend on when he makes his move. Those aliens are 'made' guys from Sicily, real old country Mafiosi, mostly young. They've got papers of recognition so they get the same respect in this country that an American 'made' guy has, but they aren't members of the mob in this country. They're well trained, well disciplined. Lillo and [*others*] are bringing them in across the Mexican and Canadian borders. The old Mustache Petes (traditional rural Mafiosi) and a few of the smart bosses are recruiting them for just one thing—to bring back respect and honor in the honored society.

"These Sicilian Mafiosi will run into a wall, put their head in a bucket of acid for you if they're told to, not because they're hungry but because they're disciplined. They've been brought up from birth over there to show respect and honor, and that's what these punks over here don't have. Once they're told to get someone, that person hasn't a chance. They'll get him if they have to bust in his house in the middle of the night, shoot him, bite him, eat him, suck the blood out of his throat. They'll get him because they were told to do it."

Teresa was right about the Sicilians and Galante's ambition. Galante lost no time in surrounding himself with his own Sicilian army. Two key figures were Baldassare "Baldo" Amato, a good-looking young Sicilian with jet-black hair and a swarthy complexion, together with his cousin Cesare Bonventre, a flash Mafioso with a fondness for discos, gold chains, dark glasses, black shirts and a matching black Ferrari. Cesare Bonventre was an up-and-coming heroin dealer. In their spare time, Bonventre and his cousin, Amato, were Galante's bodyguards. Back on the streets, Galante lost no time in reestablishing his control over the heroin trade, once again putting his Sicilian connections to good use.

While he was concentrating on his business interests, Galante seemed to have forgotten the threats that he had made against the old guard. Castellano, head of the Gambino Family, didn't like Galante and in particular disapproved of his wholesale drug dealing. It was considered unseemly for the head of a Family to be so closely associated with the narcotics trade.

On July 12, 1979 Carmine Galante had just finished eating a large bowl of spaghetti and was halfway through his after-lunch cigar. His lunch guests were Leonardo Coppola and Giuseppe Turano. Sitting with him at the table in the patio of Joe and Mary's, one of his favorite Italian restaurants in Knickerbocker Avenue, Brooklyn, were Cesare Bonventre and Baldo Amato, his bodyguards. Both were armed with handguns. A half-drunk bottle of red wine stood on the table. Galante lifted his cigar to his mouth when for a split second he saw a stocky man wearing a black ski-mask coming towards him.

The man in the ski-mask emptied the contents of a double-barrelled shotgun into Galante's face. The man behind him was armed with a pump action rifle. He fired twice at Galante and then picked off the two guests who had been with Galante at his table. His bodyguards moved quickly and drew their guns, but not to defend their boss.

Cesare Bonventre delivered the coup de grace.

A car with its engine running was waiting for the hit team outside the restaurant.

According to a New York homicide detective: "Galante was into narcotics up to his ass, and narcotics and the mob is a no-no, believe it or not. Galante was killed by his own people, all New York–based people. Bonventre and Amato were part and parcel of the conspiracy; the motive for the killing was strictly his move to take over the Bonanno Family. It was ordered by Rastelli and approved by Paul Castellano—Corallo and Salerno were annoyed that he made that move without consulting the Commission, but he could pull it off because he was the boss.

"The way you make your mark in the mob, the way you survive is not necessarily by killing somebody. The main criteria is your earning power. It's what you generate, what kind of money you generate. Even if you step out of line and you're considered a top earner, you will survive. They very rarely kill an earner, unless he gets way out like Galante did. Galante wanted to start knocking people out—Commission heads.''

— 6 —

THE PIPELINE

THE MURDERERS OF CARMINE GALANTE WERE NEVER brought to trial. It was an event that continued to haunt both the mob and law enforcement agencies. The latter's attempts to prosecute those involved failed, while many of the actual perpetrators ended up in prison for other offenses or were themselves killed. Cesare Bonventre turned up in two separate oil drums.

The immediate beneficiaries of Galante's murder were the Sicilians who lost no time in expanding their heroin trade. It was the New York "Sicilians" that the FBI and many other agencies would spend years investigating, tracking and eventually prosecuting in what has now become an epic case in America's fight against organized crime. "The Pizza Connection" involved the combined resources of the FBI, the DEA, U.S. Customs and the New York City Police Department. Investigations stretched across more than half a dozen states within America and an equal number of countries outside.

The statistics were overwhelming on all counts. Conservative estimates run at two billion dollars worth of heroin in less than a decade. Because they were dealing with Sicilians, thousands of hours of wiretaps had to be translated and decoded and even then a lot of it didn't make sense. It was an immensely frustrating business, not least because there was little hope of getting any of the Italians to cooperate.

With one exception. Salvatore Amendolito.

Amendolito doesn't look like a wiseguy, or even a high-level money launderer. He dresses well but studiously avoids double-breasted suits, white crocodile shoes and gold chains. He is careful not to draw attention to himself. Not only is there the current dispute over the Mafia's missing millions, there is also a contract out on his life for betraying his former bosses in New York and Palermo. Once they heard of his defection, they sent a message. "We will kill you," recalls Amendolito. "We will scare you first, and then we'll kill you."

Today, Amendolito's life is a twilight world of hurried meetings in anonymous hotel rooms and false identities. He is still keen to regale unsuspecting businessmen with improbable schemes for making a fast buck, and when the question of his past comes up, he steadfastly maintains that he never suspected that he was moving drug money. He even claims to believe the cover story the Mafia gave him—that the money was coming from a chain of pizzerias. But ten million dollars?

"I was not surprised at all. I know the amount of business that the successful pizzeria can have here in the United States, and you would be surprised to see what kind of money they can make."

Amendolito is such a consummate con-man that it is quite likely that he may even have conned himself into believing that the suitcases crammed full of small denomination bills really did come from the sale of pizzas. Amendolito was laundering so much money (between nine and ten million dollars is his estimate) that as one of the prosecutors remarked, "There were not enough hours in the day, nor banks in the City of New York . . ." to handle the transactions.

Amendolito's extraordinary escapades began in Italy in 1980. Amendolito had become a leading light in the Mormon Church in Italy, attaining the rank of bishop before emigrating to America. On arrival in America, he moved into the international fish business. A typically improbable Amendolito venture, it involved air-freighting consignments of frozen fish from New York City to Italy and Greece. In Italy, Amendolito had a partner, Salvatore Miniati, who ran Finagest, a finance company. Finagest specialized in the discreet movement of money for wealthy Italians into the neighboring secrecy of a Swiss bank account. In the spring of 1980, Miniati telephoned Amendolito in New Jersey and asked him to help with some currency transfers from New York. The client was Olivero Tognoli, a rich young Italian businessman living in Sicily. Tognoli was the son of a respected industrialist, whose family business was an iron and steel works in Brescia. Their interests spread from the Mediterranean to South America. Olivero managed the family company in Sicily—Ferriere Acciaere Sud.

Amendolito's ears pricked up. The fish business was in the doldrums. He telephoned Olivero Tognoli.

"Tognoli had a client in Italy," says Amendolito, recalling their initial conversation. "He needed $9 million to build a hotel. And he had found financing out of several pizzerias in America." Tognoli's story was that the money was needed as a loan to finance construction and that, on completion of the project, the loan would be repaid to the backers in Sicily.

On the telephone Tognoli sounded smooth, well educated and persuasive. "The Americans can't make the transfer themselves," he explained to Amendolito. "They can't do it because their money is in cash. They don't want to have to report the deal to the IRS. They don't want to do that."

Amendolito was in a line of business where you don't ask too many questions. He accepted the offer.

The deal? One percent commission. Ninety thousand dollars in cash for moving the money.

Amendolito was then given the telephone number of the Roma Restaurant in New Jersey and told to contact Frank Castronovo, the owner.

Castronovo was a small, stocky middle-aged Italian with curly gray hair who spoke broken English. And if the amounts of money that he began to hand over to the Mormon bishop were anything to go by, Frank Castronovo was running the most successful restaurant business in America. In his first two months Amendolito collected $3,490,000 from Castronovo.

The Roma Restaurant was in the center of a concrete shopping mall in Menlo Park, New Jersey. Amendolito drove his station wagon down a ramp to a basement storage area beneath the restaurant where cardboard liquor boxes stuffed full of cash were loaded into the boot. "I used to go into the restaurant, and we'd have breakfast together, we'd chat a little bit then he suggested to go back to pick up my car and go to the delivery door at the back which is a little under the ground level."

Amounts under $10,000 could be deposited in banks without filling in the required Internal Revenue Service forms but Amendolito soon realized the amounts were too large to traipse around all day converting the small bills into cashier's checks. Salvatore switched to another method. He transferred the money into his own suitcases, hired a bodyguard, booked himself on to commercial flights and hand-carried the cash to Nassau in the Bahamas. There he found a banker, Peter Albissor, a manager at BSI, Banca Swizzera Italiana. The Bahamas arrangement was convenient—from Nassau the proceeds could be wire-transferred to accounts in Switzerland. The funds were sent to BSI in Mendrisio at Account 27971: Codename "Stefania," and to Credit Suisse in Bellinzona, Account 871: Codename "Smart."

Returning from one Bahamas trip, Amendolito got another call from Miniati in Milan. Amendolito was to wait for a telephone call. The name of the person calling him could not be divulged.

The next day Amendolito was telephoned by a man who identified himself only as "Sal." He instructed the startled Amendolito to meet him on a street corner in Queens the following afternoon. Amendolito drove to the rendezvous and waited. After a while two men came up to him and introduced themselves as "Vito" and "Sal." Amendolito was beginning to feel increasingly nervous. Sal shepherded him into a nearby doorway and said, "Not to worry." Sal borrowed a piece of paper from a notebook that Vito was carrying, wrote down a number and gave it to Amendolito. Sal told him that he would be contacted about a money transfer and then left.

Amendolito returned to his Madison Avenue office and absentmindedly stored the scrap of paper with Sal's number away in the Rolodex which sat on the top of his desk. There had been something very scary about Sal and the way they had met. Amendolito was unhappy about street corner transactions. He called Tognoli in Italy to complain.

"Salvatore, don't worry," soothed Tognoli on the telephone. "This 'Sal' is a man of great respect."

Amendolito was told to ring the number he'd been given and ask for "Sal" as they had some money that needed moving. Amendolito tried the number. A gruff voice answered saying he'd never heard of Sal or Vito. Then the mysterious Sal called back. A meeting was arranged for seven-thirty in the morning on the same street corner in Queens.

Amendolito stood and waited nervously by his car. It was at moments like these that he began to wonder what he was doing.

He didn't have to wait long. A car drew up and a short, stockily built man got out and opened the trunk of his car. "Reverse your car back to mine," Sal instructed. Amendolito opened his trunk and Sal deftly heaved two enormous suitcases into the station wagon. Sal jumped back into his car and drove away.

The cases contained over one million dollars. Pizzas were selling well in New York City.

Amendolito had been told to drive to the Waldorf Astoria, one of New York's smartest hotels in midtown Manhattan. A Swiss "banker" was waiting. Driving the money 50 blocks across Manhattan earned Amendolito $30,000. "I went up to the hotel and in the hotel I met with the banker who came from Switzerland and he took the money." From his hotel suite, the Swiss businessman telephoned a Wall Street bank who obligingly sent a security guard to accompany the man in a yellow cab to deposit the cash.

Although Amendolito did not know it at the time, the short, muscular man with close-cropped hair and narrow eyes who dumped the suitcase at his feet was Salvatore Catalano. Also known as "Toto" and "The Baker," Catalano was the ruthless Sicilian Mafia capo who acted as the New York ambassador between the separate Mafia organizations of Sicily and the U.S. Catalano was also the alleged leader of the hit team that had murdered Carmine Galante. His reward was an exclusive license to import Sicilian heroin to New York City.

The astonishing thing was that the law enforcement agencies of the United States knew virtually nothing about him. But inside the mob, particularly among the Sicilians of the Bonanno Family, he was well known. They had even wanted to make him head of the Family after the Galante hit.

There was one problem. Catalano couldn't speak English!

One Mafia contract killer with 11 murders to his credit witnessed the quiet rise of the Sicilian baker. Luigi Ronsisvalle combined a successful career as a hit man with a sideline as a drugs courier. He crisscrossed the United States by car, train and plane carrying suitcases crammed full of heroin for Catalano. Luigi Ronsisvalle remembers Catalano as the manager of a record shop in Brooklyn. Ronsisvalle watched Sal Catalano strutting up and down Knickerbocker Avenue, in time-honored mob tradition. "He was just interested in buying coffee, talking with people, or the people of the Bonanno Family. I never saw him busy. A very, very quiet man."

Ronsisvalle confirms that the man that Amendolito met on the street corner was a key figure in the heroin trade: "He was in charge of the United States. He was the boss about that." Although Catalano would rarely touch the drugs, Ronsisvalle's own exploits testified to the sheer scale of the trade that Catalano was controlling.

Ronsisvalle is one of those colorful characters from the underworld of organized crime that one can't help liking, irrespective of the awful deeds that such a person may have committed. Prosecutors, judges and agents alike fell for his charm and wit. Ronsisvalle came across like a character from a Marx Brothers movie, with a thick Italian-American accent and an often unintentional sense of humor. For all the laughs he provoked there was no doubting Luigi's credentials or the deadly nature of his profession.

Ronsisvalle had joined the Witness Protection Program along with other Mafia traitors. He was a star witness before the Presidential Commission on Organized Crime where he appeared surrounded by armed U.S. Marshals. Until his death from natural causes in 1993 Ronsisvalle's evidence played a crucial role in revealing the extent of the heroin trade and its control by the Bonanno Family. It is worth remembering that Ronsisvalle was just one of a number of couriers. He himself recalls frequent trips to Miami and Chicago, sometimes literally riding shotgun, as well as local deliveries in Brooklyn: "I'd deliver over a dozen times from Knickerbocker Avenue to 18th Avenue, Brooklyn. Forty pounds of heroin on each trip. We took billions and billions of dollars." Even allowing for exaggeration, Ronsisvalle's estimate was not far off. The heroin, as evidenced by DEA chemist samples, was of the highest purity.

Ronsisvalle's involvement with the heroin dealers of the Bonanno Family was centered around Knickerbocker Avenue in Brooklyn. It was here that various members of the Bonanno and Gambino Families congregated to set up their heroin deals. Restaurants like the Cafe Scopello, Cafe del Viale, Cafe Valentino and the Castellamare del Golfo (the Sicilian birthplace of Joe Bonanno) were all fronts for multimillion-dollar drug deals.

One night at the Castellamare del Golfo, Luigi met his contact Felice Puma. "Hey, any news about what we were talking about?" asked Luigi.

Puma leaned forward in conspiratorial fashion and spoke in a whisper. "Luigi, do you know the pipe from Canada coming into the States, the one that brings the oil?"

"Yeah," replied Luigi, uncertain what his friend was on about. He'd never seen the Alaskan pipeline but he could imagine what it looked like.

"We have the same thing with heroin coming to the United States from Sicily."

The pipeline ended in Knickerbocker Avenue, Brooklyn.

This source of limitless wealth drew other high-ranking mobsters to the Avenue and they weren't just paying their respects. Catalano's growing stature was reflected in a "sit-down" that Ronsisvalle attended. Luigi had complained that he was being done out of his rightful share of the proceeds from a million-dollar diamond heist. The haul came from a robbery at the diamond center on West 47th Street in Manhattan. Catalano hosted the sit-down—an official mob arbitration session—at a Manhattan restaurant, along with Joey Gallo, then consigliere of the Gambino Family. During the sit-down several of the larger diamonds were given away. One of the largest was offered as a "gift" to Paul Castellano, head of the Gambino Family—a fascinating anecdote as Castellano was the boss who had approved the murder of Galante and who disapproved of drugs. Luigi was furious that the fruits of his labor should just be given away to the "big bosses." In the end, Catalano decreed that when the remaining diamonds had been fenced, Luigi should be paid $30,000.

On another occasion Ronsisvalle was introduced to Neil Dellacroce, underboss of the Gambino Family. Inappropriately nicknamed "Neil the Lamb," Dellacroce was a brutal old hood who thought nothing of smashing a baseball bat into a man's face. Dellacroce was also the mentor of an up-and-coming mobster called John Gotti, then a captain in the crew that Dellacroce supervised. Despite Paul Castellano's edict against drug deals, Dellacroce and Gotti's friends turned a blind eye to Big Paul's distaste for the narcotics trade. Although just as Catalano would donate large diamonds, so did the Dellacroce crew ensure that their envelopes of tribute to Castellano contained substantial amounts from their drug profits.

Most of the heads of the New York Families were getting money from the narcotics business. Whether they knew where the money came from was another question. It was certainly one that they were not going to ask too often— and if the money was good, they could afford principles.

After all, it didn't cost anything to say they were against the drug trade. It was only when people got caught and they ran the risk of being informed on that the bosses would really become principled.

The disapproval of bosses like Paul Castellano and Tony Corallo was political. They knew that drugs were bad for the image of the Mafia and they knew it intensified the efforts of the law enforcement agencies to crack down on them. For those reasons they didn't like it. They went so far as to ostracize the Bonanno Family—barring them from Commission meetings. But they never attempted to take on Catalano and the Sicilians. That would have meant all-out war. Instead Castellano used them to get rid of Galante, and if the Sicilians continued to trade heroin, well, there wasn't much they could do about that—the Sicilians were a law unto themselves. All the Commission could do was to try and discourage their own soldiers from getting involved in the trade and in that they would be singularly unsuccessful.

Within the Gambino Family the issue ultimately became a matter of life and death. Next to the Bonanno Family, the Gambinos had the second largest number of Sicilian relatives—some of whom had moved to New Jersey. Inevitably, they dealt in heroin as did some of the American members of the Gambino Family. The philosophy was "Ask no questions and get no lies." If Castellano didn't find out, it was OK. It was when he did find out that the problems would really begin.

Some of Ronsisvalle's heroin deliveries began on Knickerbocker Avenue and ended a few blocks away at the Cafe Mille Luci on 18th Avenue and 71st Street. The heroin was packed into a large wooden crate which was then nailed shut and driven to the Mille Luci. There, it was hauled out of the boot by some tough young Sicilians who manhandled it down into the restaurant basement. Ronsisvalle made the run 15 times at $5,000 a throw. Each crate contained 80 pounds of heroin. From the time the heroin was parceled up in the Knickerbocker Avenue basement, delivered to the dealers where it would be cut, to the time it hit the streets, its value would multiply several hundred times.

On the street, average purity levels were between three and five percent. Sal Polisi, a former heroin dealer for the Mafia, connected to the Colombo and Gambino Families, and a couple of rungs up the ladder from Ronsisvalle, explained to me just how easy the money was and how the bosses managed to distance themselves from the trade: "New York is the hub of the heroin business in this country. There must be a million heroin addicts in this country and about three hundred thousand of them are based in New York. [*The heroin*] would be assigned on a consignment basis . . . you wouldn't have to pay for it. It would be like an honor system. Most of the time the bosses in the Family wanted no connection with the heroin business, so there would be guys that were away from the Family that were running the drugs as a front for the mobsters."

Polisi himself was an associate of wiseguys in the Gambino and Colombo Families but never actually became a made guy. "The guys weren't mob members but were allowed to run this drug business and kick back the mobsters a piece of the action, profits, okay. My connection was simple. I had an Irish guy that I was dealing with that was a big importer. I mean he would bring in kilos by the month, okay, but his partner was Dominic Cataldo, a Colombo member, and so they would give me a kilo of heroin. At that time I was paying $175,000 for one kilo, 35 ounces. I could make 350 ounces out of one kilo and sell each ounce for $10,000. That's $3.5 million! It's a lot of money! You could easily make $25,000 or $30,000 a week. That's what I made a week, every week. And I never had to touch the drugs after a while. I just had a man do it all. I'd give him the drugs and he'd give me the money. Just meet him at a diner for lunch and give me a bag of money! It was so much money that it would take shopping bags full to bring back the amount of money I had to give these guys. I couldn't give it to them in small bills, it had to be big bills. So I'd find a bank and I'd pay a girl off and she'd change the money. I mean she'd make some money, I'd make some money. Everybody would, you know!"

The only losers were the desperate half million junkies

on the streets of New York fighting for a fix and dying of AIDS.

The volume of the trade was breathtaking. Ronsisvalle admits to 12 flights from New York to Los Angeles carrying one kilo of heroin per flight. On another occasion Luigi flew to Miami and was told to go to Miami Beach at the intersection of Collins Avenue and 64th Street. Standing in front of a coffee shop on Collins Avenue was his Brooklyn friend, Felice Puma. Puma was a soldier in the Bonanno Family who took orders from Sal Catalano.

"Hey, Felice!" cried Ronsisvalle, greeting his friend in Sicilian.

"Let's go, Luigi," replied Puma, looking around in case they were being watched. He walked over to his red sports car that was parked on the corner. Puma got in the driver's side and motioned Ronsisvalle to take the passenger seat. He put the keys in the ignition and bent down to pick something up from the floor of the car. He tossed a .38 into his friend's lap and handed him a shotgun. Puma started the engine and headed north.

"Where are we going?" asked Ronsisvalle.

"We're going back to New York," Puma told the startled Sicilian. In the trunk of the sports car were 100 kilos of heroin. Luigi found himself literally riding shotgun. The weapons were no joke. The street value of the powder that Ronsisvalle was protecting was $70 million.

Puma and Ronsisvalle drove from Miami Beach to Brooklyn. When they arrived in Knickerbocker Avenue, Salvatore Catalano was waiting patiently for them outside the Cafe del Viale.

Puma motioned Luigi to stay in the car for a couple of minutes. Catalano and Puma spoke briefly on the sidewalk. When he came back to the car he told Ronsisvalle: "It's okay, Luigi. Leave everything in the car. Go home. I see you tomorrow!"

Luigi left the revolver and shotgun on the floor of the car and as he was walking away heard the noise of the engine being revved at high speed. Someone else was driving it away. Another "barrel of oil" had been struck.

The comparison to the Alaskan oil pipeline was no exaggeration. The secret heroin refineries of Sicily were working overtime. Their mass production capability was confirmed during an undercover investigation by Frank Panessa, one of the DEA's most experienced agents.

Panessa is a balding well-built man with a dark, trim moustache. Standing over six feet tall, Panessa's height would seem to rule him out for undercover work. But the combination of his Italian looks, natural charm and the unspoken power of his physique made him a formidable opponent. Frank Panessa emerged as one of the few DEA agents who succeeded in infiltrating the Sicilian Mafia.

Panessa teamed up with a group of Sicilians who dealt with Catalano. Working undercover in Europe, Panessa set up a string of front companies in Germany and offered their services to the mob. "I tried to interest the Sicilians in using my company to launder money. And they said, 'Well, we already have it established. We have it set up where we can launder $5 million a day.' They laundered over $300 million through Switzerland, in one year! The Sicilians said every seven hours they would put suitcases on the Alitalia flights going to JFK airport in New York. Whenever a plane took off, going to JFK, they would put suitcases on it."

Back in Sicily, the second highest-ranking informant to betray the Italian Mafia in the early Eighties witnessed at first hand Catalano's operations in Palermo. After 12 months of intensive arrangements, I met Salvatore Contorno in New York City where he revealed to me some of the innermost secrets of the Mafia's control of the heroin trade.

Many of the crucial meetings took place at Fondo Favarella, a remote farmhouse surrounded by a stone wall just off a country road bordering the picturesque mountain village of Corleone. The name given the fictitious Family of *The Godfather* has its origins in a real Family whose exploits and reputation for violence make Michael Corleone and Don Vito look like a pair of Sunday School teachers. Fondo Favarella was the home of Michele Greco, head of the Sicilian Mafia. Greco was also leader of the Corleonesi, the most powerful Mafia faction in Italy.

Contorno was flown into an undisclosed location which was only revealed to me 30 minutes before the interview. Detailed security checks had been run before I even got to the building. There I was met by the DEA agents who were baby-sitting Contorno.

I was introduced to a short stocky man with dark, black hair and a large roman nose. He seemed ill at ease, chain-smoked cigarettes, spoke no English and talked in a thick Sicilian dialect that even those who spoke fluent Italian were incapable of understanding. Fortunately the DEA supplied a translator who could understand Contorno's guttural and rapid-fire Sicilian.

The events which led to his decision to betray "The Honored Society" were as dramatic as any fictional scene from *The Godfather*. Contorno was caught in the crossfire of a bloody civil war fought between two factions of the Sicilian Mafia. At its height the body count from the feud left three corpses a day on the streets of Palermo. It was the Corleonesi, led by Michele Greco, which gained the upper hand. Tommaso Buscetta and Contorno were aligned with the losing faction. Contorno himself narrowly escaped death when he found himself staring down the wrong end of a Kalashnikov wielded by Pino "Scarpazzedda" Greco, the Corleonesi's chief executioner.

Pino Greco was a ruthless killer and psychopath. (Despite sharing the same surname as Don Michele they were not related.) After murdering one rival Mafia boss, Pino Greco kidnapped and tortured his son to preempt any thoughts of revenge. At one point, the bloodthirsty executioner cut the unfortunate adolescent's arm off and waved it at him with the taunt: "You will no longer be able to avenge your father with this!"

Early one morning after visiting his parents, Contorno drove off from the Via Ciaculli in Palermo in his Fiat 127. He was giving a lift to one of his son's friends, Giuseppe, a five-year-old boy. As he pulled on to one of the overpasses leading into town, he noticed a Mafia friend driving slowly in front of him. Contorno overtook and waved at him. His friend waved back. Driving past a six-story block of flats Contorno was surprised to see another familiar face leaning out of a top floor window. Then Contorno spotted a high-powered motorcycle driving towards him closing fast on his Fiat. Now he knew that something was up. The motorbike drew alongside and Contorno recognized in a flash that the man riding pillion was Pino Greco. The Corleonesi assassin greeted him with a burst of machine-gun fire from his AK-47. Contorno had just enough time to slam on the brakes, let go of the steering wheel and throw his body across the child in the passenger seat. The bullets flew over their heads.

The motorbike sped past. Contorno regained control of the car and checked his rearview mirror. He saw the bike coming back from behind. Rapidly starting the car again, he drove a hundred yards and stopped. Noticing that the child's face was bleeding, Contorno pushed him out of the car and leapt after him. He crouched down behind the front of the Fiat and aimed his .38 revolver at the approaching motorbike. Just as he was about to shoot, Contorno saw a BMW reversing towards the Fiat. There was no time to worry about the car as at that instant Greco fired a second burst from his machine gun. Simultaneously Contorno fired his revolver and saw Greco recoil backwards firing into the sky, the shots ricocheting off the building behind him. To his relief, Contorno saw Greco fall off the back of the bike; seizing the moment, Contorno grabbed his son's friend and fled.

Later, Contorno discovered that although he had hit Pino Greco, the wily assassin had been wearing a bullet-proof vest and survived the attack.

After his narrow escape Contorno went into hiding in Rome. But the Corleonesi didn't give up. "Scarpazzedda," furious at being outwitted, slaughtered half a dozen of Contorno's relatives and would have undoubtedly caught up with him if Contorno had not been arrested by the carabinieri in Rome.

When he was later visited in prison by the legendary Tommaso Buscetta, whose family had also been decimated by the Corleonesi, Contorno knelt and kissed the hand of one of the few leaders to survive the war. Buscetta, who had already decided to violate the sacred oath of Omerta and revenge himself by talking, placed his hand on his old friend's head and said: "It's alright, Totuccio. You can talk."

Contorno took Buscetta's advice and using the codename "White Lightning" started to unburden himself under heavy guard to Giovanni Falcone, Sicily's Chief Examining Magistrate who was spearheading the country's onslaught against the Mafia. The testimonies of Contorno and Buscetta were an invaluable breakthrough for both the Italians and the Americans and a devastating blow against the seemingly impregnable empire of the Sicilian Mafia. It was Buscetta's testimony at the beginning of 1993 that precipitated the political crisis in Italy. Buscetta and other Sicilian supergrasses gave evidence of the long-suspected links between the Mafia and the leading politicians of the Christian Democrat party.

Contorno knows that the Corleonesi are still trying to kill him. "They will search for me like a needle in a haystack," he told me. "But I am not afraid of them, you can only die once."

Contorno's inestimable value to both the Americans and Italians was his photographic memory. He was very close to the head of his Family, a man he worshiped and who was also murdered by the Corleonesi. But the friendship had given him a ringside seat at some of the most important meetings of the Sicilian Mafia. And few meetings were more important than those with their American cousins.

7
A HEROIN DEAL IN PALERMO

VISITING AMERICAN MAFIOSI WERE LAVISHLY ENTER-
tained at Fondo Favarella, the agricultural estate
owned by Michele Greco. Don Michele, a Sicilian
"Godfather" if ever there was one, was a distinguished
looking man, with thick, white hair swept back off a proud
forehead. Greco positively radiated an aura of arrogance
and power. Whether he was wearing a well-cut suit or the
casual clothes of a Sicilian country gentleman Michele
Greco was a commanding presence. His demeanor was that
of a powerful politician or wealthy businessman, which in
many ways he was.

Known as "Il Papa"—"The Pope," the white-haired
Godfather was the supreme head of the Sicilian Mafia,
heading both the "Cupola" ["The Crown"], the Sicilian
name for the Commission, and the Corleonesi. Greco, in
alliance with Salvatore "Toto" Riina, presided over the
bloody war that was being waged with an unprecedented
brutality and with equal ferocity against their enemies
within the Mafia and those in the Government who dared
challenge their supremacy. Policemen, magistrates and politicians were assassinated with impunity if they were

judged to be a threat to the ambitions of the Corleonesi. "The Pope's" power was such that the tone of his voice or a dismissive wave of his hand could signal the end of a man's life.

Greco's home, Fondo Favarella, served as the rural headquarters of an international empire of crime. It was a vast estate with three separate courtyards and a main house with smaller cottages scattered around the property. American guests, "Amici Nostri"—"Friends of Ours," were entertained at the farmhouse where they dined on the finest Sicilian food and wine. Fondo Favarella was also the meeting place for the Commission. Executions, conspiracies, alliances with politicians, bankers and businessmen, arrangements for heroin shipments and money laundering were all decided around Don Michele's dining-room table.

In the stone-floored kitchen a concealed trapdoor led into a secret cellar equipped with table and chairs which was used as a hideaway either by the Commission or Greco himself. Astonishingly, Sicily's top Mafia bosses were able to live quite openly even when there were national manhunts launched against them. Salvatore "Toto" Riina was on the run for 22 years until he was suddenly picked up in what was said to be a routine roadblock in Palermo. Riina was discovered on January 15, 1993 and the news was immediately relayed to the leaders of the Italian Government in Rome where the announcement was greeted by a round of applause. Cynical observers concluded that Riina's whereabouts had long been known and that he could have been arrested at any time had he not had high-level political protection. Similarly Greco's farm was well known to the authorities but local carabinieri would not have dreamt of disturbing such a powerful man until some high-ranking politician in Rome gave the signal.

Salvatore Contorno gave both the Italian and American authorities a graphic description of life at the farm. This is what he told the author: "At Fondo Favarella there were several meetings, several feasts with a lot of people and food. In Fondo Favarella there was everything. There were meetings of the Commission, there were meetings for 'andare a tiro' [to order an execution], to talk, to converse with all the other 'Men of Honor.' However, when there were Americans, and therefore matters concerning drugs and their export to America, which meant a lot of money being brought, it was always there that the meetings were held."

Contorno was known as "Coriolanus of the Forest," with the reputation for being a "Brave Man"—a Mafia euphemism for a tough soldier or more usually an efficient killer. One morning Contorno was making his way to the barber's shop when he met a friend, Emmanuele D'Agostino, a fellow Mafioso. "Where are you going?" asked D'Agostino.

"I am going to the barber," replied Contorno.

D'Agostino, who was on the run, asked Contorno to give him a ride in his car. "We have to go to Bagheria because there is a load of drugs," he explained.

Reluctantly Contorno agreed to give him a lift. Their first stop was at an iron warehouse belonging to Leonardo Greco, a local Mafia chieftain. Greco gave Contorno's friend some instructions about the drug shipment and then introduced the two men to his brother, Salvatore Greco, a visitor from America. D'Agostino and Salvatore Greco got into Contorno's car and the three of them drove to a country house on the outskirts of Palermo. (Although bearing the same name these Grecos were not related to Michele Greco. Leonardo was a powerful Mafia boss in his own right and his brother was one of the organizers of the Pizza Connection. Sal Greco, a small, thin man with a taste for brown suits and narrow ties, had gray hair and an aquiline nose. He was Leonardo's younger brother and had emigrated to America to set up a small pizzeria in Neptune City, New Jersey. On introduction Contorno was told that he was "La Stessa Cosa"—"The Same Thing," the code for Mafioso.)

"We went into the house and moved on to a terrace. On the terrace there were eight or nine people. One of them was Salvatore Catalano. They took out some envelopes from some rubbish sacks. From some of these envelopes they took white powder: heroin.

"They carried out some sort of test: they put it in a pan

in which there was some oil. The stuff really stank and at that point, not being able to bear the stench, I went out to the car. Forty-five minutes later Emmanuele D'Agostino came out and said: 'We have finished.' Then I said to him, 'I'm going to say good-bye to all the people up there and let's go.'

"And that's what happened. On the drive home, D'Agostino told me how things had gone: the merchandise was good but that on other occasions they had had problems because the merchandise they offered was said to be good and afterwards it had turned out not to be so good. And since it was being sent to America, he checked its quality first so as to avoid problems later with the purchasers."

Sal Catalano had traveled to Sicily to oversee a deal of some importance—not least to ensure quality control. There had been problems and complaints about an earlier shipment. This eyewitness account which placed Catalano directly with a source of Sicilian heroin was a vital piece of evidence for the prosecution of the Pizza Connection ring back in New York.

If there were occasional problems with quality there were certainly no problems with quantity. Contorno himself knew of four heroin refineries operating in Sicily capable of producing between 50 and 80 kilos a week. There was even one secret laboratory at Michele Greco's estate at Fondo Favarella.

The phenomenal sums of money pouring into the coffers of the Sicilian Mafia from the New York buyers had transformed the fortunes of the Italians. It was this wealth which was generating a new wave of violence. Both Buscetta and Contorno told me that it was the continuing violence in Sicily, orchestrated with a psychopathic intensity by Pino "Scarpazzedda" Greco, that persuaded them to betray the Mafia. The claim has to be taken with a pinch of salt but there is probably an element of truth in it.

Contorno believes that: "The Corleonesi did not carry on in the old way of thinking. They were only concerned with billions and they made drugs their business and they killed anyone who affected their interests. They no longer had any decency towards people. They killed people like dogs, only for money. It was no longer the 'Cosa Nostra' as was once said but only personal interest—there have been many traitors who sold the Cosa Nostra."

Contorno's analysis was confirmed by Tommaso Buscetta. Neither was exactly a saint—Buscetta himself had been deeply implicated in several major drug deals—but there was more than a grain of truth in what they said.

For all the untold riches that drugs were bringing in for the Mafia in America and Italy, they were creating some serious problems as well. The vast amount of narco-dollars would be recycled into the Italian economy, deepening an already dangerous level of wholesale economic and political corruption which allowed the Mafia to spread its tentacles even further into the heart of the State.

Rumors of the "Third Level," the links between the Mafia and Italy's political leaders reached fever pitch following the arrest of Salvatore "Toto" Riina, successor to Michele Greco and fugitive boss of the Corleonesi. After his arrest, an élite unit of carabinieri revealed that they had been videotaping him for three months. Among those seen beating a path to his door, it was alleged, were several top political figures. Other more cynical commentators thought that Riina's arrest was a rather contrived affair. The links between the Men of Honor and the worlds of finance and politics were too enmeshed to ever be untangled. Close political links had been forged ever since the Americans backed Mafiosi in the postwar elections, preferring their tough stance on Communism to that of their more principled opponents. The billions that flowed from the heroin trade helped cement the relationship and gave the Mafia unprecedented economic power. It was that power which enabled them to gain high-level political protection.

Drug couriers and killers like Luigi Ronsisvalle were small parts of a machine that endlessly recycled drugs into money, money into drugs and power into influence. Money couriers like Salvatore Amendolito were the dispatch riders of the enterprise, delivering the raw material which fueled the Mafia machine.

8

THE MONEY-GO-ROUND

BACK IN NEW YORK CITY SALVATORE AMENDOLITO continued happily recycling the millions of dollars that flowed between America and Sicily. Business was going so well for him that he was able to wrap up the frozen fish business and elevate himself to full-time "International Financial Consultant." His new company was "Overseas Business Services," OBS, complete with a prestigious Manhattan address on 575 Madison Avenue. Amendolito celebrated by hiring a bodyguard and a secretary. Convinced of the importance of his new status, Salvatore looked to other methods of moving the money.

Amongst the most accommodating recipients of the Mafia millions were the giant blue-chip money-broking houses of Wall Street. Merrill-Lynch took nearly three million dollars in cash in three days while similar amounts were deposited at E.F. Hutton by Swiss couriers traveling through Manhattan. When the FBI discovered the deposits and began to make inquiries, E.F. Hutton decided their first loyalty lay with their wealthy customer rather than the U.S. Government. The bank tipped off their Swiss client. When the investigators heard about it, they were devastated. If the money men reported back the whole trail could die out. U.S. Customs were beginning to make real headway by following the money trail but it was proving virtually impossible to find any of the heroin. That made it all the more imperative to construct a watertight case from the bank accounts.

"We nearly got blown out of the water by E.F. Hutton," recalls one Government investigator through gritted teeth.

When the news reached Giuliani, the U.S. Attorney with jurisdiction over both the Commission and the Pizza Connection case, he was speechless with rage. Prosecutors from Giuliani's office pored over the criminal statute books, trying to find a charge they could bring against the bank which had chosen the wrong side. To Giuliani, the ethics of Wall Street in the 1980s seemed little different from those of the mob. (Giuliani would follow his success against the Mafia with a moral crusade against corruption on Wall Street, targeting the likes of Ivan Boesky and Dennis Levine once his triumphs over the Mafia had slipped from the front pages. Other prosecutors and the press thought he had gone too far when some Wall Street brokers were paraded and photographed in handcuffs and chains after one much publicized arrest!)

Back in Sicily the services of OBS were highly appreciated. Amendolito was delighted to receive an invitation from Olivero Tognoli to a celebration dinner party in Sicily. He flew out and was chauffeured to a five-star restaurant on the Palermo waterfront. There he was given VIP treatment. Realizing the company he was keeping, black-tied waiters hovered in respectful attendance, filling golden goblets with ice-cold champagne. Fresh lobster and seafood were served while Amendolito was fêted as an honored guest.

There were two tables of well-dressed men, among them a man who was introduced to Salvatore as a wealthy Sicilian businessman in the steel industry, Leonardo Greco. Amendolito was sitting close to Greco at the dinner table and struck up conversation with him during the meal. To his surprise, Greco asked Amendolito for his help and advice. The industrialist might need to travel to America soon on business and was worried that he might have some problems with his U.S. visa. Amendolito, somewhat intoxicated by the heady atmosphere, was quick to reassure his new friend that it was nothing to worry about and that he, Salvatore, could sort it all out if the need arose. "If there's anything I can do just call me," he said, handing over his business card.

The Mafia boss took the card and nodded in appreciation. Amendolito was enjoying himself. He felt at home in Sicily, business was going well and he had made some influential new friends.

Leonardo Greco was the capo of the Bagheria Family, from one of the districts surrounding Palermo which are the territorial preserves of the main Mafia clans in Sicily. Through his business front, Leonardo Greco had developed close links with Christian Democrat politicians, financiers and businessmen.

Olivero Tognoli, the originator of the plan to move the money out of New York, was Leonardo Greco's partner in a variety of business deals, including the iron warehouse in Palermo which was sometimes used for secret Mafia meetings. Although there may have been some legitimate enterprise between the two men, it was little more than a cover. The profits came from heroin. Greco controlled supplies of morphine base arriving by boat from Turkey, as well as a number of secret refining laboratories in Bagheria.

The main supplier of morphine base to the Sicilian Mafia was "Musullulu the Turk," a shadowy but immensely wealthy Turkish businessman who numbered Leonardo Greco among his clients. His real name was Yasner Avni Karadurmus. Musullulu surfaced in a secret DEA intelligence report which noted that he was operating out of Zurich. The information was passed on to the authorities in Zurich where the Turk had set up a network of front companies to charter freighters to transport his morphine base. These freighters, chartered by his own company, Oden AG Shipping, made secret rendezvous with small fishing boats some miles off a deserted stretch of Sicilian coastline. Sacks of morphine base would be humped on shore and thrown into the back of a truck or trailer and driven off to the laboratories.

Musullulu was also a well-known Middle East arms

dealer—a trade in which an international barter between drugs, guns and money was always possible and a trade which for years had been the speciality of Bulgaria, aided and abetted by corrupt officials and the intelligence service. The Turk often bought morphine base that the Bulgarians had confiscated and then sold it on to his Sicilian clients.

For an inclusive price Musullulu guaranteed delivery of morphine base in 500-kilo consignments to an area within 70 nautical miles of Sicily. He had agents working at Mazzara del Vallo, a dusty village near Trapani in Sicily where a refining laboratory belonging to the head of the Sicilian Mafia was located. The favored transfer point was the island of Marittima between Sicily and Sardinia.

Payment for the shipments was made in Zurich, where most of the cash that Amendolito laundered ended up. Other consignments consisted of couriers hand-carrying heavy suitcases bulging with small denomination bills. One courier regularly arrived with an entourage of six fellow Sicilians carrying suitcases containing between $3 million and $45 million in $50 and $100 dollar bills. The courier made 15 trips with his bodyguards, accounting for $45 million worth of morphine base. Translated to New York wholesale prices that was $500 million worth of heroin; at street level it worked out as $5 billion worth of heroin. It was a serious business.

The Musullulu connection ended when his Mafia contact arrived with his usual escort and $5.2 million in suitcases. The money was payment for a 500-kilo consignment of morphine base. The Sicilians were actually in credit for over a million dollars and were paying $13,000 a kilo for the base. Shortly after the meeting, Musullulu disappeared, absconding with over $6 million of Mafia money. He has never been heard of since. One report suggested that he was lying low but was keen to return to Turkey and was offering $750,000 to an agent of the Turkish intelligence service for a safe passage. Another report indicated that he had fled from Zurich to Bulgaria where one of his henchmen had set him on fire but that he had survived. Either way, stealing that amount of money from the Mafia was not conducive to life expectancy.

Such was the network that Amendolito was helping to sustain. Whatever he says now, his visit to Sicily must have rung alarm bells over the nature of the business that he had got himself involved with. One of the first things he did when he got back to New York was to contact Tognoli and ask for a rise in his commission. Now it would have to be 5.5 percent. He was running all sorts of risks, he didn't know who he would be dealing with from one day to the next, he was expected to drop everything and meet sinister people in deserted doorways, he was in constant danger and at times he was short of cash to run the business. Then there were fees to the banks to count the money, bribes to officials in the Bahamas and all the other expenses of laundering huge sums of money. Tognoli listened patiently to Amendolito's stream of complaints and agreed to his pay rise. He informed Amendolito that he had to visit Venezuela on a business trip and to be ready for more cash deliveries.

As with other money launderers, cover stories can easily be concocted to support the claim that they genuinely believed the money had nothing to do with drugs. For the investigators it is a constant headache; they treat the claims with a weary skepticism but it is difficult to prove otherwise. The RICO legislation allowed the prosecutors to charge the money men with being part of the overall conspiracy, "the spokes in the wheel," as one U.S. Attorney described it. But to acquire the necessary proof to confront a money launderer with the certain knowledge that he knew the source of his funds was virtually impossible.

With the expectation of additional funds, Amendolito set about the further streamlining of his business operations. One of his best investments was the purchase of an electronic money-counting machine. He opened three bank accounts in Bermuda, the quiet British offshore tax haven, which had all the advantages of the Bahamas and less of the corruption. He took his money to the Bank of Bermuda, the Bank of Butterfield and Barclays. He told the banks that he represented a group of Italian restaurant owners who were investing in a hotel in Sicily.

"I explained to them that I had reached an agreement

with a group of pizzerias who needed to transfer some money into a little place in Sicily and that I was going to make some out of it." So were the banks—no questions were asked.

In Manhattan, OBS collected the money and stored it in the new safe until there was enough to fill several suitcases. Then, accompanied by his bodyguard, Amendolito would book a flight to Bermuda or the Bahamas. On one occasion he was stopped at JFK airport as he was about to board a flight for the Bahamas. An official politely asked him to fill out a form for the $500,000 that he was carrying, which he duly did. After that Amendolito swapped the public inconvenience of the commercial airlines for the discreet luxury of chartered Lear jets. In Bermuda, the banks were so grateful for his business that the Bank of Butterfield thoughtfully provided an armored van and security guard to meet the jet and transport the money from the airport direct to the bank vaults in Hamilton. Once in the vaults, the money was simply wire transferred to a numbered account in Switzerland, part of the millions of daily transactions between the offshore banks of the Caribbean and the financial centers of Europe. Of course any delay could earn the depositor or the bank several thousand dollars in interest.

It was in the Bahamas that it all began to go wrong. Amendolito now professes to be shocked by the corruption of the small Caribbean island. At the time it is unlikely that he regarded it as anything more than a business expense. Bank tellers would deliberately miscount the dollar bills and pocket the proceeds, a widespread tax inflicted on lone operators. One way of bypassing the system was to buy political protection. On one of his visits to the Bahamas, Amendolito was introduced to a proprietor of a Bahamian company who promised him access to high-level political contacts and the chance of making even more money by investing in a fishing project. Amendolito was intrigued— to the tune of $250,000. The only problem was that the money belonged to the Sicilian Mafia. When they discovered it was missing they wanted it back.

Amendolito had also decided to invest some more of the Mafia's funds in "Italia Presenta," one of his numerous moneymaking schemes. Italia Presenta was set up as a food, gift and novelty distribution company to distribute Italian produce all over the Caribbean from the Miami free trade zone. According to Amendolito, it was going to be "a great initiative for Italian industry—which needed exports around the world." Once again the unwitting financier, the sleeping partner, was Olivero Tognoli, and behind Tognoli was a more sinister paymaster—the Mafia boss from Bagheria who was contemplating a trip to America. Amendolito was in trouble.

As the delays between the payments and transfers began to get longer and the explanations shorter, Olivero Tognoli became seriously concerned. Salvatore is someone who can talk his way out of practically any situation. His tactics are a beguiling cocktail of charm, naivete and sophistication. A façade of injured pride confronts the skepticism, exasperation and the cynicism with which most of his schemes are greeted. But whatever his abilities it was unlikely that they would cut much ice with the Sicilians.

Salvatore had succeeded in fobbing off an increasingly exasperated Tognoli with a bewildering variety of excuses for months. When the question of the missing money— some half million dollars in total—was raised, there was never a straight answer. He had even appealed to Tognoli's patriotism and that of his backers. Amendolito explained to the long-suffering Tognoli that the "Italia Presenta" export project could be vital for the "economic renewal" of the Italian economy. Such appeals were accompanied by Amendolito's vastly inflated optimism for the export prospects of the company. Awkward interruptions about the $500,000 shortfall were skillfully deflected by the suggestion that Tognoli and his associates should put their country first. Their country would be eternally grateful if they would only invest in such a promising export-led scheme. If he hadn't been a con-man, Salvatore Amendolito would have made rather a good politician.

Inevitably, Tognoli's clients lost their patience.

Amendolito's prevarication, delays and excuses seemed to lose something in the translation. A Sicilian does not like losing money, still less will he favor the prospect of being hoodwinked. A loss of face might be perceived as something far worse than the loss of the money.

For the second time Salvatore Amendolito was invited to Sicily. But this time there were no grand waterfront restaurants, no bottles of champagne, smiling waiters and expensive women. The Mormon bishop from Salt Lake City owed the Sicilian Mafia half a million dollars. And they wanted it back.

Amendolito was such a consummate confidence trickster that he seemed to have convinced himself that he could somehow ride out the storm—a conviction that was not shared by his long-suffering friend and business associate. Miniati, his erstwhile partner from Milan, was beginning to lose his nerve. Living in Italy, he felt too close to the situation for comfort. Under Mafia ritual, the person responsible for introducing someone into a business deal which later turns sour, or for vouching for someone who may turn out to be an undercover cop, will always be held accountable. It is regarded as an act of betrayal, even if the person was entirely innocent of any deception. Such mistakes could rarely be rectified but they could be punished. Usually by death.

"Miniati was in shock," recalls Amendolito. "In his opinion, I had already been sentenced to death. They had to get rid of me."

Similarly, Tognoli was almost out of his mind with fear. He was screaming with rage when Amendolito spoke to him on the telephone to discuss the trip. Fearing he had little choice, Salvatore reluctantly agreed to the meeting. He arranged to visit Tognoli before going on to Palermo.

Face to face, the young industrialist appeared to have calmed down. He even seemed subdued, resigned almost, except that Amendolito noticed that when he spoke his hands were shaking. Amendolito agreed he would have to go back to Sicily and explain about the missing funds. They discussed the timing of the trip to Sicily. Tognoli didn't see any point in beating around the bush any longer. "Are you going to return the money?"

Amendolito looked at him. He felt sorry for him. "Listen, I have no money," he confessed.

Tognoli turned white.

"It is MY problem. Not yours. Your neck is not in danger. Are they ready to talk about my company, Italia Presenta?"

"Yes," replied Tognoli who was probably as desperate as Amendolito to subscribe to some faith in the fictitious export scheme. "They are investors—but they want the money."

"Don't worry," soothed Amendolito. "Don't worry."

Tognoli's nervousness was contagious. The young man's naked fear was a clear signal that they were dealing with an organization of considerable power and ruthlessness. Amendolito was beginning to feel distinctly uneasy himself. Nevertheless, whether through bravery or stupidity, he decided to make the trip to Sicily with Tognoli.

"Someone comes to pick us up. One car after another. We change cars several times. First of all we drive for miles, coming to a deserted country road and we arrive at a small villa which has all its windows boarded up. The first person to arrive is Leonardo Greco. I looked straight at him, taking the attitude of someone who is not scared. He smiles. He's a nice guy! Right after he arrives, comes 'The Boss.' He is a smaller man, looks Spanish and he is introduced to me and I started talking—mainly small talk, setting the pace of the 'business meeting.' I say to them: 'Listen, I know there are two subjects on the agenda. First, let's start with Miami. It's a great opportunity for people like you who control the economy!' "

A combination of audacity, flattery and changing the subject coupled with an apparent immunity to fear began to work. The Mafia bosses had been forewarned by the nervous Tognoli that their American friend was engaged full-time in establishing Italia Presenta in the Miami free trade zone. It was all part of a carefully worked out strategy. Whilst Amendolito's pleas for patriotism may have fallen on deaf ears, the potential of a Miami-based export business which could be used as a front company was not lost on his captive audience.

"I let them believe everything could be arranged. They were so enthusiastic! They said 'When can we start?' "

Salvatore had succeeded with the first part of his plan. He had successfully sidetracked Leonardo Greco and his taciturn companion with his scheme, but he knew he was only buying time on borrowed credit. Their apparent enthusiasm might be nothing more than a ploy to lull him into a false sense of security. Then again, maybe they were genuinely interested.

Leonardo Greco certainly appeared to be amenable. Amendolito sensed he was making headway. It was the man sitting next to him that worried Salvatore. His cold eyes betrayed nothing and his blank expression signaled neither approval nor anger. The small man with the narrow moustache gave nothing away. But Amendolito realized he had seized the initiative; he just needed to keep going.

"Listen, there are two debts," explained the con-man, continuing to control the discussion by making sure that he himself raised the issue. "One, a check which bounced. The other is $300,000."

Amendolito felt that he had got a great weight off his chest merely by introducing the subject of the missing cash. He then launched into a lengthy explanation of how he had been ripped off in the Bahamas, how you couldn't trust anybody nowadays. Now was the time to play his "injured innocence" card. He recounted to Greco the sorry tale of his encounter with the proprietor of the Bahamian company and how he had been sold on the need to cut through the petty local corruption via a strategic alliance with crooked Caribbean politicians. Greco listened and nodded. This they could understand only too well.

The man with the thin moustache continued to sit in silence. His demeanor suggested he was more powerful than Greco, yet Greco was a capo and there were only one or two positions that could outrank a boss. Perhaps he was a wealthy investor, a shareholder in the drug business, looking to claim his dividends. Perhaps he was a hit man or a torturer.

Amendolito's thoughts were interrupted by a voice. "Edwards is your problem," said Greco after listening to Amendolito's endless litany of complaints about corruption in the Caribbean. "We want our money back," declared the Mafia boss, glancing over his shoulder at his silent companion. Amendolito breathed a silent sigh of relief. It wasn't over yet, but there was hope.

Leonardo Greco interrogated Amendolito about a sum of $100,000 which had disappeared from a consignment delivered to some Italian furriers from Naples. Amendolito had come prepared. He laid the blame on Castronovo, the New Jersey restaurant owner who had been his initial contact. Amendolito claimed that he must have confused two separate boxes containing different amounts of cash. Somehow, he explained, these had got muddled up.

"No one knew where it went," says Amendolito, disingenuous as ever. "But fortunately, Castronovo backed me. The Mafia bosses looked at each other as if to say 'Why bother me with this? He is a good guy.'"

Amendolito was on a winning streak. He couldn't believe his luck. "I was out. It was all smiles and friends!"

The atmosphere inside the claustrophobic and dusty villa in the Sicilian countryside visibly relaxed. Amendolito breathed a huge sigh of relief. What's more, Leonardo Greco seemed genuinely interested in Amendolito's Italia Presenta project, no doubt calculating in his own mind the dividends it might pay for his own international import-export trade. As Tognoli and Amendolito were leaving the villa, Greco summoned Tognoli back inside: "Tell Salvatore to forget about the $100,000. It's our fault."

Amendolito deserved an Oscar. It might be argued that the Sicilians were moving so much money around that actually they couldn't care less whether $100,000 here or there went astray. In reality, as Tognoli knew and Amendolito had begun to suspect, the Sicilian code of honor dictated that if losses were the result of a betrayal or a double cross, they would eliminate that person whether it was ten dollars or a million dollars.

Returning by as tortuous a route as he had arrived, Amendolito was driven back to the airport to catch his connecting flight from Rome and thence to the United States. On the flight back he felt that a large weight had been removed from his shoulders. He arrived in New York with a renewed sense of optimism. He was on a roll and, like any gambler, Amendolito was too intoxicated by his success to give much attention to anything else. It never occurred to him that the net might be closing in. All his energy and powers of concentration had gone into fending off his immediate problems. Nothing else mattered.

Apart from his accidental brush with officialdom at JFK Airport, Amendolito believed that he was leading a charmed life. A man who had just succeeded in facing down the Sicilian Mafia could be forgiven for neglecting to worry about American law enforcement agencies. They had rarely bothered him in the past; it was unlikely that was going to change.

Salvatore was picked up in New Orleans on a hot summer's night. News of his arrest was flashed to the World Trade Center in Manhattan, the headquarters of the U.S. Customs team that had spent more than a year tracking the Pizza Connection's million-dollar money couriers round the globe. Mike Fahy, the supervising agent, packed an overnight bag and took the first available flight from La Guardia to New Orleans. The resourceful U.S. Customs officer, in charge of the Pizza Connection case, was sticking to the money trail with the tenacity of a highly trained sniffer dog.

In a New Orleans prison cell, Fahy encountered a somewhat crestfallen Amendolito. Following his escape from the Sicilian Mafia, Amendolito had flown to New Orleans to put the finishing touches to a $100 million loan: Salvatore's company, Overseas Business Services, was acting as the intermediary between a group of oil sheiks and the Government of Costa Rica! Instead Amendolito found himself being rudely awakened in his hotel early one morning by the FBI. He had escaped the clutches of the Sicilian Mafia only to find himself threatened with charges of "currency violations" and money laundering.

Mike Fahy lost no time in stressing that the charges carried serious penalties. Fahy then ran through some additional charges that they may bring. "How about laundering the proceeds of narcotics to start off with?" suggested the Customs agent.

Amendolito was still high on the brilliance of his escape from a fate worse than death in Palermo; there was no way that he was going to jeopardize all that for some two-bit Customs charge. Fahy left him to stew overnight in the cell. He liked what he saw and realized they had a potential star witness.

Sure enough, it didn't take long for Amendolito's instincts for survival to get the better of him. He made a deal. In exchange for dropping the charges, Amendolito gave Mike Fahy an undertaking to cooperate and testify. His decision resulted in a starring role at the 1987 trial where he appeared as the Government's most valuable witness. Amendolito's intimate knowledge of the multimillion-dollar transactions of the heroin trade could provide the detailed evidence to convict Catalano and the other Mafiosi in America who ran the Pizza Connection.

When the case eventually came to court, Amendolito proved an excellent witness. In the OBS office, the FBI had discovered the piece of paper that he had carefully filed away in his Rolodex address machine. It was the scrap of paper that Catalano had given him on the street corner in Queens. It became the prosecution's prize exhibit. Even the defense lawyers privately admitted it was the most devastating piece of evidence against the lead defendant. More than anything else it helped to clinch the 40-year sentence that Catalano received for his drug trafficking career.

Once they were confident of gathering some of the financial records, providing the requisite hard evidence to put before a jury, the FBI could move in on the heroin traffickers, the money launderers, the couriers and the hit men. With Salvatore Amendolito as a cooperating witness they had the vital evidence of the money trail on both sides of the Atlantic. It was priceless intelligence about the operations of the Sicilian and American Mafia, information that was then circulated on secret reports and fed into the NADDIS computer system of the DEA with cross-references to major Mafia figures all over the world.

Amendolito's odyssey through the global connections of money laundering and his adventures in Sicily helped the prosecutors to identify the key players and to make additional sense of the fast accumulating database of tape-recorded telephone conversations both in Italy and America. Many of the Pizza Connection tapes were so cryptic as to be useless and some were so surreal that it was thought that not even the Mafiosi themselves knew what was going on. But in some cases, the tapes offered a tantalizing glimpse into the men who were sometimes known as "The Godfathers of Two Worlds."

— 9 —

THE GODFATHERS OF
TWO WORLDS

BY THE END OF THE PIZZA CONNECTION INVESTIGATION thousands of hours of secret tape recordings had been accumulated. They represented the fruits of a four-year investigation. Most of the tapes were the result of telephone intercepts and all the conversations were conducted in Sicilian. The geographical scale of the tapes was immense. Calls were monitored in New York, Chicago, Detroit, Miami, New Jersey, Rome, Palermo and Rio de Janeiro.

Behind the coded conversations and the obscure vocabulary used by those who were setting up the deals, the interpreters could occasionally detect a glimpse of the landscape of violence. Ironically, the war being waged by the Corleonesi in Sicily would bring unexpected benefits to the American investigators. Whilst the spoils of victory included the unchallenged supremacy over the heroin trade between New York and Palermo, some of those who survived lived to tell tales that were immensely damaging to the victors of the Mafia wars.

Although the informant and the supergrass had long been a common phenomenon in America, such people were extremely rare in Italy. The Sicilians took the oath of Omerta and its enforcement far more seriously than their American cousins. The Corleonesi, led by Michele Greco and Salvatore Riina, with Pino "Scarpazzedda" Greco as their chief executioner, changed all that. When a Mafioso survived only to discover that his children, wife, nephews, brothers and cousins had all been slaughtered by his enemies, even the strong pull of Omerta began to fade.

Tommaso Buscetta's epic act of betrayal gave new meaning to the ancient Sicilian proverb that "revenge is a dish best eaten cold." For the Italians and Americans, Buscetta provided the inside story of the postwar machinations of the Mafia in Sicily and America. He revealed the names and positions of all the top Mafia bosses, including a detailed account of the crimes of Michele Greco. He gave the investigators an account of how the Sicilians took over the heroin trade, the key players who arranged the American exports and the location of some of the heroin refineries. After he spent months being debriefed by the Italians in Rome he was flown to America.

When the FBI in New York ran into problems interpreting their hours of telephone intercepts, Buscetta was helpfully on hand to translate arcane Sicilian codewords. But there was one mysterious figure whose name was beginning to emerge from the telephone intercepts about whom Buscetta was being strangely reticent. The FBI knew he was one of the main heroin suppliers, but there was very little hard information on him. He had become a shadowy figure moving across Europe and South America. He would occasionally surface in the odd intelligence report attending some secret summit of the heads of organized crime meeting in Rome or Marseilles. He was known to have several aliases and a multitude of passports. The only thing that anyone could be sure of was that he had once been head of the Mafia in Sicily and had been ousted in mysterious circumstances, a loss of power which created the vacuum so brutally filled by the Corleonesi. His former position and a childhood friendship with Buscetta put him right at the center of the Mafia war but like Buscetta he survived.

Another mystery was that, given he was persona non

grata with the Sicilians, the New York buyers still seemed willing to do business with him. Or was it all an elaborate charade to try and draw the mysterious Mafia capo out of hiding so that he too could be murdered to satisfy the Corleonesi bloodlust? Alternatively it may have been that business was business. Mafia politics were all very well, but money was more important.

The figure was identified as Gaetano Badalamenti from Cinisi in Sicily. Despite his ability to evade capture, surveillance and his enemies it was, ironically, Badalamenti himself who led the police into the final act of the Pizza Connection case. Badalamenti was commuting between Europe and Brazil, where, along with Buscetta, he had sought refuge from his enemies in Palermo.

The Pizza Connection gave new meaning to the phrase "Family business." As well as the interlocking Mafia Families there were myriad connections of blood relatives involved in the trade. Badalamenti's point man in America was his nephew, Pietro Alfano. If Badalamenti had ever heard the saying that you can choose your friends but you are stuck with your relations, he seemed to have ignored it. Pietro "Pete" Alfano came dangerously close to being a congenital idiot. A small man with a pinched face and a long hangdog expression, his only family resemblance to his uncle were his prominent black eyebrows. If Badalamenti had not been on the death list of the Corleonesi and if the heroin trade had not been so dangerous, then he might have lived to see the funny side of his nephew's incompetence. As it was the wretched Alfano was a constant source of irritation and exasperation to his long-suffering uncle. Not only did Alfano have to endure his uncle's insults, he was also treated with contempt by Catalano's men in New York.

If the commodity they had been dealing in had not been so deadly, then the elaborate code that the Pizza Connection members used in their dealings with each other would have been almost comic. Heroin was "shirts," "cheese," "ovens," "tomatoes" and "suits." When the purity was low, the "clothing," the merchandise, was described as having a certain percentage of "acrylic"! Sometimes the codes were obvious, at other times the conversations were indecipherable. When the messages were being relayed from New York to Alfano in Chicago and then on to Badalamenti in Brazil, and then all the way back to New York, it was hardly surprising that misunderstandings occurred and tempers became frayed.

Although the Pizza Connection dealt in prodigious quantities of heroin, there were times when deals fell through. The FBI agents listening in would be as frustrated as the traffickers to find that weeks of surveillance and wiretaps came to nothing. Supply problems in Sicily could dry up the streets of New York City, while money problems in Manhattan could delay shipments from Palermo. That was what seemed to be happening in the New Year of 1984.

Pete Alfano, the small-time pizzeria owner from the Midwest, was caught in the middle. Alfano was mediating between his increasingly irascible uncle, hiding out somewhere in South America, and the New York buyers. With some trepidation, Alfano dialed their number to break the bad news that he had received from his uncle. The deal they had been setting up had fallen through. He tried to reassure them with the news that they were pursuing two other sources of supply. He pleaded with Catalano's men to be patient, begging them not to lose their tempers. "It's the bosses who are causing these problems," he wheedled, hoping to invoke sympathy for the common man.

New York told him to get his uncle on the line as soon as possible. Alfano duly made the arrangements. It was a thankless task as his uncle was not only trying to avoid the Brazilian police but also trying to keep out of the way of any Mafiosi affiliated to the Corleonesi. The order had come from Palermo that Badalamenti should be shot on sight. He was suspected of organizing yet another attempt on the life of Pino "Scarpazzedda" Greco. Greco had lived up to his nickname—meaning "Fleet of Foot"—and escaped unscathed. The Mafia's most efficient emissary of death either had a charmed life or was under the protection of even darker powers.

As one of the New Yorkers waited by a public pay phone

on Queens Boulevard for the expected call, he noticed a group of New York City housing officials approach the phone booth. In exasperation he saw one of them pick up the phone and make a call. Worried that it might be a surveillance team, the nervous Mafioso scuttled away.

The next day the message reached New York that their Sicilian chemist was now ready with some "cheaper paint." The cheap stuff could be delivered immediately. The more expensive material—the "good stuff"—would not be available for another three months. To the listening FBI it was apparent that there was a quality control problem. The available heroin was of low quality and therefore more difficult to sell.

The New York buyers were not happy. They protested to Sicily that they would not be able to satisfy their "big contractor." But the Sicilians were adamant—there was nothing they could do about it.

The American Mafia were desperate. That was where the hapless Alfano came in. Alfano could be the answer to their problems. They got back to him and told him they needed a large shipment—immediately. Another call was set up with Badalamenti. The New York buyers told the Brazilian fugitive that they could take care of the "little jobs" with the "cheaper paint" but that they would need his help with regard to the "more important matters."

Pete Alfano was dispatched to New York with samples of the merchandise. This was followed up a few days later by a phone call from Badalamenti to the New York buyers. Waiting by the pay phone in Queens were Salvatore Lamberti and Sal Mazzurco, Catalano's two main henchmen in New York. The phone began to ring.

Mazzurco, a diminutive but unusually good-humored Sicilian, looked around before picking up the receiver. "Hello . . . ?" said Mazzurco, speaking in the Sicilian dialect. The line was bad, full of cracks and hisses. "Hello?"

"Hello!" shouted the erstwhile head of the Sicilian Mafia.

Mazzurco pressed the phone closer to his ear. "How is it going?" inquired Mazzurco, nodding at his friend to indicate that they had made contact.

"But we are here," explained Badalamenti in one of the frequent non sequiturs that only seemed to make sense in the tortured vocabulary of the Sicilian Mafia. "You guys?"

"Well, thank God!" replied Mazzurco, presumably relieved that it was indeed the Mafioso he was hoping to speak to.

"Heh, what do you say?" said Badalamenti.

"Well, always the same old stories. And you?" inquired Mazzurco.

"Well, we are here," repeated the Mafioso, who in his heyday had controlled the small town of Cinisi, a lucrative freehold as his district included Palermo airport. Badalamenti had grown rich from the construction of the runway and the buildings and later from having the pipeline for international smuggling operations right on his doorstep.

Feeding a pocketful of Brazilian escuderos into his pay phone, Badalamenti continued with this apparently meaningless small talk before getting down to business. "Fort Lauderdale," he said, "you know where it is?"

"Eh!" said a puzzled Mazzurco. "Sure I know."

"Eh, from there they will go over there. Will that be fine with you guys?"

"Well I think so . . ." said Mazzurco.

"Eh . . . I think that by the beginning of the next week," continued Badalamenti, "they will come with 22 parcels and with 11 parcels, whatever you guys prefer."

"Uh, uhm," said Mazzurco.

"But since with him," continued the Mafia boss, "it also depends on . . . with the Customs there that they have to give him the answer for thing about the clearance."

"Yes," said Mazzurco.

"It's his opinion to come with all 22 parcels . . . or containers, no?"

"Uh, uhm."

"That would be alright for you guys, no?" asked Badalamenti.

"I don't know about the 22," said Mazzurco.

"We have to do it in a way because . . . and that's one," said Badalamnti. "In any case give me an answer."

"Alright," agreed the small Mafioso, shivering from the biting wind gusting down Queens Boulevard.

At least Badalamenti was somewhere warm. "Now there's another thing. I met the guy with the shirts of four years ago."

"Uhm," replied the man from New York City.

"But there's a little problem. But there is another guy here that had, there's ten percent acrylic. I understand little about this."

Mazzurco clearly did. "But ten percent is not bad," he said, seeing a potential solution to their problems in Sicily.

"However, I showed it to . . ." Badalamenti coughed and cleared his throat. "To a competent individual, more competent than I . . ."

"Yes . . . ?" inquired Mazzurco.

"And he told me," continued the old man, " 'Nothing,' he says, 'it's good . . .' he says, 'it contains ten percent acrylic.' "

"Uh, uhm," said Mazzurco, trying to sound noncommittal while freezing to death.

"Now and that practically—nothing," continued Badalamenti becoming more businesslike. "The cost over here is about 45 cents. And over there it will cost about 60 cents."

"Uh, uhm," repeated Mazzurco once more with appreciation.

Badalamenti coughed and cleared his throat again. "The price is good, and it seems to me, it seems to me that the things are not—what price is there right now?"

Mazzurco had already made the calculations. Perhaps it had been unwise for his distributor to discuss the wholesale prices. "Well, ah . . ." The wily Mafioso hesitated, giving himself time to think.

Out of all the Pizza Connection defendants, Salvatore Mazzurco was one of the more engaging. Mazzurco was in his early fifties, lived in Long Island, drove an expensive Mercedes and was the wealthy partner of a roller-skating emporium, clothes boutique and the Pronto Demolition Company. With receding, short, brown-gray, curly hair and reading glasses he was one of the less sinister looking defendants. When I met him briefly before the trial, he struck me as the most approachable of them. He displayed an amused interest in the portable electric typewriter that I was working with outside the courtroom. Yet according to the prosecution, Mazzurco was one of the ringleaders of the billion-dollar heroin ring and whatever personal charm he possessed was countered by the FBI surveillance pictures of Mazzurco collecting money and drugs from various locations. With Badalamenti he was nothing if not ambivalent and for a person who was normally talkative Mazzurco was being uncharacteristically quiet.

". . . to really tell you the truth really . . ."

Whatever it was Mazzurco was about to tell "The Old Man" was never revealed. He was interrupted by Badalamenti. "It should be good as soon as we talk again, you can tell me, because since now I will continue, this is one thing. Closed."

From reviewing the tapes the FBI were able to decode much of the conversation. Badalamenti was offering heroin at $90,000 a kilo. In New York they could get as much as $200,000 wholesale so there was money to be made. His supplier of the pure heroin wanted to keep half of the consignment to himself but realized he might need to work through the New York buyers because "he does not have an importer's license." Badalamenti emphasized that the "ten percent acrylic"—cut heroin—would cost New York $60,000 whereas "pure cotton" would be an additional $30,000. FBI agents were particularly intrigued by this comment to Mazzurco: "You guys already know the trademark because you have sold it over there." Either Badalamenti had done a similar deal with them four years ago or his supplier knew them of old.

The long distance telephone call ended with the traditional Sicilian greetings.

Mazzurco: "Many beautiful things."

Badalamenti: "I embrace you."

Mazzurco: "Bye-bye."

Badalamenti: "Many things."

From the thousands of pages of intercepts harvested from the wiretaps and Title 111's of the investigation, agents point to this one as being the most crucial. It provided an insight into past deals between Badalamenti and New York and it put the investigators on full alert for what appeared to be an imminent and massive shipment of heroin. FBI surveillance teams mounted a round-the-clock surveillance on the pay phones at Queens Boulevard. Using a blacked-out van, the FBI watchers kept shifts peering through a periscope which gave them a wide field of vision. Unable to turn the van heater on for fear of arousing suspicion the FBI agents waited, watched, listened and froze! Their patience was rewarded. Over the next week there were several more calls relating to the Badalamenti deal in Florida and the logistics of taking delivery of the 22 containers.

Another crucial call was arranged for February 14. A U.S. Customs surveillance team monitored Alfano's arrival at La Guardia Airport while an FBI team observed Mazzurco arriving with one of his colleagues for a summit meeting at Catalano's bakery in Queens. Although their discussion was not recorded, it was thought that the meeting was to discuss their response to the Badalamenti deal and what they would say to Alfano and his uncle when he telephoned.

The pay phone started ringing at 3:55 P.M. Alfano picked up the receiver.

Badalamenti then gave his nephew a list of instructions. "They told you the town over there, no?"

"No," answered Alfano. "They still haven't told me."

"Aren't they with you?" inquired Badalamenti.

"Yes," said Alfano.

"Ask them if they know, or else I will tell you. Listen to me . . ."

"Tell me," said Alfano.

Badalamenti spelled it out for his nephew. "Bring with you a hundred . . . then I will give you the name of the hotel. Friday night you will go to sleep over there. Saturday morning they will call you. They will look for Mr. Rossi."

Badalamenti, displaying a deep skepticism for the competence of his nephew, repeated the instructions several times. He asked Alfano if he understood clearly. Alfano promised that he did. As usual he deferred to his uncle, calling him "sir." Neither Badalamenti nor Mazzurco and his friends seemed to hold the hapless Alfano in much esteem. Badalamenti preferred to deal with Mazzurco, knowing that they were closer to the man who wielded the power. Later in the call he revealed his frustration to Mazzurco. "But why doesn't the boss ever want to come?" complained the old man. "What is it? What? What does he have? Does he always have things to do?"

"But what do you mean 'things to do'? Eh, he has a tail going after him," replied Mazzurco.

"Hah," said Badalamenti, apparently satisfied. "Anyway, you know the town, right?"

"Uh, uhmm," grunted Mazzurco.

"Tell it to my nephew," commanded the former head of the Sicilian Mafia.

When the FBI reviewed the tape later that day they were convinced that the deal was nearing completion. According to Badalamenti, it was "on the road." There was talk of the price being rather high due to a 15 percent transportation cost, but Badalamenti explained that this money was payment for the courier in Florida handling the shipment.

This is how the conversation ended.

"We will hear each other, okay?"

"So then you will call your nephew?" asked Mazzurco.

"Give him some money, to my nephew, now, because he has to leave it over there. Because I don't have any more; therefore or else . . ."

"Hah," replied Mazzurco. "He has to give it to them. Eh . . . those samples that, that he brought to me . . . I gave them to an individual. And day by day I am waiting for them to give me the result."

"Listen, he has to leave it there," said Badalamenti. "Therefore, there is nothing to be done. And I don't even have any to be able to send from here. But from here what can I send?"

"I tell you . . . at this exact moment, today . . . it's the same as if, if . . . as . . . squeezing a rock!" replied Mazzurco.

"You guys have to prepare it. Many regards."

"Thank you," said the ever polite Mazzurco.

"Good things," said Alfano's uncle.

"Bye-bye, bye."

"Good-bye."

Badalamenti was instructing the New York buyers to come up with $100,000 for the Florida shipment—money in advance which they were to give to his nephew. The money that was needed to pay off the courier in Florida— "Mr. Rossi." The demand for this advance payment and the arguments it provoked would precipitate the downfall of the multimillion-dollar drug network which had functioned with such efficiency for the last five years.

Alfano never got the $100,000.

Somewhere in Brazil was an increasingly exasperated Badalamenti. "What am I going to do with you?" chided the infuriated uncle. In a final phone call Badalamenti pleaded with the New Yorkers to give his nephew "eighty" for "samples." When the reply came that it was very difficult to do that at the moment, Badalamenti quietly pointed out that he would be "embarrassed" if the money was not handed over. The arrangements had already been set in motion. "That guy is on the road," he reminded them. "He has not learned that payment was not made. That guy is on the street with 22!"

What had happened was that one of the investors in New York was getting cold feet which meant that Mazzurco and associates were having a temporary cash flow problem. Then there was an argument about who was going to pick up the drugs in Florida and bring them to New York. Mazzurco claimed it was Alfano's responsibility, while Badalamenti insisted that it was Mazzurco's.

The New York dealers were increasingly concerned about surveillance and didn't want to risk being caught with the drugs. Alfano relayed the problem to his uncle who promptly ordered him not to deliver the drugs to New York. "Those are not your affairs, it's their affair," he instructed him. "You don't take the walk: they have to."

The FBI watched and listened with glee as the pizza men began to fall out with each other. Even "honor among thieves" seemed to have fallen out of fashion. The New

Yorkers were increasingly frantic to get their hands on the heroin for their "big contractor" while the former head of the Sicilian Mafia on the run in Brazil was increasingly desperate for cash. In the end he became so frustrated that he summoned the hapless Alfano to a meeting. In Madrid.

It was the break the investigators had been waiting for. For months they had been trying to pinpoint the whereabouts of the elusive Gaetano Badalamenti. Using satellite technology and with the help of an élite Brazilian police intelligence squad they had once pinpointed the area from which Badalamenti was making his calls. On another occasion they had actually discovered the exact telephone booth, but by the time a police car had arrived the Sicilian had vanished. The sense of mystery and the aura of power that surrounded the man tantalized the investigators.

What if they could turn him? Who knows what secrets could be unlocked?

Now came the biggest break of all—but it presented the FBI, U.S. Customs and the DEA with a quandary. Should they wait for the shipment of drugs or move in and arrest the New York dealers and hopefully Badalamenti and risk losing the shipment? Both options offered equal advantages and both carried equal risk.

Mike Fahy, leading the Customs investigation, had no doubts when Assistant U.S. Attorney Louis Freeh asked him: "Do we want the heroin or do we want Badalamenti?"

"Louis, anybody can get heroin," the Customs agent pointed out. "Get a shot at Badalamenti."

They took Fahy's advice. In 1972, the young Fahy had begun working for U.S. Customs while still a student. A lucky break led to him discovering 82 kilos of pure heroin packed tightly inside 169 cellophane packets stuffed inside the door frame of a Ford Galaxy shipped over on an Italian ship, the SS *Rafaello*. It was one of the first shipments of the Pizza Connection. The car belonged to Gaetano Badalamenti. Fahy realized with a grim determination that its rightful owner now stood a chance of receiving the justice which he had successfully evaded for so long. But first they had to catch him.

"We just keyed in on Alfano's phone," recalls Fahy. "The Bureau out in Illinois keyed in on his phones when we knew that he was leaving. When Alfano left, we knew exactly where he was going. He was going from Chicago to Madrid. So we figured that Badalamenti was in Madrid and we had the DEA set it up with the Spanish cops and they followed him."

From the moment that Alfano boarded the KLM flight in Chicago he was under surveillance. At Madrid's Barajas Airport the FBI and DEA team was discreetly met by the Spanish police.

Alfano was met by Badalamenti's son. They were then trailed to an apartment in a wealthy suburb of the city—11 Santa Virgilia Street. Once the building was identified plainclothes agents from the Spanish police accompanied by their American counterparts surrounded it. After a night of waiting and watching, two men were observed leaving the apartment. On Sunday, April 8, 1984, at 11:30 in the morning the former *capo di tutti capi* and his nephew were arrested taking a quiet stroll through a street in Madrid.

Back in New York City, at the FBI control room headquarters, the tension was as noticeable as the thick smoke that was filling the air, despite the no-smoking signs on the walls. Semicircular desks faced a large computer display screen and smaller monitors which simultaneously displayed the output of the three U.S. networks, CNN and microwave links from FBI surveillance vans. The signs on the desks indicated the importance of the occasion. Special Agents from the DEA, U.S. Customs, the Bureau, the U.S. Attorney's office and the New York City Police Department, all had ringside seats. A row of clocks above the monitors gave the time in the different capitals of the world. But everyone's eyes were fixed on the time in Europe. They were five hours ahead. The head of the FBI got the news first. Badalamenti was claiming to be a Brazilian businessman, Paolo Barbosa, but they had made a positive ID and he was now in custody. The news triggered a wave of relief and elation around the room. Now they could arrest everyone else. The Pizza Connection was about to be disconnected.

The massive arrest operation began at dawn the following day. It was the culmination of an investigation which reached back more than a decade. Standing by in locations all over America were armed arrest and search teams made up of agents from the FBI, DEA and U.S. Customs. Each squad had a photographer and an agent in charge of the team's physical security.

"I used every dog team that we had," recalls Mike Fahy with pride. "Twenty-two dog teams running around to different locations. As soon as we locked everybody up here the Italians just moved in and locked everybody up in Italy. Everybody that we were looking for was locked up in a couple of days. There were 32 people between Switzerland, Italy, Spain and the United States. It was like a well-organized pincer movement the way everything was coordinated. It was good. And then they were all arraigned. We had everybody locked up by four A.M. and then we had a couple of drinks."

While Alfano languished in a jail cell in Madrid, agents searched his pizzeria in Oregon, Illinois. They found a rifle, a submachine gun with a silencer, three automatics and two bulletproof vests. Later events gave an indication as to why the slight and ineffectual looking Sicilian might have needed such a sizable armory.

On February 14, 1987, as the Pizza Connection trial was entering its final stages, Pietro Alfano and his wife had just finished buying some groceries at Balducci's deli in Greenwich Village. As they headed downtown laden with four shopping bags crammed full of pasta and cold meats, a red Chevrolet screeched to a halt. Two men leapt out and started emptying their guns into Alfano's back. One of the gunmen fled down the street and jumped into a waiting blue van. His accomplice calmly hailed a yellow cab and disappeared into the afternoon traffic. They had been paid $40,000 for the contract. Although the police later caught up with the hit men, the reason for the shooting was never satisfactorily explained.

Could it have been that the exasperation induced by dealing with Alfano may have contributed to the decision to try and kill him? Possibly. Could the fact that he led the authorities to Badalamenti and precipitated the mass arrests of the other members of the world's largest heroin ring be the motive? Perhaps. Or was it the case, as the leading Defense Attorney suggested at the trial, that being caught in the middle of the Mafia power struggle in Sicily meant that there was an outstanding death warrant against Badalamenti and the rest of his Family? The Corleonesi had shown a ruthless lack of discrimination in the past when it came to murdering the relatives of their enemies. With Badalamenti locked up in the Manhattan Correctional Center just behind the courthouse at Foley Square, he was untouchable. Alfano was a close relative and an easy target.

Unusually in the case of mob hits and contract killings, the police identified not only the actual shooters but also the man who had given the orders. Working on a tip-off from an informant, the police arrested Philip Ragosta, Giuseppe Amico and Mario DeGraza, A fourth suspect in the shooting was Frank Bavosa, aged 41, from New Jersey, who confessed to the police about his role in the shooting and gave details of the "contract." The information led them to the alleged mastermind behind the hit. He was Pasquale Conte, a multimillionaire businessman from Roslyn, Long Island. Conte was picked up nine days after the attempted shoot-out as he was about to board an American Airlines flight to Puerto Rico at JFK airport.

Conte was an alleged capo in the Gambino Family. He was also a member of the board of directors of the Key Foods supermarket chain, the sixth largest food chain in New York, and president of Conte Supermarkets which owned more than a dozen stores in the metropolitan area. In 1983 the Conte firm with head offices at 39–42 59th Street, Woodside, Queens, had grossed more than $51 million. Pasquale Conte had never been arrested before. When they searched Conte's home, police discovered ten guns, a bulletproof vest and a large amount of cash.

It was alleged that the hit men had been paid $10,000 each plus $10,000 for expenses—a total of $40,000.

It was rumored that Conte was the ultimate boss of the Pizza Connection, receiving a payoff on every kilo of heroin smuggled into America but when the case came to court witnesses and informants mysteriously lost their memory. The charges against Conte were dropped.

The presence of a high-ranking member of the Gambino Family was significant. Catalano was a capo in the Bonanno Family but his activities were well known to the Gambino Family. It is inconceivable that he would have been allowed to operate without their sanction. Despite the edict forbidding drug deals within his own Family, Gambino boss Paul Castellano tolerated the "zips" and their heroin dealing. When it came to his own "soldiers" it was a different story.

10

TRIALS

THE ATTEMPT ON ALFANO'S LIFE LEFT HIM PARALYZED. **I**t was also a depressing reminder to law enforcement officers that there were those right at the top of the international heroin trade who had probably evaded capture and would continue to do so. Nevertheless, the breaking of the Pizza Connection was a considerable success and the subsequent court case was a historic occasion on a number of counts.

Appropriately, the world's longest Mafia investigation was succeeded by America's lengthiest court case. The trial was held in the somber, wood-paneled surroundings of Federal Courtroom 506, Foley Square, Manhattan. It began on October 29, 1985 and closed on June 22, 1987. It had lasted a mind-numbing 20 months. The trial cost the taxpayers $50 million. It made fortunes for some of the 22 defense lawyers and brought others to the verge of bankruptcy.

When the long-suffering jury finally retired to reach their verdict they had to recall events stretching back more than 18 months. Each juror was given a 59-page verdict sheet, a 100-page copy of the judge's instructions, a copy of the indictment which ran to another 129 pages and a 410-page notebook summarizing the prosecution case.

In summing up, the Government prosecutors described the defendants as "one of the most efficient and dangerous criminal groups in the world." The lead prosecutor, Richard Martin, had devoted six years of his life to just one case. It made his reputation and earned him a position with the U.S. Embassy in Rome as legal attaché. He had seen enough of the inside of a courtroom to last him a lifetime. For his boss, U.S. Attorney Rudy Giuliani, the trial was a triumph and a vindication of the RICO statute which had been used to justify the mass trial.

"I think that there has to be a recognition that when you're at the level that Mr. Badalamenti was at and Mr. Catalano and the others in this enterprise, you are basically running something akin to 'Murder Incorporated,'" said Giuliani. Despite the frequent complaints from defense lawyers about the infringement of their rights through a mass trial process, Giuliani had no such doubts. "You are directly making your millions of dollars from the death of other human beings. These people are running an enterprise that leads to murder and destruction. That has to be recognized at the time of sentence."

It was.

Salvatore Catalano got 45 years which he is now serving at Leavenworth Federal Penitentiary in Kansas, a prison with a strong Mafia tradition which had once housed another notorious Mafia drug lord—Carmine Galante, the former head of the Bonanno Family allegedly executed by Catalano.

Gaetano Badalamenti is serving 45 years in Marion, Illinois, reputed to be the worst prison in America. He is occasionally heard muttering darkly in Sicilian about how he will soon be sent back to Italy where he believes his "power" will once more be in the ascendant. There is also a chance that the Italians will extradite him to face charges and there is still the hope that he may one day decide to cooperate.

Salvatore Mazzurco was sentenced to 20 years on narcotics conspiracy charges and 15 years under RICO, the sentences to run consecutively.

Carmine Galante's former bodyguard, Baldassare

"Baldo" Amato, fared somewhat better. His lawyer earned the admiration of his fellow attorneys by plea-bargaining his client into an admission of guilt on a RICO charge in return for the dropping of the narcotics conspiracy case. In May 1988 the judge gave Amato a five-year sentence. Following parole Amato was freed in 1993.

Ironically, Amato owed his lenient sentence to his murdered boss, Carmine Galante. Galante's ghost had haunted the proceedings. Originally the 1979 murder was part of the Pizza Connection indictment until defense lawyers successfully moved for it to be struck out of the proceedings. Subsequently, Amato's lawyer was able to present a strong argument for a mistrial on the grounds that the Galante killing had been used at the beginning of the case to besmirch his client only to be struck from the record later. In law it was a valid point. It was a sign of the strength of his motion that the judge agreed to a deal.

The murder of Carmine Galante in the summer of 1979 had been approved at the highest levels of the Mafia. Gambino boss Paul Castellano had personally approved the hit. Galante had been "whacked out" because of his open hostility to the other mob bosses. True, they didn't like his blatant involvement in narcotics, but that was a secondary motive.

As "boss of bosses," Castellano was responsible for the spiritual welfare of those within his parish, which included the Bonanno Family. However much he protested about narcotics to the members of his own Family he had been powerless to stop the wholesale involvement of Catalano and the other Sicilians servicing the heroin pipeline to America. Equally Castellano would have received money from drug deals, the difference being that those who offered the tribute would have disguised its origin. Castellano's disapproval was motivated by self-preservation and his ambition to expand the Gambino Family's legitimate interests. Or at least "legitimate" businesses based on extortion and corruption, which in his eyes amounted to the same thing.

Joe Coffey, from the New York State Organized Crime Task Force, who had followed "Big Paul's" career with avid interest, confirms his prohibition on drugs. "He was dead against narcotics and the reason for that was he felt that it brought heat to his so-called legitimate enterprises. They have no moral commitment here whatsoever and the only thing they are concerned with, and that includes Paul Castellano and every other guy who ever preceded him or followed him, their only God is the almighty dollar."

It was a doctrine of faith followed by "The Pope" with a devotion that would have done credit to his namesake. Ultimately, it was a religion that he would die for.

Whilst Castellano failed to enforce his prohibition throughout the Mafia he did succeed in excommunicating the Bonanno Family. They were barred from the innermost workings of the Commission and denied a seat on the supreme council. But when their leader Phil "Rusty" Rastelli wanted his position formalized he appealed to the Mafia's Supreme Court for their old seat back. Castellano was surprisingly sympathetic but the others were firmly against it, as the tapes show.

FBI bugs installed in the headquarters of Fat Tony Salerno provided a fascinating insight into the effect of Commission disapproval of Bonanno involvement in the narcotics trade. Disapproval of the "junk dealers" had the full backing of fellow Commission member Tony "Ducks" Corallo, the foul-mouthed head of the Lucchese Family. Like Castellano, the boss of the Lucchese Family feared the "heat" it was bringing on Mafiosi like himself: the "legitimate" wiseguys. Corallo had also issued an edict in his own inimitable style. "Anybody fucking with junk, they gotta be killed. That's all. Fuck this shit."

The Mafia bosses knew that the federal agencies were increasing their budgets by targeting drugs and that meant more heat for organized crime. The problem was that outside their own Families there was not much Corallo or Castellano could do. Mob rules made it difficult to kill members of other Families unless agreed by the Commission. The only effective step they could take was to give the Bonanno Family a wide berth—particularly their leader Phil "Rusty" Rastelli.

An FBI microphone hidden in the ceiling of the Palma

Boys Social Club picked up a conversation which revealed the arguments raging within the Commission over what to do about the Bonanno Family.

"There's a meeting Friday over the union, Paul, Tony, and another guy, uh, Gerry Lang. Just the four of us. For what?" complained Fat Tony Salerno. "About Rusty. Meet me at Strang Clinic. I won't go there with Rusty if it was a million-dollar deal. I won't go there for nothing. First of all, it's a Friday, I'm never around here on a Friday. Second of all, what is this meeting that Paul is talking about? Tell them to take care of it themselves. Because I told Paul four times what to do. He kept telling me, 'What are we gonna do about Rusty? He's so interested in the title, must be an angle someplace.' So I tell him, I said to Paul: 'That's the boss if the Family wants him. But, as far as the Commission, he cannot be on it.' Well now, what is he trying to prove? This Commission, them guys don't want to deny that they aren't switching. First they wanted to go before the Commission. The Commission tells them who's gonna be the boss. Don't you see? I don't want to answer. They're all junk men, all junk men."

Salerno was outraged that they should have tried to schedule a Commission meeting on a Friday afternoon. Didn't they know that was when he went to his upstate country residence? "On a Friday! I ain't been in this town. I never was here for 30 years on a Friday. Meet with this guy on a Friday!"

In Rhinebeck, New York State, Salerno had a large house and a stud farm. Wealthy residents were intrigued to receive invitations at Christmas to lavish parties and banquets where Fat Tony held court. Upstate, Fat Tony Salerno was a pillar of society. In downtown Manhattan, Salerno's only interest in the community lay in its wholesale exploitation. His "office" and the headquarters of the Genovese Family was a dilapidated building in a rundown area at 416 East 115th Street on the borders of Harlem.

If Paul Castellano was the "boss of bosses" on the Commission, then Fat Tony was its elder statesman. Every morning without fail Fat Tony Salerno could be found shortly after ten sipping coffee and holding court at his social club. Like his fellow bosses Fat Tony didn't have a lot of time for the "junk men" or their leader Phil "Rusty" Rastelli. As far as he was concerned the whole lot of them were drug dealers.

"Yeah," said Micky Generoso, a Genovese sidekick, agreeing with Salerno's dismissal of the Bonannos. "Most of them, yeah."

"Yeah, number one," said Salerno, grateful for the endorsement. "Number two, they should take care themselves. They make him, they make him the boss . . ."

"Rusty, if the Family wants him. They present it to somebody and then . . ." Micky Generoso was referring to the fact that it was normal practice for a Family boss to be elected by the members of his own Family.

Salerno interrupted his observation to continue his complaint: "I told the Commission, 'Ah, hey, listen, this guy wants to be the boss. He can be the boss as far as I'm concerned,' I said, 'but he *cannot* be on the Commission. One vote is enough to throw it out.' 'Cause that, ah, the Commission thing, it's supposed to be such a sacred thing." In his elder statesman role Salerno saw himself as keeper of the sacred flame of the Cosa Nostra—"This Thing of Ours."

In the New Year of 1984 Salerno found himself at odds with Paul Castellano. "The Pope" seemed to be having second thoughts about the exclusion of Rastelli from the Commission. Rusty had been making overtures to the "boss of bosses," pointing out the difficulty he was having within his own Family, where his own recognition as head of the Family was compromised by his failure to have a voice on the Mafia's ruling council. Salerno was equally adamant that they had to keep Rusty away from their meetings. In one conversation that the FBI secretly recorded at the Palma Boys Social Club, it appeared that Castellano might have changed his mind.

"Now I told him up there, 80 times. I says, 'But he cannot sit on the Commission.' So he came back about four weeks ago and he said uh, 'You know, uh, Rusty likes to meet us. Let's meet him,' he says, 'and we'll straighten it out.' Well there's nothing to straighten out. 'He wanted to be the boss, make him the fuckin' boss,' I said. I said, 'As far as the Commission, they don't want him. That's all.' Now if we meet, we see what goes on. Whether they come to the meet, who the fuck knows?"

Fat Tony was talking to the underboss of the Lucchese Family, Salvatore "Tom Mix" Santoro and Lucchese consigliere "Christie Tick" Furnari. The Lucchese underboss had also heard that Castellano was about to allow Rastelli on the Commission and that he had the support of another Commission member "Gerry Lang," the acting boss of the Colombo Family. "I don't know how they feel about it," retorted Salerno, "I don't want to see him on the Commission."

"They took too many junkies," added Santoro.

"I know all these guys from Canada. They're all in the junk business. Now they'll be coming down here to meet with us. We'll be meeting them and we'll be able to get into this fuckin' shit."

Furnari expressed his surprise to Fat Tony. Only yesterday he had met Gerry Lang of the Colombo Family who had just come from a meeting with Castellano. Gerry Lang indicated that Fat Tony had given the go-ahead for Rastelli's membership on the Commission.

"What a cocksucker this guy is!" exclaimed Salerno. "I can't make it out."

The Lucchese underboss probed further. "Did he mention the word 'Commission'—Gerry Lang?" asked Santoro. "That he okayed him to be a boss?"

The issue revolved around the distinction between being a "boss" and the head of a Family. While everyone on the Commission agreed Rastelli was the rightful head of his Family, he was not formally recognized as a "boss" because he did not have a seat on the ruling board of organized crime.

"Did Gerry Lang want him on the Commission?" inquired Salerno.

"No, he okayed it. To be a boss. Now he spoke to Paul . . ." replied Furnari.

"But not the Commission," added Santoro. "Now who threw the word 'Commission' in?"

There was a certain amount of confusion over Rastelli's exact status. Salerno needed to know whether there was a genuine misunderstanding or whether there was a serious dispute within the Commission. Hence the need to establish the position of Gerry Lang who, as an acting boss, had both a seat on the Commission and a vote on matters of strategy. Misunderstandings like this could get out of hand and lead to all sorts of problems. Even a war.

"No, no, pay attention to what I'm saying," Santoro told his consigliere. "Gerry Lang said that it's okay for him to be a boss. Did he say it's okay for him to be on the Commission?" Furnari didn't know.

"Do youse guys want him on the Commission? Do you?" asked Fat Tony in a rare spirit of democracy.

"Does Gerry want him on the Commission?"

"I don't know," the Lucchese Family's consigliere admitted, "but he says it's alright with him. And I says, 'Well I gotta get back to you.'"

"Okay," said Santoro, attempting to sum up the situation, "so in the next ten days he could be the boss of the Family, but he can't sit on the Commission."

"Paul wants him to sit on the Commission?" muttered Salerno in shock.

"And he's the one that says you okayed it," interjected Furnari.

"No, he can't say that," said Salerno, beginning to get agitated. "I got two witnesses! I'll make them tell . . ." Salerno was puzzled, he thought that the issue had been settled. What was Castellano playing at? "I really don't understand," Salerno confided to his friends, "why he's so insistent, Paul, on why, number one. Number two, he wants him on the Commission. Why? What does he wanna do with these guys? There's nothing but trouble in it for us. It's an open book."

Eight weeks later the Bonanno issue still hadn't been resolved. Just before five in the afternoon Fat Tony was talking to Genovese capo Matty "The Horse" Ianiello. In a conspiratorial whisper Salerno confided in the fellow mobster that he had boycotted a Commission meeting. Salerno related how he had met with Tony Corallo, head of the

Lucchese Family, and told him in no uncertain terms that he was sticking to his guns.

" 'Count me out,' I says. Just like that. 'Count me out.' You don't plan to go to the meeting, why the fuck should I go and sit down and bust his balls? You go there, Tony, tell him, 'You cannot be on the Commission. I'm against that.' "

Fat Tony Salerno shared Corallo's conviction that drugs were redoubling the Government's efforts against organized crime, hence their need to dissociate themselves from those known to be involved. They also knew that using RICO the prosecutors could ask for heavy sentences and if drugs were involved the chances were that they would get them. The underboss of the Cleveland Mafia had just been given one of the heaviest sentences in the history of the mob. "One hundred twenty-five years to the Cleveland underboss," lamented Fat Tony one afternoon in the Palma Boys Social Club. "A hundred years and the judge gave him another 25 to run consecutively!"

Salerno was complaining to Joe Zingaro, a mobster worried that both he and an associate were about to be arrested. Zingaro had turned up at his friend's house to suggest that they "go on the lam"—hide out until the heat had died down. "Fucking guy," complained Zingaro. "Go over his house. Duck in a car. He didn't want to go to the fucking country with me."

Salerno sympathized. "He should stay in Miami and forget about everything for about a month or two anyway. We know this guy's on your ass, this fucking Giuliani."

"Go away," mused Zingaro, "I mean go, go someplace for four weeks. Go away, go away for some time."

"They made another pinch over here," Salerno told him. "Three buildings away from here, 30 people selling junk. The whole building!"

Being so close to Harlem, the Palma Boys Social Club was surrounded by the wholesalers and dealers of the black-dominated heroin trade. In the rundown tenements that surrounded the club, there were crack houses and "shooting galleries" where strung-out junkies could buy a fix for a few bucks and hire a needle by the hour. In hot,

windowless rooms, women stripped to the waist cut the
precious commodity with milk powder or detergent. But
the dealers, traders and users knew better than to drop in
at Number 416. The Palma Boys could have been in another country.

Zingaro expressed surprise at news of the bust and
pressed Fat Tony for more details.

"No, I didn't know nothing. We never seen no bulls
around there, or agents. When they went in there and took
everybody out . . . I never saw an agent around here.
About four buildings from here. Right downtown."

The next problem Salerno had to deal with was a request from Rastelli to "make" some new members for his
Family. Worried by the arrests in the Pizza Connection and
struck by a high mortality rate, the Mafia's compulsory retirement scheme was creating staff shortages in the middle
ranks of the Bonanno Family.

In an attempt to tighten up security Castellano and
Salerno had forbidden the recruitment of new members. To
undergo the full initiation rights now required Commission
approval.

The message was relayed by Ianiello. "Rusty, he wants
to know if it's okay to make these guys. He gave me a list."

"What is this? He ain't got nothing to do with . . ."
groused Salerno.

"Well, he's got something but he don't like that . . ."
replied Ianiello.

"I don't even know what to do with this thing," said
Salerno.

"Wait a second . . ." said Ianiello.

"Listen, we don't recognize him down there," repeated
Salerno. "He's too tired and then he wanted to meet. Paul
didn't want to meet. Tony Ducks didn't want to meet. Tony
Ducks told Rusty, he said, 'Listen,' he said, 'Take care of
your Family first. Straighten out your Family and when you
straighten them out, then we talk about the Commission.'
He wants to be on the Commission. But there are too many
junk guys. They got a crew of 80 guys like that."

Fat Tony suddenly saw the funny side of it. His massive
frame began to rock with laughter. "How could they meet

The Ravenite Club before it was bricked up to deter break-ins by the FBI.

The club after it was bricked up.

A surveillance still of John Gotti (*right*) and Frankie
De Cicco, the underboss of the Gambino Family who
betrayed news of Castellano's appointment at Spark's
Steak House. For Castellano it became a rendezvous
with death.

John Gotti and Angelo Ruggiero (*right*).

GOVERNMENT
EXHIBIT
771-B

Anthony "Fat Tony" Salerno (with hat and cigar),
boss of the Genovese Family, photographed by the
FBI outside his Harlem headquarters, the Palma
Boys Social Club. A bug inside recorded Fat Tony
expressing his incredulity that the FBI could have put
a microphone inside his fellow boss's car—Tony
Corallo's Jaguar.

A surveillance picture of Benito Zito greeting the daughter of Guiseppe Ganci, Catalono's right-hand man in the "Pizza Connection." Zito is holding a package of heroin concealed inside a box of chocolates.

Ralph Scopo (*left*) having a business meeting with his underboss, Gennaro "Gerry Lang" Langella, from the Colombo Family.

Ralph Scopo under surveillance in the Queens parking lot. He holds an envelope containing a construction-contract payoff.

Neil "The Lamb" Dellacroce outside the Ravenite Club on Little Italy's Mulberry Street. John Gotti's mentor held court in the dingy social club until his death in December 1985.

Sammy "The Bull" Gravano, Gotti's underboss. Described as a serial killer by Gotti's defense lawyer, he is the highest-ranking defector in the Gambino Family (*New York Post*).

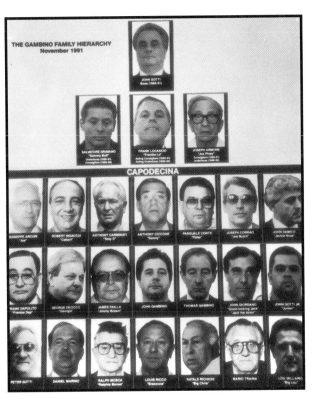

An FBI composite of the Gambino Family.

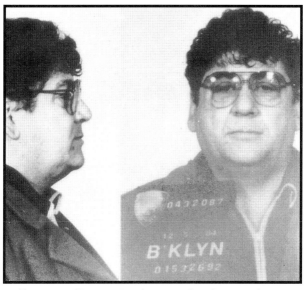

William "Willie Boy" Johnson, the first mafioso to betray John Gotti. He became an FBI informer and Gotti had him killed.

John Gotti (*left*) in conversation with his underboss, Neil Dellacroce.

A surveillance picture of Angelo Ruggiero (*far left*), a major heroin trafficker and Gotti's right-hand man and confidant.

John Gotti conferring with Bruce Cutler (*center*), his
defense lawyer who won him three acquittals.

Anthony "Tony Roach" Rampino, one of Gotti's crew, a heroin addict and hit man in the Castellano execution.

John Gotti, boss of the Gambino Family, leaves his Ravenite Club headquarters. The bearded man is Gerald Shargel, a high-powered Mafia defense attorney. Conversations between Gotti and his lawyers were picked up by the FBI bugs.

Frank Sinatra (*third from left*) with Carlo Gambino
(*third from right*) and Paul Castellano (*extreme left*).

An FBI surveillance picture of a "Commission"
meeting. The man in the check jacket is Tommy
Bilotti, Paul Castellano's driver and underboss.

A crime scene picture of Paul Castellano's murder.

Tommy Bilotti murdered by John Gotti.

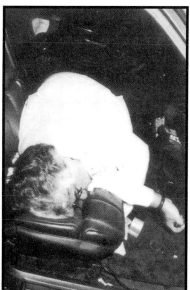

The corpse of Louie Di Bono, murdered by Gotti for "challenging the administration."

The "White House," Castellano's Staten Island mansion, which was bugged by the FBI.

Salvatore Mazzurco and Guiseppe Ganci (*right*) who set up their million-dollar drug deals on pay phones that were tapped.

with this guy?'' he chortled. Salerno turned his attention to the request to make some more wiseguys. "First of all did the guys die?"

"I don't know, Tony," confessed Ianiello. "I just should bring a message to you."

"He's only supposed to make guys that died," said Salerno, referring to a Commission ruling which stated that the only new members allowed were direct replacements for those who had passed away.

"We got to find out," replied Ianiello, joining in the laughter.

Salerno glanced down at the list he had been handed. "I don't know none of them. They don't put the nicknames down there." Salerno thought it was all a bit of a joke. "But anyway, I'll leave this up to the boss," he laughed.

Ianiello took the list back. "Frankie Cheech from Brooklyn . . . do you know these guys?"

"We have no authority. He could do anything he wants."

"Yeah, but he wants to make sure he don't put nobody in there that a guy's got something against," explained the messenger.

"Yeah, but he should . . ." continued Salerno. "He doesn't know that he's only supposed to make guys that are dead like that, in other words if he would have had the dead guys. When you make them guys, you got to have dead guys."

"Call back there and tell him," suggested Ianiello. "Let me ask you something. Here's what you do. Go back, tell Gerry. Tell him put the nicknames of these guys. Tell him to put the nicknames."

"He could make guys that died," added Salerno helpfully.

"Replace them?"

"Replace the guy that died if he wants," confirmed Fat Tony.

"In other words," said Ianiello, speaking slowly to make sure that he was getting it right. "Get the names of these guys, whose place the guys taken that died, and the nicknames of these guys."

"That's all," said the ever reasonable Salerno, "and the guy's name, like his name, now let me give the name of the deceased." As the mob's most senior undertaker, Salerno was a stickler for formality.

"Right, and nicknames of the guys, the nicknames also," said Ianiello, acting for all the world like the club secretary of some exclusive members-only organization—which was more or less what he was.

Joe Coffey had followed Fat Tony Salerno's criminal career with interest from the days when he was a New York City street cop. Working as a uniformed sergeant, Coffey's duties had included patrolling the zone around 115th Street, the area which contained the Palma Boys Social Club. Although organized crime investigations were off-limits to the uniform cops of NYPD, Coffey began to take a keen professional interest in the activities of the brick-fronted building in East Harlem. He was intrigued by the expensive cars illegally parked on the sidewalk and the stout man with the Homburg hat who shuffled along the pavement surrounded by fawning admirers. Sergeant Coffey and his fellow patrolmen jokingly referred to the club as "Mafia World Headquarters."

The young sergeant would cruise past in his patrol car and take down the details of the cars outside the club. At the end of each day Coffey sent detailed reports to the NYPD intelligence division charting the day's comings and goings at the club.

Word soon reached Fat Tony that an overzealous street cop was taking an unhealthy interest in his visitors. One day Coffey was sitting behind the wheel of his patrol car when he noticed the fat gangster waddling towards him. Coffey lowered the window. With a sneer on his face, Salerno addressed the handsome young policeman as if he was a form of lowlife trespassing where he didn't belong. "If you keep sending those reports to your bosses downtown, you're gonna get a transfer!" growled the head of the Genovese Family and strode off. From that moment Coffey made a point of stepping up his observations on 115th Street and filed even more reports. Coffey realized that Salerno's warning was made in the secure knowledge that the Genovese organization had several corrupt cops on its payroll. Such knowledge merely made Coffey redouble his efforts against the millionaire from Rhinebeck.

Sergeant Coffey became a familiar face to the inhabitants of Harlem. Salerno would occasionally saunter over to his patrol car and trade insults. On another occasion during City elections for the District Attorney, Salerno approached Coffey and pointed to an election poster stuck on the wall of the diner next to his club. "See that man there?" said Salerno, pointing to a picture of Frank Hogan who was running for the D.A.'s office. "A great man, but his assistant—we hate him." With that Salerno walked back to his "office." Coffey was unimpressed with Salerno's political endorsement of the candidate for District Attorney. When Coffey was promoted to detective he drove up to Rhinebeck to get records from the local telephone company relating to Salerno's phone calls. He came away empty-handed. The local company was firmly in Salerno's pocket.

"The Genovese Family were the originators of political and police corruption. In fact they were probably the most sophisticated. They were the ones who really brought in political and police corruption as a major force in organized crime," says Coffey.

Salerno's empire had been built on illegal gambling and loan-sharking, the two traditional mob activities that were being rapidly eclipsed by narcotics. In the past Fat Tony had thrived on a system that was openly for sale. It was the reason for his long-term survival. Police, judges and politicians were little more than necessary expenses. Everyone had their price, from the uniformed patrolman on the streets of Harlem to the corrupt Congressman in Washington and the ambitious politician running for the office of District Attorney whose campaign would gratefully receive contributions from respectable sounding Italian-American associations dedicated to keeping crime off the streets. It was a system which had guaranteed the survival of the older generation of mobsters represented by Salerno, Corallo and Castellano. It was the main reason why the elderly triumvirate disapproved so strongly of the younger generation's obsession with the easy profits that came from drugs.

When a U.S. Attorney like Giuliani appeared on the scene, they all knew that the old world which had tolerated their presence was giving way to a new order. To keep their place in the new world they would have to clean up their act. One thing was for sure—if they didn't move fast enough Giuliani would do it for them! The Mafia Commission in New York was living on borrowed time.

The Commission's bid for legitimacy depended on their control of the labor unions in New York City. It was through them that the Mafia had succeeded in insinuating its tentacles into virtually every facet of the mainstream economic life of New York City. Their control extended from the Fulton Fish Market on FDR Drive to some of Manhattan's finest five-star restaurants, from the smallest of building sites to the largest construction projects in New York City. The key to it all was the unions.

As Salvatore Avellino steered the Lucchese limousine through the streets of Manhattan, Organized Crime Task Force investigators were tracking his route and monitoring the sounds coming from inside the Jaguar on a mobile radio relay system. The agents picked up one conversation between Avellino and his passengers which revealed exactly how the mob could sink their hooks into a union.

"This is what I'm looking for, you see," began Avellino. "Ahh, let's designate somebody. I don't want 813. You notice how I threw in 813 A? Now, let me be able to pick somebody for that office. Do you follow what I'm bringing out?"

"Yeah," said Tom Ronga, one of his passengers.

"We want to put a delegate," said Avellino. "You got me?"

"Yeah," said his other passenger, Emedio Fazzini.

"You see? Like we want, he puts a president out there. See?"

"Right."

"Then it's our fuckin' union. Not that it's Jimmy

Brown's union, not that it's Paul Castellano's union. It's, it's, it's theirs and ours, in other words. You understand. What . . . ?"

"We got the 'A,' " said Ronga.

"They're claiming 813," replied Avellino.

"They're claiming 813 A, 813 B."

"Right," agreed Avellino, "they're claiming . . ."

"One guy got this one, one guy got the other," Ronga interrupted.

"Now you got it. You're claiming 813 . . ."

"You want 'C,' you want 'C'?" offered Ronga.

"813 is yours, 'A' is ours and yours together. But not that we, now it's the dog waggling the tail. 'Cause if we gonna go to work and we're gonna put these ah, ah, 200, 300 people in it. Now let's take somebody, let's take a son, a son-in-law, somebody puts them into the office. They got a job. Let's take somebody's daughter, whatever, she's the secretary. Let's staff it with . . ."

"Our people," added Ronga, proving himself familiar with the traditional Mafia methods of union control. They handed out favors to Family and friends by giving them jobs in their unions. They got a union salary and the mob got a man or woman on the inside.

"With our people," continued Avellino. "And when we say 'Go break this guy's balls . . .' "

"They go!" enthused Ronga.

"They're there seven o'clock in the morning to break the guy's balls," said Avellino, proudly citing one of the mob's greatest skills in industrial relations.

What Avellino was driving at was an agreement over the control of the unions which ran the construction industry. The Lucchese Family wanted to split their share of this union with the Gambino Family.

"Let Bernie have all the five boroughs. Nassau, Suffolk is 'A,' but we gotta have the strength, we have to have the strength, that when a fuckin' Bob Morga comes along and bids 71 county fuckin' buildings, that tomorrow he's got four gold tooths in front of him saying, 'Okay, now that you've built all, took all these buildings, where's all the men? Huh?' "

Avellino was talking about exercising power to add muscle to a bid. If they controlled the workers then no rival bid
had any meaning because the Lucchese Family would
merely instruct the workers not to go to the construction
site.

"You've got to control the men," agreed Fazzini.

"That is the power," said Ronga.

"That's the power!" emphasized Avellino.

"You gotta control the workers here. Right now you
control the employers . . . well you got . . ." said Fazzini,
moving the conversation back to the garbage disposal business.

"Right," said Avellino. "Right, now we as the Association are, we control the bosses, right? Now, when we control the men we even control the bosses even better now,
because they're even more fuckin' afraid. Right?"

The Lucchese Family's dominance of the carting industry was breathtaking. Even The Carter's Management Association (the Private Sanitation Industry Association of
Nassau and Suffolk Counties, Inc.) had been set up by the
Family. But the ambitions of Corallo and Avellino didn't
stop there.

"Sal, please don't let my men walk backwards, let them
walk ahead," pleaded Fazzini, in a show of concern for his
labor force.

"Do you understand me?" continued Avellino, ignoring
him. "Now when you got a guy that steps out of line and
this and that, now you got the whip. You got the fuckin'
. . . This is what he [*Corallo*] tells me all the time. 'A
strong union makes money for everybody including the
wiseguys. The wiseguys even make more money with a
strong union.' "

Avellino was no follower of Marx but even the Mafia
could appreciate the power of labor. A union controlled by
the wiseguys that could twist their employers' arms allowed
the mob to "guarantee" harmonious industrial relations by
going straight to the employer and demanding protection
money in return for a docile union. A weak union was no
good to the mobsters. A union strong enough to pose a

threat to their employers and corrupt enough to be on the Mafia payroll was the dream ticket.

"True," murmured Fazzini.

"Because the envelopes could be bigger and better!" said Avellino. "In other words, whatever is to be, every dollar that is made is 50–50. But the only people that tell the office what to do is us. 'Cause we, do you understand me? And then let's go to town . . . if there's gonna be ten of us, four of us pickin' up all the fuckin' garbage. I got to tell you, who's gonna pick 'em up? We're gonna knock everybody out, absorb everybody, eat them up! Whoever stays in there is only who we're allowing to stay in there."

Fazzini was impressed by the Lucchese plan to carve up the garbage industry. There was a lot of money in waste disposal. "You've got big plans," said Fazzini admiringly.

"Well isn't that the truth?" smirked Avellino.

Avellino negotiated a traffic snarl up as he drove down the Brooklyn-Queens expressway. "Look at this traffic over here!" he exclaimed at one of the few aspects of modern life that the mob was unable to control. Then he revealed his cynical dislike of union power—when it was in the wrong hands. "I don't want to be union because I don't like the union fuckin' telling me what to do. I don't wanna be controlled by somebody, say, you're not allowed to fire this guy . . . I don't like somebody telling me how to run my business—see? That's the bad thing. But, if I could have the union at the right wages, getting the right prices but I got the guy that's not going to tell me that. Then it's . . ."

"Gonna pay pension?" inquired Ronga, wondering if any vestige of a legitimate union had a place in the Mafia's plans for the garbage industry.

"Sure," replied Avellino generously. "We're going to have a union. A real legitimate one!"

"Got to be legitimate," replied his passenger.

"No, we really, right. We're using it for a totally different reason," explained the Lucchese representative.

"Different reason," Fazzini chipped in, "we want to control the employers, the employees."

"Let me tell you something," said Avellino.

"Then you got it made," answered Fazzini.

"Whoever controls the employees controls the bosses. The fuckin' Association don't mean a fuckin' thing. Do you know what I'm pointing out?"

"That is the power," agreed Thomas Ronga.

"Because the power is, if you got 20 people and they're not gonna come to work tomorrow pick up that fuckin' garbage, who you going to listen to?" asked Avellino.

It was a question which didn't need an answer, but Fazzini obliged anyway. "You—of course!"

Avellino felt secure in the driving seat of the Jaguar; controlled, assured and an essential part of an organization which was functioning as smoothly as the three-liter high-performance engine that was purring under the sleek black bonnet.

Unions in the construction industry, the garment center and garbage disposal were all firmly in the pockets of the mob. This was the vision of the future that Avellino shared with Castellano, Corallo and Salerno. An organization receiving its illicit millions through its control of legitimate business. The further the mob moved away from the traditional street crimes of loan-sharking, numbers running, prostitution and drugs, the more untouchable they would become.

All they had to do was to keep their distance from the junk men.

11

FAMILY BUSINESS

IN REALITY THE MAFIA'S STRATEGY WAS DOOMED TO FAIL-
ure. Their successful infiltration of legitimate business
was regarded by the law enforcement community as the
prime reason for renewing efforts to bring them to justice.
By the mid-Eighties the Presidential Commission on Organized Crime estimated that $65.7 billion was being illegally
extracted from the economy. Paul Castellano was overheard saying: "If the President of the United States, if he's
smart, if he needed help, he'd come, I could do a, some,
favor for him." It was not an idle boast.

The Mafia had sunk its hooks into New York City's
unions for over half a century. In the 1930s one of the first
unions to be taken over was the waterfront workers.
Through the International Longshoremen's Association,
the Cosa Nostra ran the docks. By the 1980s the Port of
New York-New Jersey processed more than $40 billion
worth of freight. The Manhattan-New Jersey docks were
controlled by the Genovese Family while the Gambinos had
Brooklyn.

Talking to his right-hand man, Tommy Bilotti, a vicious
thug whom the Gambino boss was grooming to be his successor, Paul Castellano was heard to reminisce: "In my first

year the Longshoremen's Union was theirs [*Genovese*], we had Brooklyn."

The front man down at the docks was Anthony Scotto, a full-time captain in the Gambino Family. Scotto had been a protégé of Carlo Gambino, the soft-spoken, stoop-shouldered old man who had founded the Family that inherited his name. "Give the International Presidency to Anthony Scotto," the old man had instructed Castellano. Castellano took his father-in-law's advice and supported Scotto: "We respected him . . . it was our union. We were making him advance in our union. Go up, up, up the ladder. And what it was, what's gonna happen, we're gonna have a president!"

Scotto was extorting payoffs from anyone and everyone who did business on the waterfront. Castellano's aspirations for him to become union president were only curtailed by an FBI investigation.

By the 1970s the ILA had a membership of 69,000 and assets approaching $30 million. It was a powerful organization in its own right and Scotto was a man with connections in high places. When he was eventually tried on labor racketeering charges he was able to summon as character witnesses Hugh Carey, the Governor of New York, two former New York City Mayors and a Justice of the New York State Supreme Court! His high-powered friends couldn't get him off but they seemed to have impressed the judge. The sentence was a mere five years for a lifetime of corruption.

Scotto's power directly descended from one of the most feared Mafia figures in history, Albert Anastasia, the founder of "Murder Incorporated" and one of the early Cosa Nostra figures who helped lay the foundations for the organized crime empire which flourishes to this day. Anastasia had muscled in on the docks in 1937 by sinking his hooks into the six locals that ran the labor force on the waterfront. In the words of Joe Valachi, the first Mafioso to become an informer in America, Anastasia was the "absolute ruler of the Brooklyn waterfront."

Anastasia appointed his brother Anthony "Tough Tony" Anastasia as the head of Local 1814. Tough Tony was eventually succeeded by the man who married his daughter, Anthony Scotto.

Albert Anastasia's career came to a premature end. He was enjoying a wet shave, covered in hot towels sitting in the barber's chair at the Park Sheraton Hotel in 1957. He never saw his killers. They unleashed two double-barrelled shotguns while his face was still covered in white flannel.

His successor was one of his most loyal followers, Carlo Gambino, a man who politely described his occupation to police as "labor relations consultant." It wasn't far from the truth. One top mobster was picked up on the FBI microphones openly admitting the "labor relations" strategy for tightening their grip on the economy: "In order for the scheme to work across the country you have to have the cooperation of the union that is involved, the company that is involved and then our company. It has to be all three or it won't click. . . ."

The Presidential Commission on Organized Crime attempted to estimate the cost to society: "The costs of labor racketeering, although often hard to trace, are staggering. They are not just borne by union members, but by society as a whole. Millions of dollars of workers' dues and benefit monies have been siphoned off by organized crime through outright embezzlement or more sophisticated devices, such as loans or excessive fees paid to corrupt union and trust fund service providers. Workers can be denied the full benefit of their collective bargaining agreements when corrupt union officials trade their rights for payoffs or other advantages in mob-run businesses.

"The highest costs are, however, borne by the public. Because organized crime's exercise of market power is usually concealed from public view, millions of consumers unknowingly pay organized crime what amounts to a surcharge on a wide range of goods and services."

Joe Coffey, who has stalked the Mafia all his life, agrees: "They're the second government in this country, in the United States. You cannot walk into a restaurant where you're not paying a tribute to the Mafia. You can't go into a catering establishment, a laundry, a car dealership; show business even has a great influence in the mob. They are economically destroying this country because of their input and what they do to business."

Restaurants, clubs, pizzerias, food wholesaling, trucking, construction, the docks, there was no facet of the city's economic life and no business that the mob didn't have some control over. It was a network of influence and income that afforded the American Mafia an extraordinary degree of power. "Our job is to run the unions," confided Paul Castellano to one of his associates.

"Paul Castellano was lord of the manor," says Giuliani, the U.S. Attorney who would ultimately be responsible for Big Paul's nemesis. "He got a certain percentage out of all of the hundred or so businesses that the Family members were involved in and there was a system for how that money came up to him, through the capos, through the various underbosses. All of them would get a percentage and then each week or each month depending on the period of time, a tribute would be paid to him in cash. Envelopes would be given to him with five thousand dollars, ten thousand, 15, 20, 100 for himself. He lived in a house which looked like a manor house in Staten Island; he called it 'The White House.' I don't know if he gave it that name or it always had that name, but the people in the Family kind of enjoyed the idea that he lived in a place that they could call The White House and he ran what would be equivalent to either a major business or a Government enterprise, since it also had one of the powers usually reserved to Government—the power to execute, to take human life when Paul Castellano determined that someone was in his way or not following the rules."

Giuliani felt just as strongly about the damage that the unseen hand of organized crime was inflicting on New York: "It damages New York City because the cost of doing things here is considerably greater than elsewhere; it costs more money to build buildings in New York because organized crime takes a percentage out of the cost of construction. It costs more money to ship goods into and out of New York because organized crime exacts a tribute and requires the doing of business, the transportation business, in a way that is very unprofitable, so that people elect to ship their goods through other ports rather than the Port of New York. New York is deprived of jobs as a result of that. If we took a tour of the Port of New York 30 years ago, you would see an awful lot of people working. You would see a great deal of activity, you would see an awful lot of jobs, people who were working and earning a good deal of money. The Port of New York today is inactive. You see very little going on and the jobs have been decreased enormously and organized crime has a major share of the responsibility for that because of extortion."

As a prosecutor with political ambitions, Giuliani realized that the ultimate victims were the citizens of New York. "What it means is that the cost is passed along to the consumer. So that it costs more to build in New York. It costs more to buy food in New York. If an organized crime Family is shaking down a food distributor, it is then passed along in the cost of buying food in New York, or the cost of eating or drinking in a restaurant. It contributes to a very large extent to the cost of living in New York and the reasons why the cost of living is so high and so disproportionate to many other places in this country. It also contributes to the lack of having the kind of resources available to deal with our social problems—with the problems of rebuilding and modernizing the infrastructure in New York. The problems are exasperated by the presence of organized crime in New York and the corruption that it brings with it."

The moral consequence of all this corruption was not something which entered the calculations of the ruling head of the Commission. Castellano saw himself as a "businessman." According to James La Rossa, his wealthy New York attorney and family friend: "He was gentle, soft-spoken, self-educated, loved business in every respect, loved to talk about it, would read *Forbes, Fortune,* would read *The Wall Street Journal* on a daily basis. Very interested in the complexities of American business." Castellano did indeed look like any other millionaire businessman in his dark suits, sober ties, silk socks and well-polished shoes. As chairman of Dial Poultry, Castellano headed one of the country's biggest chicken wholesaling operations. As "the boss of bosses," Castellano was the chairman of the world's most powerful criminal organization. For good measure, he had inherited New York City's most powerful Mafia Family: the Gambino Family.

Although there were some who resented Big Paul's style of leadership, criticizing him for his remoteness and detachment from the "men on the street" who had to pay tribute to the mansion on the hill, by the early 1980s Castellano's reign was at the height of its success. Most of the members of the Gambino Family seemed to be obeying his edict forbidding the trade in drugs, apart from the odd wiseguy and the Bonannos whom he had written off anyway. Money from construction and the garment center was pouring in to the Gambino Family coffers, while the more traditional mob activities of loan-sharking, gambling and hijacking were ticking over nicely, supervised by the strong-arm enforcers of the Gambino Family.

While Castellano padded around his spacious sitting room in his silk dressing-gown the real work was being done on the streets by Gambino captains. These were the tough street hoods who supervised the activities of a crew of half a dozen or more wiseguys and associates. The captains were the middle management of the mob hoping for promotion, keen to catch the eye of those above them and ready to slap down those below them. Wiseguys like John Gotti and Roy Di Meo were captains. Both men were in charge of street crews whose skills ranged from busting limbs to breaking and entering luxury cars.

Roy Di Meo, one of Castellano's most trusted lieutenants and hit men, ran a hugely successful international stolen car business. Junkies and car thieves, many of them highly skilled in their art, would be paid a few hundred dollars or even given free drugs to go and steal luxury limousines. The cars were then driven to a Gambino-controlled "chop shop" in Brooklyn where the Mercedes or Porsche could be cut up and given a new identity, with a new engine number, new plates and a different color. The car was then safely driven down to a Gambino-controlled freight terminal, put on a ship and exported to the Middle East where it could be sold to an oil-rich Arab for as much as 90 percent of its real value. It was just one of the hugely lucrative divisions of the Gambino "corporation"—each one of which was a profit center.

In the fashion trade, Gambino interests were well protected by Tommy Gambino, son of Carlo and nephew to Paul Castellano. His headquarters consisted of a small office on West 35th Street, the cramped and crowded cross-street in the heart of Manhattan which is the bustling center of the garment industry. Thirty-fifth Street is a dark, dusty and long, narrow road interspersed with dingy shop-front windows at the bottom of tall and aging buildings that reach up into the sky and block out the light. Behind warehouse windows are the occasional plastic mannequins, some naked, some clothed; rails of dresses and suits covered in polythene wait to be shipped out to the fashion stores of Manhattan and all over the United States. The street is a cacophony of noise: truckers shouting to get a parking bay, drivers shouting to get out, New York City transport officials harassing those who are parked and those who are trying, loaders loading merchandise into the vast caverns of the empty trucks. Cursing workers, Hispanics and blacks, noisily trundle garment rails on castor wheels along the sidewalks, some packed tightly with clothes, others empty. They disappear into loading bays or the backs of the garment trucks. Inside the entrances along the street are cardboard boxes, packing cases, clothes hanging on rails, thousands of wire and wooden coat hangers, accessory shops selling zippers, buttons and fasteners. Lining the sidewalks on both sides of the street are giant trucks, belching smoke into the shadows and gunning their engines before moving off to their destination. Many of the trucks have the same names emblazoned across their sides or on top of the cabs, names like "Dynamic" and "Consolidated." The trucks and the companies belong to Tommy Gambino. On 35th Street, nothing moves in or out without the say-so of the slender, dark-haired son of Carlo Gambino.

Those who have seen pictures of his father can spot the family resemblance. Like father, like son, Tommy inherited the Family business.

Andris Kurins used to work on 35th Street and knows

Tommy Gambino well. He used to watch him for the FBI. Pointing up to the sign over the storefront, Kurins runs down the reasons for mob control of the area: "The Gambinos and the other organized crime Families run a monopoly. They're able to control this garment industry because of the unions and the various associations that have been formed over the years in the garment industry. This area is where most of the garments in America are manufactured and this right here happens to be 'Consolidated Carriers' which is one of ten trucking companies owned by Tommy Gambino and his brothers and his Family. Their income is really fantastic. Tommy Gambino himself admits to making about $30 million just from Consolidated—legally! So you can see that combining ten companies the money's just astronomical."

It's not just trucking companies; the Gambinos and the other Families have successfully diversified into the other parts of the clothing industry. From manufacture through to retail, there is mob involvement somewhere along the way. Thirty-fifth Street does not look like an avenue of wealth, compared to the fashion stores and shop windows of Fifth Avenue, but like so many Mafia operations many of the shop windows are just a front. The source of enormous wealth has to remain hidden. In amongst the backstreet tenements in the poorer parts of the city it is estimated that there are 3,000 sweatshops where non-union, immigrant employees work in appalling conditions stitching fabrics and cutting cloth. Many of them are controlled by the mob.

With a stranglehold on the trucking companies and the Teamsters Union, to which the drivers belong, the Mafia has such a deep hook into the garment trade that it is doubtful that anyone will ever be able to get it out. "Whoever controls the trucks controls the garment center. Nothing moves without your consent. You have it by the throat," says a former union leader who once tried to defy the might of the mob and ended up only being able to walk down 35th Street accompanied by two bodyguards and wearing a bulletproof vest.

According to another businessman in the industry, you have to toe the line. "Don't cheat on your trucker unless you want big trouble. It would be better to cheat on your *wife* than cheat on your trucker. I can have all kinds of trouble. Things don't get delivered or they get damaged. The ability to move the merchandise is the heart of the business, it's the pump that keeps the whole industry going. Nobody's a free agent in trucks. You have two choices: you use the truck line you're married to or you truck yourself. You can complain to your trucker about lousy delivery and high prices, you can bitch and you can moan, and the guy might make the deliveries better for you, but you can't say, 'I'm gonna get XYZ to truck for me because he runs a real snappy service and we're gonna use him instead' because there is no XYZ service. And XYZ would take his life in his hands to service you so he doesn't do it. The territory is all carved up."

And no one was better at a carve-up than Big Paul. A former butcher by trade, Castellano knew exactly where to put the knife and how much pressure to apply. Castellano knew how to get the best cut—whether it was a piece of prime beef or a slice of a legitimate business. Despite the elegant suits and patrician air, the hawk-nosed Castellano was a vicious gangster. His elevated position allowed him to distance himself from the day-to-day brutalities which kept the empire going and the underlings in line, but in order to maintain his position, Paul Castellano had to be as ready to kill as any other Mafia boss. He had been quick to authorize the contract on Galante when word reached him of the latter's territorial ambitions.

Castellano's ruthlessness was displayed in another family dispute. Of all his immediate family Big Paul was closest to his daughter, Connie. Tall and attractive with long, blonde hair, Connie would have been quite a catch for any aspiring Mafioso. Instead, she disappointed her father by marrying a low-life thug and small-time hood who had worked for her father's chicken company, Dial Poultry, as a butcher.

Castellano tolerated the marriage until the news reached him that her husband had been playing around with another woman, the wife of a Mafioso from another Family. While it was accepted Mafia practice to have mistresses and girlfriends, it was expressly forbidden in the oath of initiation to fool around with the wife or girlfriend of another wiseguy. It was also extremely inadvisable to double-cross your wife when she happened to be the daughter of the "boss of bosses."

To make matters worse, Connie became pregnant during the course of her husband's affair. Rarely home, when her husband did appear there were hysterical rows which usually ended with the former butcher beating his wife. Eventually the strain became too much for Castellano's daughter and she had a miscarriage.

At this point the Godfather intervened and ordered his son-in-law's execution. In time-honored tradition, a friend invited Connie's husband out for an evening drink at a local Gambino social club in Brooklyn. After a few drinks they adjourned to a nearby apartment, accompanied by Roy Di Meo. As the unsuspecting son-in-law opened the door to the apartment, a man stepped from the shadows and pushed a knife expertly through his heart. The murder had been carried out with surgical precision to minimize the flow of blood. In view of the importance of the killing, one which had been personally ordered by "The Pope" himself, Roy Di Meo was especially careful to remove all traces of evidence. The killers dragged the corpse of Connie's husband to the bathroom and dumped it on the floor. They switched on the shower to wash away the blood and calmly proceeded to cut up the corpse.

Roy Di Meo, who was supervising the contract, became annoyed with his underlings for the time they were taking to cut up the body: "Listen," he said impatiently, "I'll cut—you wrap." The pieces of body were then placed in a couple of garbage bags and probably disposed of by a Mafia-controlled garbage company. For Roy Di Meo and his crew it was a routine night's work; an estimated 200 murders were carried out at the same location using the same method. For the man with the elegant suits and gold spectacles in his Staten Island mansion, it had been a question of honor. Family virtue had been restored. His daughter might have lost her husband, but then there were more important things in life. Word of the killing soon spread to the streets but the police could never prove it and without a body there was no case.

Although it was one of many murders that he got away with, some of the other divisions of the Gambino "corporation" were under intensive investigation. An FBI squad had been formed to specifically target the Gambino Family.

Andy Kurins had nothing personal against Big Paul, apart from the fact that his job was to make a watertight case against the most powerful mobster in America and to put him in jail for the rest of his life. Along with his partner, fellow FBI agent Joseph O'Brien, Kurins felt he was getting to know Mr. Castellano. The hours spent in surveillance vans outside the house of the "boss of bosses," the pumping of street informants and the study of the intelligence profiles of his top associates gave the agents a detailed picture of their target. But at the beginning it seemed a fairly dull assignment. Castellano gave all the appearance of being semiretired. He rarely stirred from the creature comforts of his house on the hill.

In reality, Castellano was far from inactive. It was simply that he liked to do business from home. He didn't feel that it was fitting for such an accomplished businessman to frequent the dingy social clubs that were the traditional meeting places of the mob. It was there that the real Mafia activities took place. It was in the social clubs that you found men like Gambino underboss Neil Dellacroce, the vicious gangster who practically lived in the Ravenite Club on Mulberry Street, or John Gotti, his rising capo who commuted between the Ravenite and his own Bergen Hunt and Fish Club in Queens.

Castellano was rarely seen in such places. Not for him the seedy surroundings of the Palma Boys Social Club where his fat friend Tony Salerno could be seen every day hobbling along the sidewalk with the aid of his walking stick and being helped up the steps by some obliging minion from the Genovese Family. If the weather was warm, Fat Tony would hold court on the streets in true Mafia tradition, with his Homburg jammed down tight on his head and a fat cigar chomped firmly between his teeth. But that wasn't Paul's style. He was a businessman, he had standards to maintain. His position was such that he could call all the shots.

If there was business to be done, a union man to be brought in line, a Family wrangle to be adjudicated, then they must come to him. His word was law and the mountain must come to Mohammed, not the other way round. Which was why Andy Kurins and his partner were being forced to spend long days and lonely nights on the private driveways of Benedict Road, Staten Island, patiently noting down the registration numbers of the Mercedes, Lincolns and Cadillacs that drove through the electrically operated, wrought-iron gates that led to the head of the American Mafia's front door.

In addition to the mind-numbing boredom, hunger and discomfort, the agents had to put up with the obscene insults from Castellano's driver, bodyguard and right-hand man Tommy Bilotti.

Bilotti was a curious choice as the Godfather's most trusted assistant. Not renowned for his intellectual attributes, Bilotti was a wide-shouldered hood with a ducklike gait who showed a surprising gentleness in public while steering the old man through the crowded streets of Manhattan and shepherding him through the doors of restaurants. In private Bilotti had a reputation as a vicious, strong-arm man who was capable of wielding a baseball bat with a ferocious intensity, smashing an opponent's face into a bloody pulp. The contrast between the tall, imposing frame of Castellano and the short, fat Bilotti, whose bizarre dress sense favored yellow trousers and loud check jackets, was almost comic.

Despite his reputation for physical violence, Bilotti also displayed traits which were highly valued by the Godfather—not least an unquestioning loyalty and obedience. In his private life Bilotti had been touched by tragedy. His first wife had died of cancer and their son suffered from autism. Although the boy lived in a home, Bilotti loved him and apparently visited him regularly.

In the company of his boss, Bilotti displayed the watchful demeanor of a Presidential Secret Service bodyguard. On the street, Bilotti was known as a hothead. Woe betide any mobster who chose to laugh at his dress sense or ill-fitting black toupee. If a loan-shark victim was behind on his payments, Bilotti would chase up the back-payments with the aid of the baseball bat he kept under the front seat of his mauve Buick. Bilotti had boasted that he had 11 hits to his credit. His police record showed numerous arrests for assault and possession of weapons.

The agents had been warned about Bilotti's short fuse and it wasn't long before they were exposed to it. "We were sitting just a few feet from here [*Castellano's front door*] and watching the house and we noticed a big black limousine coming round the block and go round real slow. It had tinted windows on it so we had a hard time seeing who was there. But we suspected it was somebody that was coming to the house. We didn't know at the time it was Tommy Bilotti but he actually pulled right up next to us, rolled the window down and started screaming at us—about sitting here, what we were doing here, why we were bothering to sit around the neighborhood and just wasting our time . . . just going on and on into a tirade about us being here."

On another occasion on a Sunday morning O'Brien trailed Bilotti to a local beauty parlor and was waiting for him to reappear. Suddenly the fat gangster appeared alongside in a different car, startling the agent out of his wits by shouting: "Hello, asshole!" As Bilotti began to taunt the agent with the FBI's inexpert surveillance, the Godfather's bodyguard began to work himself up into a rage. He was going into overdrive.

It soon became apparent to O'Brien that the reason for Bilotti's incoherent fury was that he thought that the FBI agents had been making rude remarks about his beloved hairpiece which Bilotti vainly believed few people had noticed. For an undercover FBI surveillance operation to reveal the existence of the hairpiece seemed to Bilotti to be the ultimate insult—never mind that they might be discovering the existence of some evil criminal conspiracy which could put him away for life. To publicize the presence of his hairpiece was unforgivable.

* * *

One of captain John Gotti's crew was a man called Angelo Ruggiero. An FBI bug in Ruggiero's home recorded a variety of derogatory references to the overlord of the American Mafia. Castellano, with his fondness for silk dressing gowns and pajamas, was a "pansy" and a "milk drinker." His sons were scathingly referred to as "the chicken men" while his Wall Street aspirations were openly mocked and his business advisers called "The Jew Club." In one blasphemous remark Gotti's crew joked that "The Pope" probably spent his evenings "whackin' off with Tommy. . . ."

The Gotti crew's contempt for the man they saw as the fool on the hill was in large part due to their open disdain for Castellano's edict on drugs. Known as The Two Commandments, the first stated that anyone caught dealing drugs since 1962 could not become a made member of the Gambino Family. The second commandment made it a capital offense to bring the Family into disrepute by either being caught dealing in drugs or closely associating with dealers. If you dealt drugs or implicated other Gambino soldiers in narcotics, you would be "whacked."

No one was more aware of this than Angelo Ruggiero and Eugene Gotti, two of the Gambino Family's largest heroin traffickers. It was inconceivable that their activities were not known to their crew captain, John Gotti. If he knew then so did his boss, Neil Dellacroce. Both of them would have received their share of the profits, some of which would have been passed on to Castellano.

The blind and unswerving loyalty to the boss shown by the faithful Bilotti was openly scorned by the Dellacroce faction. Originally Dellacroce had been an arch-rival of Castellano but by making him underboss the two men had reached an accommodation. Although Dellacroce was outwardly loyal, the crew he supervised were less bound by mob protocol. For them, there was far too much money to be made from the drugs business to pay any attention to The Two Commandments. They were a different generation operating under a different set of rules: "Don't get caught."

Although Gotti managed to distance himself from the actual deals, those who knew him suspected he was deeply involved. It was inconceivable that he didn't know what his brother was up to and almost certain that he was investing in their deals. Sal Polisi, who mingled freely with the Colombo and Gambino Families, knew Gotti from the heady days of hijacking and gambling down at the Bergen Hunt and Fish Club in Queens. Polisi, who has dabbled in the trade himself, soon noticed that Gotti was surrounded by high-level drug dealers. "The people that he [*Gotti*] recruited to build his army in the mid-Seventies and early Eighties," recalls Sal Polisi, "were all major drug dealers. Even his brother Gene was a drug dealer. So he would get a piece of the action. They would give him piles of money. When you're making so much money, when you're making a couple of hundred thousand a month, it's nothing . . . over $25,000, like a gift. Just give it away."

In the early days of Gotti's rise to power Polisi would hang out in the Bergen Hunt and Fish Club in Queens. With his ear to the ground, and as an associate of the Gambino Family, he too heard the order come down from Castellano. "They send the word down through the boss of the Family to the underboss to the various captains and 'This is what we don't want you doing.' No drugs, no paper crime, no counterfeiting, they didn't want us involved in this type of thing. Don't hijack certain trucking companies, I mean, these particular orders would come filtering down to us, it would work its way from the Ravenite right down to the Bergen Hunt and Fish Club, I mean from Manhattan to Queens and it would be carried by various members of the Family and at that point it was, 'No Drugs. Hands Off Drugs.' Anybody caught doing drugs was dead, that's what they claimed the penalty would be."

John Gotti's closest friend, Angelo Ruggiero, was up to his neck in drug deals. Ruggiero, who was also Dellacroce's nephew, together with John's brother, Eugene Gotti, and a Gambino soldier, Pete Tambone, were the main dealers in the Gambino Family. In 1982 the FBI were given permission to place a bug in Ruggiero's Cedarhurst, Long Island, home on suspicion of drug dealing. The bugs captured the garrulous Ruggiero more or less openly discussing drug deals. The narcotics activities of Gotti's crew were common knowledge in mob circles and it was only a matter of time before word circulated up to Paul Castellano's mansion on Staten Island.

On April 22, 1982, Castellano chaired a meeting to decide the fate of Pete Tambone, the Gambino soldier who had been caught dealing heroin. It didn't take long to reach a decision. "Clip him," was The Pope's terse response.

"It's a different story now," Ruggiero warned Eugene Gotti two days after hearing the news. "Not even Neil no more. It's Paul."

"Oh, Paul's thinking about doing something?"

Ruggiero explained the situation to Gotti's younger brother, adding that Castellano had made an agreement with Vincent "The Chin" Gigante, underboss of the Genovese Family about getting rid of drug dealers. "Him and Chin made a pact: any friend of ours that gets pinched for junk, or that they hear anything about junk, they kill 'em. No administration meetings, no nothing, just gonna kill him. They're not warning nobody; not telling nobody because they feel the guy's gonna rat. And your brother says he meant that for Neil."

That meant they couldn't even rely on Ruggiero's uncle, Neil Dellacroce, to tip them off because Paul wanted to ensure that no one would be warned.

Gene Gotti realized that as one of Pete Tambone's closest associates the contract could well be given to him. "I don't want to kill this guy. I know the guy 20 years! He knows my family. I know his family and everything."

Three days later, going against all the unwritten rules of the Mafia, Angelo Ruggiero warned their mutual friend about the hit. "You don't know what the fuck I'm going through, Pete. I'm going through so much over here. I feel like crying. I swear on my mother!" Ruggiero warned Tambone that the situation looked pretty bad. He had been fighting his corner but in the process was laying himself open to suspicion. "I'm protecting you so much that they think maybe I'm your partner. All that was said is that you're a junk pusher. Somebody came forward and said that you pushed junk, that you gave them something. That's the worst thing." Someone had "ratted" on Tambone and signed his death sentence. "Pete, listen to me," implored Ruggiero, trying to impress on his friend the seriousness of the situation. "Listen to me like a brother. I'm tellin' ya, worse comes to worse, get your wife and take off."

Tambone listened to Ruggiero and did precisely that.

By tipping him off Ruggiero was himself risking the wrath of his boss but he gambled that he would never be found out and carried on with his own drug deals. Ruggiero had a lot of chutzpah. At one point while all this was going on he even arranged a $200,000 loan from Castellano, claiming it was for a pornography deal whereas in fact the cash was being used to finance a major heroin transaction.

One week after the death sentence was pronounced on Tambone, Ruggiero and Gene Gotti were overheard discussing another drug deal involving another member of the Gambino crew, Eddie Lino.

"He said the one he's getting from Canada ain't no good. He says, if you can get me them, I'll pay 100,000, but I want a sample."

"Give 'em one," said Gene Gotti.

"He says, 'I've got coke coming in,'" said Ruggiero, lowering his voice. "He says, 'I'll give you first shot. If the figure's low, I'll pay them.' They put it on the plane together."

Even the agents monitoring the bugs were surprised at how openly Ruggiero and his fellow mobsters were discussing drug deals. Even when they thought they were safe from bugs, wiseguys usually spoke in a cryptic code, especially on drug deals. But not Angelo Ruggiero.

Information from the tapes was coming into the Brooklyn-Queens Resident Agency Office of the FBI which was where the FBI's Gambino squad was based. Reading the transcripts of the Ruggiero tapes, Kurins and O'Brien realized it presented them with a golden opportunity. Combined with the intelligence they were accumulating from their Staten Island surveillance and information from street informers they had enough evidence to apply for a Title III, a court-authorized affidavit that would allow them to force an entry into Castellano's White House and plant a hidden microphone in the "holy of holies"—the room where the most secret deliberations of America's most powerful Mafia boss took place.

The order was duly approved by a judge. That was the easy part. How on earth would they get inside the Staten Island home of Paul Castellano, plant a bug and get out again? Plus the court order only gave them 30 days in which to accomplish a break-in which in itself could require months of planning. However, the potential rewards were so great the FBI thought it was worth a try.

The first problem was to find premises near enough to The White House to set up an FBI monitoring station. It would have to be close by to be within the range of the transmitter. As Castellano lived in the richest neighborhood on the island that would be difficult. By a stroke of good fortune they discovered an apartment for rent on Todt Hill which put them well within range of Castellano's house at 177 Benedict Road. Wearing a disguise, Joseph O'Brien would pose as a commuter and move into the apartment. They still had to break into the house, conceal the microphone transmitter and get out again without being caught.

By this time the original court order had expired and been renewed twice. When they presented the third one, a sympathetic judge gently reminded them that there was a limit to the amount of times that they could keep coming back. His warning helped to concentrate their minds on the urgency of the break-in but, as their surveillance had shown, there was always someone at the house. There was nothing they could do but wait and pray. Even if Castellano was out of the house, they still had to contend with vicious guard dogs, alarm systems, electric gates, a private security firm, to say nothing of a psychopath in the shape of Tommy Bilotti who would like nothing better than an excuse to blow away a couple of FBI agents he had mistaken for cat burglars.

It would help if Castellano would leave the house for a period of time but he seemed to be a man firmly wedded to the creature comforts of home—until one morning the agents observed the departure of a rather odd entourage from the Castellano mansion. The party consisted of Big Paul, Tommy Bilotti and the Castellano housemaid from Colombia, Gloria Olarte. The unlikely trio were going on holiday to Pompano Beach, Florida, where Castellano kept a luxury condominium.

The FBI break-in began at 1:31 A.M. It was a night that Andy Kurins would never forget.

"Castellano had the most elaborate security system that money could buy. He had security on all the doors and the windows. He had alarm systems, he had cameras, you can see are still mounted on the house." Andy Kurins directed my gaze in the direction of the front roof directly above the enclosed porch which housed the front door. "In addition to that," recalls the agent, "he had Doberman pinschers on the premises and those had to be neutralized before the FBI could gain entry to the house." Earlier in the day two FBI agents disguised as local gardeners had flung some of New York's finest sirloin steak laced with tranquilizers over the fence. Kurins and O'Brien just had to hope that the Dobermans had eaten it and that the drugs had the required effect.

"The alarm systems were neutralized and we were able to gain access through a back door right here, behind the garage that leads into the main building, and the alarm system was deactivated.

"Going into the house is a hair-raising experience, believe me. All we could think about is getting in and getting out of there, because naturally you don't want to get caught in a situation like that. No matter how long you've prepared for it, something could go wrong, somebody could be alerted and then everything would go down the tubes; all those months of preparation. We go in through the entrance there by the garage and then there's another door there so that the lock had to be picked and we had to deactivate the alarm system. And all this had to be done in a very short period of time because we know that the alarm would go off if it had not been deactivated. We were successful in that and we proceeded into the area where

Castellano held his meetings. We knew the area from information that Joe O'Brien had obtained through interviewing a number of people. We knew exactly where to put the microphone. It was installed and we were able to get out of there.

"There were a lot of agents that were prepared as backup if anything went wrong. This is always the case, no matter how much you prepare—something could go wrong. But you have the knowledge that you have some help if things go sour. Luckily they didn't and we were able to get out of there and not get detected."

The whole operation took less than 15 minutes. There were more than a dozen FBI men staked out in the area in various guises. A garbage truck circled the area around Benedict Road, ready to develop engine trouble at a moment's notice and block the approach road to any passing security patrol or mob visitor. On that night its services were not needed. Paul Castellano's four-million-dollar mansion had been successfully bugged.

The sacred privacy of The Pope was about to be violated. Ironically, the Commission's worst nightmare was about to begin. A drug case was leading investigators into the heart of organized crime.

— 12 —

THE KING IS DEAD

"**F**UCKING MORON," COMPLAINED CASTELLANO. "I GOT A headache. Gloria, bring me some aspirin. That cheap jerk. He don't know what the fuck he's getting involved in. Pain in the ass."

The reason for The Pope's headache was money. "He gotta pay," ordered the Godfather. "And he gotta be clued in. Over two, forget it, he sits out. That's 'Club.' Under a deuce, we talk. Maybe he gets some. But he pays the two points. First. None of this 'You'll have it in a few days' bullshit."

"You want I should talk to the fat guy?" asked a concerned member of the Gambino Family.

"Talk to the fucking President for all I care," replied his boss dismissively. "Just get me my money."

The "fat guy" was Tony Salerno, the overweight head of the Genovese Family. The conversation was about control of the building trade in New York. The tapes revealed that there was one man who had no doubts whatsoever as to who was in overall charge: Paul Castellano.

As the FBI began to reel in the tapes it soon became apparent that Castellano had one overriding motivation above all others—greed.

"The boys all send you their best," said one visiting Gambino capo by way of greeting.

"They send anything else?" grunted the Godfather.

"Oh yeah," said the capo. "There's nine thousand in the envelope."

Kurins and O'Brien listened in fascination as Tommy Gambino turned up one spring evening to discuss their mutual interests in the garment center. Castellano's nephew had come to complain about the presence of Chinese immigrants around 35th Street. It was an unwelcome incursion. They weren't just moving into the area—they were muscling in on the industry. Tommy was worried that it might weaken the Family's hold over the various associations they had set up to control the garment center.

But it was when Gambino explained that one of their own partners was receiving more money than Castellano on one particular deal that the multimillionaire began to show concern. "So what's the fucking story on the money, Tommy?"

"Their guy gets six-fifty a week and a car. Our guy gets four-fifty and no car."

"You're telling me that their guys get more fucking money than you and I?" asked Castellano, his voice rising on a note of outraged incredulity.

"Yeah," came the reply from another of the richest men in Manhattan. "Yeah, yeah."

"What the fuck!" exploded The Pope.

"Jesus Christ!" shrieked Bilotti as if he had never heard of anything quite so outrageous—and maybe he hadn't.

The Pope was about to deliver a sermon. "Well, here's how it seems to me," said the Godfather, doing his sums. "If it's thirds, it's thirds, and cut the bullshit excuses. Look we got a third of the jobs, and I want a third of the money. A third of the jobs and a third of the responsibility. I want a third of everything, get it? It's rightfully mine, and I want it. Fuck the Chinese, fuck the Jews, and fuck the fucking paisans who are grabbing more than their share. It's our association to reap the benefits."

Castellano's nephew seemed not the least put out by this petulant display of proprietorial interest over an entire industry in which he had never even worked a day. But at least Tommy Gambino maintained a legitimate front in the area through Consolidated Carriers.

"Listen, Paul," said Gambino in an attempt to pacify his uncle. "Lemme say something here. Just food for thought, okay? I know you're upset. I understand. But let's say you wanna make a stink about this. You wanna, you can. You got the power. So you sit down with Gerry Lang, and Jimmy Brown, you stand up for your rights, and now you're the heavy. You won but what did you win? And maybe you opened up a can of worms. Maybe Gerry says, 'Hey wait a minute, Paul—if it's thirds over here, why is it that, over in construction, anything over two mil goes to you, like automatic?' So now you gotta argue with the fucking guy. What I'm saying is, maybe you're risking something big to get something small.''

Big Paul wasn't impressed by his nephew's arguments. The discussion ended seemingly unresolved.

Whatever the problems with the clothing industry, Castellano had more pressing matters on his mind. There was a dispute between the members of the Club, the men who controlled Ralph Scopo and in turn every aspect of New York City's billion-dollar building trade. That was far more serious. Conversations from the tapes suggested it could only be resolved by a "sit-down," a meeting of the heads of the Families: the Commission.

It didn't take long for Kurins and O'Brien to realize what that meant. It had never been done before. Real-time surveillance of a Commission meeting would be the ultimate feather in the cap for the FBI agents. Not since a patrolman had accidentally stumbled on a secret conclave of Mafia bosses at Appalachin in New York State in 1957 had law enforcement ever come across concrete evidence of a meeting of the Mafia's secret government. Then the chance intervention of the State police had forced high-ranking Mafiosi, including a young Paul Castellano, to unceremoniously flee across open fields and bramble-infested woods, tearing their double-breasted silk suits and risking premature heart attacks in their attempts to escape. The result was the country's first public glimpse into the existence of the secret national institution which controlled organized crime in America.

The Cosa Nostra had come a long way since then, but the FBI and the law enforcement community had never managed to recapture that early success. They'd never even really thought about it. Until now. Kurins and O'Brien realized that all they had to do was keep listening and the date and venue of a real live Commission meeting might just fall straight into their laps. It would have been the ultimate prize in their case against Paul Castellano.

And then the bug stopped working.

Back at FBI headquarters, their taciturn boss Bruce Mouw, who was supervising all the different investigations into the Gambino Family, was considerably less exercised than his two agents. But then he hadn't been actively involved in the ball-breaking hours of surveillance outside The White House, the relentless teasing out of information from Gambino soldiers and capos, the harvesting of intelligence from street informers, the long hours spent monitoring the tape recorder as it spooled round and round recording both the mundane and the murderous mouthings of the Staten Island Godfather. So what did he know anyway? He could never have been as involved as O'Brien and Kurins who felt as if a lifeline had been cut when their beloved tape recorder stopped turning. But for the FBI desk men there were other priorities and other cases. There was good news and bad news. The good news was that Giuliani's office was definitely going ahead with their indictment against the Commission, using the RICO statute. The jewels in the investigative crown would be the bugs in the Jaguar, Fat Tony's social club and Castellano's mansion. The bad news was that they also wanted to indict Castellano on some "chicken-shit" stolen cars case, the auto-theft scam masterminded by Roy Di Meo. Joe O'Brien exploded with rage when he was asked to participate in the latter.

Using RICO, prosecutors were planning to present evidence to the jury that would tie in the activities of Roy Di Meo and his murderous crew to their ultimate boss, Castellano. To O'Brien and Kurins it seemed like they were using a sledgehammer to crack a nut that wouldn't yield. They wanted a case which would reflect the epic quality of Castellano's power—a case which would literally do him justice. Not some street-level crime from which Castellano was as far removed in theory and practice as the Chairman of Chrysler was from the paint shop on the assembly line.

There was an undeniable logic to the case—simply that Castellano was ultimately responsible for all the filthy crimes committed in the name of the Gambino Family, whether it was the vicious beating of a bankrupt business-man who might have fallen victim to a Gambino loan shark or the million-dollar payoffs from the extortion of the city's construction industry. Castellano certainly presided over the top of the pyramid. Even Kurins and O'Brien could grudgingly see the logic of that. What they didn't see was any chance of the case succeeding. They would have nothing to do with it.

Perhaps the agents had grown too close to the courtly old man on the hill. However much they objected, they found themselves overruled by their FBI bosses. Nor could they get permission to reactivate the bug. A second entry would be far too risky. Fuming, the two FBI case agents were ordered to garner the intelligence that they had accumulated up to now, which was considerable, and process it into a shape which could be utilized in the developing Commission case.

But first Castellano would be arrested by agents from the rival New York State Organized Crime Task Force and publicly humiliated in a carefully coordinated media blitz.

In itself the stolen car racket was a major case. It added up to a million-dollar-a-year business. Di Meo's professional car thieves had been successfully stealing to order. Make of car, engine size and even color could be specified in advance by the customers before the Mercedes or BMW was stolen and given a new identity.

Di Meo's crew had concentrated their activities on middle-class residential areas, which guaranteed a high population of expensive cars. Ironically, one of their favorite hunting grounds had been Howard Beach, the home territory of another powerful Gambino capo, John Gotti. Fortunately, no one had stolen his smart black Mercedes.

One of Di Meo's top men was Vito Arena, a short, fat and ugly specimen of humanity who wore thick-lensed glasses. Arena was a skilled car mechanic capable of getting into virtually any make of car and driving it away. He would drive it to a backstreet "chop shop" in Queens, where it could be cut up and welded to another identical model to disguise its identity, resprayed and readied for shipment to the lucrative car markets of the Middle East. Periodically, Roy Di Meo would take a long drive over the Verrazano bridge to Staten Island, where he would pay tribute to the head of his Family with a large envelope stuffed full of cash.

The car-theft scam had come to the attention of the Organized Crime Task Force as a result of a series of vicious murders. Joe Coffey, who had once been in charge of the Organized Crime Homicide Squad, had been seconded to the Southern District U.S. Attorney's Office to investigate the series of unsolved killings. His investigations led him to suspect the involvement of both the Gambino Family and star car thief and hit man Arena. A warrant was issued for the arrest of Vito Arena.

By chance an off-duty cop found himself sitting next to a fat, bespectacled man in a restaurant in Suffolk County one evening. The cop thought his dining companion looked familiar but couldn't place him. By the end of the meal the connection had clicked. He matched the description to the wanted poster and made a discreet call on the restaurant pay phone to the Suffolk County police.

Before he had even paid the bill the fat man was arrested. It was Vito Arena.

After being fingerprinted and photographed, Arena was brought to Giuliani's office where Joe Coffey was working. Easing his bulk into an office chair the Gambino Family's leading car thief looked around the room before his impudent gaze settled on the tall figure of Joe Coffey. Fixing him with a long stare, the fat man grinned and said: "I want to talk about a homicide I did."

Coffey, somewhat taken aback, but determined to remain unimpressed by the loathsome specimen of humanity sitting just a few feet away from him, said, "Go ahead, Vito."

Unabashed, the pudgy hit man began to describe a killing at which he had been present. Then another. And then some more. Even hardened detectives like Coffey began to recoil. The litany of murder that poured from his fat lips began with a detailed account of the death of Joseph Scorney, one of Arena's friends and a partner in the Gambino operation. As usual the murder was motivated by an argument over a share of the profits. His partner in crime was another lowlife, Richard Di Nome.

"Scorney and I and Richard Di Nome were walking into the auto chop shop in Brooklyn," recounted Arena in a matter-of-fact tone. "As we were walking in, I shot him in the back. He turned round and fell to his knees and said: 'Vito, what are you doing?' " "I'm killing you, you motherfucker," replied his friend. Arena shoved his gun into Scorney's mouth and pulled the trigger. Amazingly the hapless Scorney was still alive, so Di Nome grabbed a five-pound sledgehammer and crashed it down on the bleeding man's head. Arena then helped him stuff the corpse into a 55-gallon oil drum which they covered with eight bags of quick-drying cement. There was only one problem. Scorney's head was still sticking out of the top of the oil can. The resourceful Di Nome picked up a shovel, severed the head and pushed it down into the concrete so it was level. The two men heaved the oil drum into the back of their car, drove it to the south shore of Long Island and rolled it into the water's edge. They then headed for Chinatown where they consumed a hearty meal.

Keeping his composure, Coffey asked Arena if he could take the investigating team to the location where they had dumped the body. Arena said he could. They made the half-hour drive out to Long Island and Arena pinpointed the exact spot.

"Two days later we went there with a scuba team and we found the barrel with the body in it, exactly the way he described it. He described the clothing he [*Scorney*] had on, three and a half years on, and he also told us that in his left breast pocket we'd find his wallet, which we did. Not only did we find his wallet with his ID in it but we found his dentist's name in it which helped in the positive ID. He gave us the whole litany . . . he described how they cut bodies up. He went to the extent of saying that they killed two guys and they cut their testicles off and he sat there like we would talk about having a cup of coffee. He said, 'Yes, we cut his testicles off.' And he said, 'You could see the guy's balls roll across the floor like little white onions!' "

"Why did Arena turn around and why did he become an informant?" says Coffey, posing the obvious question. "He was a homosexual. He was captured with his lover who was also wanted and all he wanted was to be incarcerated with his lover. That was the whole deal."

No fiction writers would have dared to create a character like Vito Arena and when he retold his story for a New York City jury some of the more susceptible jurors visibly gagged as the gory details spilled out. Two women jurors put their heads in their hands, appalled by the horrific testimony of the overweight homosexual hit man. But to the U.S. Government prosecutors, Arena was worth his weight in gold.

As for Roy Di Meo, he had been prematurely dispatched to a higher court. His corpse was discovered in the trunk of his car with five bullet holes and a glass chandelier wrapped around his head. No one ever could work out the significance of the chandelier but he was almost certainly whacked on the orders of the head of the Gambino Family. It was both insurance against the possibility that Di Meo might talk and punishment for dragging his boss into such an unseemly court case consisting of low-life defendants like Vito Arena.

Although Castellano had to attend the court every day, accompanied by the ever attentive Tommy Bilotti, the Godfather maintained a physical and mental detachment from his codefendants in the courtroom. His expensive attorney, James La Rossa, made sure that his client was seated as far as possible from his fellow accused. Castellano himself was careful not to acknowledge their presence or exchange pleasantries with them.

La Rossa remained confident that his client would beat the rap. "He was on the periphery of the case," maintains La Rossa, "and it was obvious that the Government was stretching to put him in the case and the witnesses had been debriefed over a period of three or four years and suddenly put him in after hearing our openings in court—so it was obviously an 'add-on.' "

James La Rossa was equally unimpressed by the gay hit man and another low-life Government witness called Dominick Montiglio. "There were two major witnesses that testified with him," recalls La Rossa. "One was a man by the name of Arena and the other a man by the name of Montiglio. Between the two of them they had been accused of 15 various crimes, multimurders. Montiglio was an ex–Green Beret who would hook up hand grenades to cars and by wiring them kill them. Arena had done just about everything that one could think about. The jury didn't like both of them, obviously.

"Arena was a very peculiar character and a very interesting one. Once he began to cooperate with the Government he became something of a movie star. He made demands upon the prosecutor and without the prosecutor being aware of it, the penal system had hooked up a recording device on the phones to ensure that no criminal activity occurred, so Arena constantly called the prosecutor and asked for things like larger steaks, a barber's chair in his cell—they kept his homosexual lover in jail for two months after his release date so that Arena would have company!"

In court, La Rossa did his best to impress on the jury the fact that his respectable client, Paul Castellano, was a pillar of society and respectable businessman, frequenting social circles that were a world apart from the sick universe of homosexual hit men, psychopaths and drug-crazed car thieves.

Arena was convinced that the part he was playing in the downfall of the head of the American Mafia would guarantee him celebrity status. He was eager to discuss his publicity potential with a distinguished firm of literary agents and suggested that his role in the inevitable movie would best be played by Tom Selleck. He was quite open in his admissions that he was cooperating with the Government to get leniency for his live-in lover. The whole affair degenerated into black comedy when Arena admitted under cross-examination that in addition to demanding Bruce Springsteen records, larger steak portions and plastic surgery for his homosexual partner, he had also requested an operation to have the fat sucked out of his cheeks, chin and neck. James La Rossa couldn't resist the opportunity this presented in court. Donning a pair of gold-rimmed, half-moon spectacles, the urbane lawyer approached the witness box and, looking over his glasses, continued his cross-examination.

"Did you say you needed a nice profile because you look like a Cyclops?"

"I felt that my appearance was awful," came the dead-pan response from the gay mutilator.

"Is that the word you used?" pressed Castellano's defense attorney.

"Yes," replied Arena.

La Rossa was careful to look at the jury before his follow-up question. "Did you say that?"

"I thought it would help my appearance," replied the witness, who was equally unabashed, whether testifying about his heinous crimes or his homosexual vanity.

"Did you further tell Mr. Mack [*the federal prosecutor*], 'La Rossa is going to dress up all the defendants, and I am going to look like a bad guy.' Did you say that?"

"If you look at the baby faces on them and you look at me . . ."

This time it was the turn of the prosecuting attorneys to put their heads in their hands. Vito Arena had already turned the proceedings in the Federal Courtroom into a field day for the tabloid press but his bizarre personal characteristics were beginning to detract from the seriousness of their case. La Rossa saw a chance to turn the psychotic and surreal nature of Arena's testimony to his client's advantage. The more unbelievable and bloodthirsty the world of Vito Arena could be made to appear to the jury, the easier it became for James La Rossa to point up the unlikelihood of his distinguished client having anything to do with the homosexual mass murderer. All Castellano had to do was to look faintly outraged and exude his carefully cultivated aura of the respectable and successful businessman.

It was a natural part for The Pope, whose whole philosophy as mob boss had been designed to distance himself from the public perception of the Neanderthal street hood with his thick neck, wide shoulders and monosyllabic grunt. (Although it has to be said that the regular attendance in court of Mr. Tommy Bilotti did not help a great deal. But at least he was wearing his smartest blazers and a collection of increasingly colorful ties.) To the unsuspecting jury members, the man sitting a few feet away from them certainly had the appearance of someone more at home in an exclusive Manhattan club reading a copy of *The Wall Street Journal* rather than skulking in a sordid Brooklyn "chop shop" where the smell of spray paint mingled with cigarette smoke and the leftovers from a pizza takeaway— to say nothing of bodies being dismembered and stuffed into rusty 55-gallon oil drums.

Even if the case was going well for Castellano inside the courtroom, in the outside world there were mounting pressures which were fast moving beyond his control. Compulsory attendance in court inevitably weakened his grip on the Family and not everyone shared his defense lawyer's desire to see him beat the rap.

13

THE RISE OF A GODFATHER

WHILE THE POPE WAS FORCED TO LISTEN TO VITO Arena's tales of mutilation and murder, certain ambitious members of the Gambino Family were smiling at the misfortune of the man they secretly loathed. In addition, those who bore a grudge against Castellano did not take kindly to the prospect of receiving their orders from "The Wig."

For anyone nursing ambitions to succeed The Pope now was an ideal opportunity. But it would require someone with ruthless charisma and a ready-made power base. Like any politician running for office, there would also have to be the vision of a better future and the capacity to deliver it. One ambitious Gambino captain who thought he could do all of the above was John Gotti.

According to his former friend, Sal Polisi, "Johnny Boy" displayed all the right qualities from the beginning of his career in the mob. "He was very popular," remembers Polisi. "Because he's charismatic, he's incredible! You know, he talks in simple language. He's very persuasive, he's clever and astute. He was respected because the bosses that were above him, they raised him as a kid, you know, and they liked him a lot. He was very effective and he could carry out a lot of orders and get a lot done on the street. He was a hijacker in the early Seventies. But uniquely enough, what John was able to do that no other mob guys did was, he put Families together. He took guys from the Colombo Family and the Genovese Family at times and put them together and sent them out on missions to rob. Hijacking was a big business in the Sixties and Seventies here. We made a whole bunch of money. He had all these connections with the cargo people giving up information about the valuable loads, diamonds, jewelry, all the valuable cargo that was coming into Kennedy from all over the world. We could get information, we could hijack the truck. Go as far as sometimes not even actually having to steal, you know, the merchandise. The driver would just give it to us! Just give it to you and make believe that he was robbed. Those were the connections that John had!"

In his rise through the ranks, those sort of connections had earned Gotti a lot of friends and also enhanced his reputation as a high earner in the Gambino Family.

Sal Polisi was a regular at the Bergen Hunt and Fish Club, the original low-life haunt where Gotti began his career and built his power base before graduating to the Gambino headquarters at the Ravenite Club in Mulberry Street. The Bergen was a home from home for a vast crowd of itinerant hijackers, car thieves, hit men, visiting Mafiosi, gamblers and loan sharks. "He was originally a thief," explains Polisi, "but he became a wheeler-dealer. He was such a good thief that the other thieves looked up to him. He was so charismatic they just followed his lead."

But Gotti's early career was also being followed with some interest by the New York City Police Department, in particular by an élite unit from the Detectives Squad attached to the District Attorney's office in Queens. Detective Bob Hernandez remembers John Gotti as a rising young hood, observing the change in his dress sense from track suits and T-shirts to designer clothes and silk ties. "Just based on your knowledge of the street, on one's involvement in working on organized crime, you had the sense that this was an up-and-coming guy. I mean, if you were sitting a block away and he got mad, you could hear him screaming at guys, you know, calling them 'stupid' and all these other names, you know. So you knew he was an up-and-coming guy, different from other people.''

Gotti certainly stood out in a crowd. He pandered to his superiors and treated those below him with utter ruthlessness. A telephone wiretap captured the essence of his style. A Gambino soldier had missed an appointment that Gotti had arranged.

"Why am I burning my fucking balls?" screamed Gotti. "I waited three days for you!"

"My wife just called me . . ." replied the trembling Mafioso.

"Your wife just called you, ha!" Gotti pounced. "I'm missing you for three days. She tells me she told you yesterday."

"She hasn't told me yesterday," replied the soldier weakly.

"She just told Willie she told you yesterday," shouted Gotti at a decibel level which miraculously didn't destroy the microphone recording the conversation. "You telling me your wife's a fucking liar?"

Faced with the choice, the Mafioso was quick to sell his wife down the river. "Well then, she lied then," he pleaded. "She didn't tell me."

"Well, let me tell you something. I need an example. Don't you be that fucking example. You understand me?"

"Listen, John . . ."

"Listen, I call your fucking house five times yesterday! Now, if your wife thinks you're a fucking dusky, or she's a fucking dusky, and if you're gonna disregard my motherfucking phone calls I'll blow you and that fucking house up." From the way he was saying it, it didn't sound like an empty threat.

"I never disregarded anything you say . . ."

"This is not a fucking game," continued Gotti. "I'm not gonna miss meets for three days and nights, yeah? My fucking time is valuable!"

"I know that . . ." said the underling, desperately trying to calm his boss down.

"Now you get your fucking ass down here and see me tomorrow," he continued without drawing breath.

"I'm gonna be there all day tomorrow."

"Well, never mind, 'you be there all day tomorrow.' And NEVER make me have to do this again, 'cause if I hear anybody else calling you within five days I'll fucking kill you. Now you make sure you get your ass out here tomorrow! Maybe you're all fucking liars."

The only sound after that was of a telephone being slammed down with sufficient force to snap it in two.

"There was a certain amount of respect that John demanded. He would use the word 'homage,'" explains Polisi. "You know, he liked for his people to pay homage to him. Because he was intelligent, okay, he was a leader, and there's very few leaders out there in the mob. He's an incredible guy. He's very clever and manipulative, you know, and he has a great personality. He's very friendly and he has a fascinating way about him. He has body language that everybody likes. Yeah, you've got to like the guy because he doesn't appear to be what he really is. He's a criminal, he's a murderer, and he's a mobster, and yet he appears to be like a polished actor."

At the Bergen Hunt and Fish Club Gotti liked to sit in the small back room where there was a barber's chair and have his hair groomed by his personal barber at least once a day. In the club itself there was always music playing and sports on the TV. There was the scent of sausage and peppers mingling with cigar smoke. Bottles of beer and wine were stacked up on the tables. Gotti's father would sometimes turn up and prepare a meal in the kitchen for his son and his cronies. At the front of the club would be the mob "gofers" and numbers runners. The more important people sat at the back.

"We would sit in there and play cards and plan robberies and burglaries and just talk about crime all day long. And there was tables in there, and you'd kind of work from one table to the next and in the back would be the mob bosses. Rarely would you get to the back table. Most of the people that come in there would meet in the front. You might get to shake a hand with John but to get in the back

you really had to be close. So there was always half a dozen
of us that would spend time in the back, you know, really
close guys, and the rest would come in and they would kind
of wave to John. But to really get a hug and a kiss, to get
this Mafia kiss, you had to be close to John, you know, you
really had to be close. When I'd come in there, we'd hug,
we'd kiss, we had respect for each other, all this kind of
thing you know."

Polisi commuted between his own club and the Bergen,
gambling and hijacking his way across Brooklyn. One
morning Gotti arrived at Polisi's club. "I've got some interesting information for you," he told his friend.

"Oh yeah?" said Polisi, trying not to sound too interested.

"You guys can go and get half a million dollars worth of
silver . . ."

Polisi was interested.

"I've got some information about a silver bullion shipment," Gotti told him.

Polisi's eyes lit up. "Well, what do you think?"

"Take Foxy and maybe Funzie and Tommy," suggested
the Gambino capo. (Tommy was Tommy De Simone, a
character played by Joe Pesci in the Martin Scorsese *Good-
fellas* movie.)

Polisi put the team together and over the next four
weeks they commuted down the freeway to Kennedy Airport to plan the hijack. On the day of the heist Polisi was
driving with Tommy De Simone, while Funzie and Foxy
were in a backup car behind. Polisi overtook the van and
jammed on the Cadillac's brakes. The bullion truck was so
heavy that it smashed into the back of Polisi's car. Tommy
De Simone was thrown forward before he could even get
out of the car. Regaining his composure, De Simone rushed
out of the car clutching a 12-inch double-barreled shotgun.
Sprinting towards the cab, he aimed the gun straight at
the driver's face. The armed guard sitting next to him put
his hands on the windscreen in a gesture of surrender.
De Simone forced them both out of the van and into the
back of Polisi's Cadillac. He then jumped into the bullion

truck and headed for a small lock-up garage in Queens which was the planned rendezvous.

Sal Polisi took the two guards out to Jamaica to a tunnel near the subway where he dropped them off. "Hey guys, thanks a lot. Here's a hundred dollars, get yourself some lunch!" said Polisi handing over a $100 bill.

After unloading the bullion Polisi reported back to Gotti to negotiate a deal on selling the silver. They were storing the bullion in a mob warehouse. As each member of the hijackers was from a different Family they could all cut their own deals and sell independently. Gotti had already arranged to buy from Foxy and had agreed to pay 25 percent of the original value of the silver. He offered the same deal to Polisi. But Polisi was smarter than this. He took his silver bars and had them melted down before selling them for 98 percent of the silver value. Polisi made nearly half a million dollars compared to Foxy's $100,000.

Although Gotti was annoyed there was not much he could do about it as Polisi was close to the Colombo Family. "John kind of laughed about that, because he was making all this money and I wouldn't allow him to make money on me because I was designated with the Colombo Family and yet Foxy was designated with him, the Gambino Family."

Foxy was younger than Gotti but had grown up with him on the streets and was treated like a kid brother. He was one of Gotti's most trusted sidekicks which was why he put him together with Polisi. But Foxy fell out with Tommy De Simone. De Simone was a paranoid hijacker with a cocaine habit. His problem was that he had fallen for Foxy's sister, a striking Italian beauty. "Listen, we're in the life together," Foxy told De Simone, "but don't you ever think that you are going to take my sister out. I don't want her involved with anybody like us."

Tommy De Simone ignored the warning and continued to date Foxy's sister. One day Foxy grabbed hold of him and half strangled De Simone, then he pushed him against a wall and screamed: "Stay away from my sister!"

One week later Tommy De Simone went up to Foxy's apartment, shot him four times and killed him.

It didn't take long for word to reach John Gotti that one of his closest friends on the streets had been hit. Gotti was in jail at the time, as was Foxy's other friend, Sal Polisi. Gotti sidled up to Polisi in Manhattan's West Street Detention Center and whispered in a low voice: "I want you to know that Tommy De Simone killed Foxy and Foxy was like a brother to me."

"I'm going to kill Tommy when I get out," said Polisi.

"No you're not," hissed Gotti. "You're not going to kill Tommy, because I'm going to kill him."

Polisi was inside for two years while Gotti did three. On the outside Tommy De Simone figured he had it made. He took part in the sensational Lufthansa hijack, America's biggest robbery, and thought he was being lined up to become a made guy in the Lucchese Family. All his life he had dreamed of one thing: the initiation ceremony which would make him a real-life wiseguy. Tommy couldn't believe his luck when a message came through that Paul Vario, a powerful Lucchese captain, wanted to see him. Tommy De Simone proudly put on his best three-piece suit and gave his immaculately polished shoes another shine, not that they could get any cleaner. His fastidious dress sense was well known to the cops and had almost given him away when a witness to the $8 million Lufthansa heist had commented on one of the robbers having unusually clean shoes.

On January 14, 1979, a distraught Mrs. Tommy De Simone reported her husband missing. His body has never been recovered and the disappearance has never been solved. Paul Vario had indeed summoned the well-dressed and aspiring wiseguy. But not to initiate him into the Lucchese Family. He was doing a favor for John Gotti.

"Paul Vario was delivering him to John Gotti," explains Polisi. "Gotti killed and chopped him up and nobody's ever seen Tommy De Simone's body. Right after that I ran into John and Angelo Ruggiero, John's most trusted friend. And he said, 'See we avenged your buddy, Foxy's death. We chopped up Tommy.' And so you know they took him out, there was no doubt. He waited four years to kill that guy to get even and he bragged about it. Never a piece of evidence found. No body, no missing clothing, nothing. No money. Killed him, took him out."

It was one of the many killings engineered by Gotti. It all contributed to his growing reputation on the street as a man who should be respected and whose fearsome temper could erupt at any moment. Detectives watching his career with growing interest in the late Seventies and early Eighties were particularly intrigued by one tragic event which was to change the life of the "Dapper Don" forever. Joe Coffey heard it on the street and later found out exactly what had happened.

"He [Gotti] had a young son who was crossing behind the driveway of his next-door neighbor. The neighbor came out, ran John Gotti's son over with the car, a pure accident, and dragged the kid several hundred feet and killed him— total accident. This poor guy's life was never the same again and ultimately John had him killed. They met him at a prearranged meet at a diner in Nassau County, Long Island, picked him up and they brought him to John live, and they took him down to a basement, where it was we don't know, and they strung him up and John cut him in half with a chainsaw while he was still alive. This was his neighbor who accidentally killed his child."

Joe Coffey heard the details from one of his informers. The neighbor's body, like Tommy De Simone's, was never found. "He was a real family man, inside his family," recalls Polisi. "John was shattered about it."

Polisi also remembers John Gotti's wife, Vicky, a formidable woman with a tongue and temper to match her husband's. When the hapless neighbor came round to their Howard Beach home one afternoon, Vicky attacked him with a baseball bat. "She actually ordered this man to be killed. A good friend of mine was involved in abducting this man, kidnapping him, and they never saw the guy again. Vicky ordered that. His wife said, 'I want this man dead,' and it was carried out."

But revenge wouldn't bring the young child back. Gotti never came to terms with the tragedy and constructed a shrine inside their Howard Beach home in memory of their lost son. Every year on the anniversary he would visit his son's gravestone and put flowers down and go into mourning. Close friends knew that it was a time when it was best to avoid him.

Even those close to "Johnny Boy" were not spared his vicious temper, but unless he was really furious or someone had done something that was a serious transgression of mob protocol or committed some act of disloyalty, his bark tended to be worse than his bite. When one of his best friends, William "Willie Boy" Johnson, was revealed in court as an FBI informer, Gotti couldn't believe it and even when he did, refrained from having Willie Boy murdered for two years.

His friends knew that Gotti was intensely loyal to those who were close to him. His crew made a lot of money and had a lot of good times. Gotti had an enormous appetite for fine food, good restaurants, money and power. But in 1985 his best friend and his kid brother, Eugene, were both in serious trouble.

The friend was Angelo Ruggiero, the overweight soldier in the Gambino Family whose life expectancy wasn't helped by his habit of chain-smoking 60 Marlboros a day. The FBI bug in Ruggiero's house had come home to roost. It had provided the FBI with sufficient evidence to bring a case against them. Angelo Ruggiero and Eugene Gotti were indicted for masterminding a multimillion-dollar heroin racket.

14

THE MAFIA TAPES

THE COURT CASE WAS THE LEAST OF THEIR WORRIES. The real problem was Paul Castellano. Not only was it merely a matter of time before he found out, it was also likely to be one of those rare occasions when a mob boss would take the word of the Feds rather than one of his own.

With the help of John Gotti and Gambino underboss, Neil Dellacroce, they had managed to keep the news from Castellano for a while. But The Pope soon got wind of the case and, even worse, learned of the existence of the FBI tapes from the bug in Ruggiero's house. Castellano wanted to get hold of them to find out what had been going on. Ruggiero knew that if his boss heard them, it would seal his fate. There wouldn't even be a trial. In addition, there were scathing references to the man that Gotti and his crew dismissively nicknamed "Nasabeak" on account of his gigantic hawk-shaped nose.

John Gotti was furious with Ruggiero for being so stupid. He had broken one of the cardinal rules by doing so much business at home. Gotti made a point of never talking about mob affairs or holding meetings at his suburban Howard Beach home. To top it all was the added disgrace of Ruggiero inadvertently allowing the FBI to get inside his home to plant the bug. If Angelo Ruggiero hadn't been a lifelong friend, John Gotti would have shot him dead in the street. But as Angelo and Eugene were part of his crew Gotti had to stick by them. No one, least of all Paul Castellano, would believe he hadn't known exactly what was going on.

If only Ruggiero had managed to keep his big mouth shut. It was something that Gotti was constantly chiding him for. On one occasion, Gotti ticked him off for discussing a Commission meeting. Ruggiero apologized. "That don't justify it, Angelo," explained Gotti. "You're not supposed to speak to every fuckin' guy about a Commission meeting. Alright, you ain't the only guy that done it, but you ain't supposed to do it. You could sit here all night an' try an' justify it, you ain't supposed to tell the guy about the Commission."

If he hadn't smoked so much Angelo Ruggiero would literally never have stopped talking. He listened patiently to Gotti's warnings but seemed unable to do much about it. For the FBI it was a gold mine. The tapes revealed Ruggiero incriminating himself over heroin deals and bad-mouthing Castellano. Although they could plead their innocence before trial, enough to grant them a stay of execution from the head of the Family, there would be little doubt once the tapes were played in court. Castellano would be able to understand the nuances better than any Assistant U.S. Attorney. But Castellano wanted to get the tapes before the case was even heard.

No way, Ruggiero decided. There was no way he would hand over the tapes, copies of which had been given to him for his trial defense. His refusal aroused Castellano's suspicions even more and The Pope finally ordered his underboss Dellacroce to get the tapes.

One summer afternoon Dellacroce summoned "Johnny Boy" and his sidekick Ruggiero to his white wooden-fronted house which was just down the road from Castellano's White House in Staten Island. There was an FBI bug there too!

"I'm gonna tell you something," said Ruggiero. "If you two never bother with me again, in the rest of my life, I

ain't givin' them tapes up. If you never bother with me
again, the rest of my life, I can't. I can't! There's good
friends of mine on them fuckin' tapes. If it was some
fuckin' asshole like Buddy, or somebody like that, I'd give it
to them in three seconds flat."

Dellacroce and John Gotti listened to Ruggiero.

"There's good guys on them fuckin' tapes," he added
pointedly. Not least Eugene Gotti, John's younger brother
who had also effortlessly moved into the Family business,
looking after what was sometimes known as the "pharma-
ceuticals" division—except he didn't display the skills of
his elder brother in avoiding getting caught.

"They're good guys," agreed Gotti.

"That's how I am," said Ruggiero. "I don't say I'm
gonna call them, John."

"Don't call them."

"I'm just tellin' you, I'm just tellin' you."

There were people mentioned or referred to on the
tapes, the "good guys," sometimes indirectly. What Gotti
wanted to avoid was Ruggiero involving them now which
could lead to more trouble with the police or Castellano—
or both. "Don't call them good guys, whatever you do,"
admonished Gotti. "Don't look for them when you're in
trouble, the good guys."

"That's right," added Neil Dellacroce, the Gambino underboss.

Castellano had suggested that his lawyer should contact
Ruggiero's attorney to get the tapes. "I'm gonna meet this
guy," Ruggiero announced. "I'm gonna meet him and his
lawyer, and I want them to tell me how these tapes could
help him."

Gotti thought that might work. "And let him tell you,
maybe he could show you how," instructed Gotti, "if he
shows you how, he's the boss, while he's the boss you have
to do what he tells you."

"That's what I'm tellin' you," interrupted Dellacroce,
"that's what we wanna hear."

Paul Castellano was attempting to get the tapes on the
pretext that they might be relevant to his own court case.
Under the rules, if the boss ordered something then every-

one else had to obey. Dellacroce and Gotti realized why
Ruggiero was hanging on to the tapes. It was in their interests as well. But as Dellacroce proceeded to try and explain
to the fat Mafioso, "rules was rules."

"You see that's why I says to you before," explained the
underboss. "You don't understand Cosa Nostra."

"Angelo," said Gotti, "what does Cosa Nostra mean?"

"Cosa Nostra means that the boss is your boss, you understand?" answered Dellacroce on his behalf.

"Forget all about this nonsense."

"La Cosa Nostra," replied Ruggiero. "I'll tell my boss,
or tell me to turn against you. I won't do that."

"Forget about it," said Dellacroce.

"I won't do that," repeated Ruggiero.

"Forget about it," snapped Dellacroce.

"I won't do that," said Ruggiero for the third time, beginning to sound like St. Peter. "That's not Cosa Nostra,
Neil."

"La Cosa Nostra, boss is the boss is the boss," murmured Dellacroce, who had his own problems—not least
the fact that he had recently been diagnosed as suffering
from terminal cancer.

"Tell me to set one of my best friends up," muttered
Ruggiero.

"And you . . ." began Dellacroce.

"I won't do that."

"Ah, you wanna make up stories."

"I don't wanna make up stories," said Ruggiero.

"Sure you do," said Dellacroce.

"I wanna say the truth, Neil."

"You ain't gonna set no friends of ours up," said
Dellacroce.

"You bet your life I'm not gonna do that. I would never
do that."

"Why don't you keep quiet?" said Gotti, fearful that his
friend might blurt something out that he would rather
Dellacroce didn't hear. While they had all been profiting
from Ruggiero's drug deals, there was an unspoken understanding between all of them that because of Castellano's
ruling they should never openly admit that any of

them knew exactly where the money was coming from. Dellacroce probably knew they had been careful not to involve him directly.

"You ain't talkin' Cosa Nostra now."

"We know I'm not," admitted Ruggiero.

"We don't need you to tell us that," rasped Dellacroce. "For Christ sake, those things were done a million times. We don't need you to tell us that, that I'm not gonna set up a friend of ours. What I'm trying to say is, a boss is a boss. Well, what the fuck good is a boss? What does a boss mean in this fuckin' thing? You might as well make anybody off the fuckin' street."

"Neil, I gotta tell you the truth, I gotta tell you from my heart. You got a different tune today that I spoke to you last week. I swear to God, I really mean it."

"Aah," said Dellacroce, deeply impressed.

"I swear on my mother," exclaimed Ruggiero.

"You don't know what the fuck you're talkin' about," interjected Gotti.

"I don't know what I'm talking about?" queried Ruggiero. "I definitely know what I'm talking about!"

"What's the different tune now?" inquired Dellacroce.

"I don't know. I'll tell you the truth, you talkin' to me different right now."

"Why don't you keep quiet and shut the fuck up?" admonished Gotti.

"How am I talking different?" persisted Dellacroce.

"You are definitely," continued Ruggiero, ignoring as usual the ritual admonishments from Gotti, "because last week, last week you agreed with me, and today, you're not agreein' with me."

"Because last week there was a problem," said Dellacroce, "I even told you, I says, 'We'll do this, we'll do that, and we'll do this.' What has last week got to do with this week?"

"You're right," concluded Gotti.

"I'm usin' a different tune. What do you mean I'm usin' a different tune?"

"Neil, I'm with you, I don't talk Chinese," replied

Ruggiero. "I'm trying to tell you the truth. You were last week . . ."

"Where's the fuckin' different tune . . . ?"

"You were different last week."

"Where's the different tune?" persisted Dellacroce. "In what way?"

Ruggiero seemed unable to answer the question, so Dellacroce attempted to spell it out for him. "I'm just sayin', why don't, why don't you listen to people a little bit, for Christ sake. No, nobody is givin' you bad advice. I never gave you bad advice in my life. I don't wanna see you or anybody get hurt. I don't wanna see no friends of ours get hurt. I'm just tryin' to tell you what's right and what's wrong."

Ruggiero didn't want to enrage his underboss by reminding him that he had appeared to support him last week. But Dellacroce kept on pressing him to explain what he meant. "Say where I use a different tune. In what time?"

"When I explained to you my situation last week, you said to me, 'You're right.'"

"And I still says you're, I'm still sayin', you're right. I mean, but what, what're we gonna do, we're arguing over these fuckin' tapes for, I told ya? I explained to you what took place yesterday. I explained to you the conversation I had, I had with him. Now, what do you want me to tell him? 'The guy says, fuck you, he don't wanna give you those fuckin' tapes'?"

"No, I don't want you, I told you, 'Stay out of it.' I told . . ."

"Right."

"I told Johnny. Please."

"I don't want nobody to get involved."

"I wouldn't, I wouldn't do that," Dellacroce assured him.

"I'll handle it myself," cried Ruggiero in exasperation. "If I'm wrong, I'm wrong."

"Why should you get involved?" answered Dellacroce, trying to be protective. "Why should you get involved over something that's, that's . . ."

"Because I'm a fuckin' hard-on, that's why . . ."

"That's not right," said Dellacroce, a stickler for mob protocol. "I mean you ain't runnin' this fuckin' borgata, you know that."

"Definitely not," agreed Ruggiero. "Definitely not. Who says I'm runnin', runnin' what?"

"Well that's what I'm trying to tell you. You ain't runnin' this fuckin' borgata. You got people over you. I've been tryin' to take your part with these tapes from the very, very beginning. That you have to give them to him. I've been tellin' him, personally. 'The guy can't give you the tapes, because his Family is on, is on there, all his . . .'"

"No excuse. There's no shame over here," muttered Ruggiero.

"I've been tryin' to make you get away with these tapes," said Dellacroce with a note of rising indignation. "But Jesus Christ Almighty, I can't stop the guy from always bringin' it up. Unless I, unless I tell the guy, 'Hey, why don't you go fuck yourself, and stop bringin' these tapes, tapes up?' Then you, then we know what we gotta do then, we go and roll it up and go to war. I don't know, if that's what you want . . ."

Dellacroce was referring to "rolling up the mattress," mob slang for hiding out with just a mattress when there was an inter-Family war in progress. You slept from house to house on a mattress so no one could find you.

"I don't want that," insisted Ruggiero, who would require a fairly large mattress. "No, I don't want that. No, I don't want that."

"I'm sure you don't want it," said Dellacroce, relieved to have made his point.

"I don't want that at all . . ."

"I mean that's what I told you last week, you say, 'What should I?' I told you, that's in the last stage. Let's wait, let's take it easy, that's the last stage. If it has to come to that, it'll come to that. But let it come to that, let's not just talk about it, because you don't wanna give the guy the tapes. I'm, for Christ's sake, I ain't sayin' you're wrong. Don't forget, don't only consider yourself. You know, you got a lot of other fellas, too, that you like. And a lot of other fellas'll get hurt too. Not only, not only you could get hurt, I could get hurt, he could get hurt," said Dellacroce pointing at a strangely silent Gotti.

But Gotti's silence wasn't due to lack of interest. He was listening intently, and thinking. In the summer of 1985 John Gotti had plans, big plans, and if he could carry them out successfully he might just be able to solve Ruggiero's problems himself.

"A lot of other fellas could get hurt. For what? For what? Because you don't wanna show him the tape!"

Dellacroce wasn't joking when he mentioned the possibility of a war. Fortunately for Ruggiero, Paul Castellano was somewhat distracted by his own impending court case for the car-theft ring. Meanwhile Joseph O'Brien and Andy Kurins had struck gold. O'Brien had been tipped off about the Commission meeting they had hoped to hear about from the bug in Castellano's mansion. The meeting was scheduled to be held at a house specially loaned for the occasion on Staten Island.

The agents staked out an ordinary looking suburban street called Cameron Avenue less than half a mile from Castellano's mansion. After waiting most of the afternoon their patience was rewarded by the welcome sight of Fat Tony Salerno swaggering out of the house with his walking stick, followed by Gerry Lang, acting head of the Colombo Family, and his sidekick Ralph Scopo. Bringing up the rear was Tommy Bilotti wearing a truly appalling loud check blazer and searching the street for any signs of surveillance.

Kurins snapped away furiously with his motor-driven Nikon, worrying that the pictures might not come out in the fading light. When the pictures were developed they were as clear as daylight. The FBI bosses and the prosecutors from Giuliani's office were ecstatic. The pictures made a powerful contribution to the fast accumulating body of evidence they were harvesting for the Commission case.

The various investigations by separate law enforcement agencies were providing a wealth of material, including audio tapes, video surveillance and photographs. So far none of the prime suspects seemed to have cottoned on to the fact that they were under round-the-clock surveillance.

Even though some of the targets were increasingly "surveillance conscious," none of them ever discovered any of the hidden microphones. Even when they suspected they were being followed they carried on their familiar routines. Better still, one of the main targets, Ralph Scopo, thought he had actually given the agents the slip when in fact they had managed to stay with him all the way.

One tape demonstrated to a delighted FBI audience that despite their target's suspicions it was still "business as usual." "I had fuckin' agents all around me," complained Ralph Scopo to Forcino and Sternchos as they sat with him in his car. "They're lookin' for me. Jesus Christ, I had the agents followin' me all day."

"Aren't you better off when you meet here—you drive away to another parking lot?" inquired Forcino. "This way you see if somebody follows you at least? Every day a different spot?"

"When they're here, there's five cars . . ." explained the Mafia's representative in the concrete industry.

"Yeah but . . ."

"So it don't matter where you . . ."

"At least you drive an' drive . . ." continued Forcino.

"And a lot of times, I mean, I meet a guy yesterday with a Mercedes Benz. He was parked in there right against the fence. I was better off just sittin' in the fuckin' car. I told him, drive into the other parking lot. I drive into the other parking lot smack into one of them fuckin' agents!"

"They probably have cars over there with walkie-talkies!" said Forcino.

They did.

It wasn't just the agents that Scopo was worried about either. He had recently read about the auto-theft case which Paul Castellano had been charged with. Scopo had got word that Roy Di Meo, the Gambino captain who had personally supervised the execution of Castellano's son-in-law for two-timing the Godfather's daughter, had himself been murdered. Di Meo's mysterious death was one of several connected with the auto-theft racket for which there was no apparent motive other than that they might have been tempted to cut a deal with the Feds in a hope of a

lighter sentence. For the head of the Gambino Family such
killings made sense as an insurance policy. They also served
as a useful warning to anyone else who might find himself
in a position where he could be offered inducements by the
U.S. Attorney's office in return for cooperation as a witness. Scopo realized that if Mafiosi like Roy Di Meo could
be murdered for what they knew, how vulnerable he was
with his extensive knowledge of the inner workings of the
Club, the Commission's most lucrative racket.

One morning as Ralph Scopo held court from inside his
car at his favored spot, at Queens municipal parking lot,
the President of the Concrete Workers District Council expressed his growing fears to one of his business associates.
"Them fuckin' names in the paper," said Scopo. "Remember? There were six guys that they mentioned that was
killed. I know five of them."

"Really?"

"Yeah, five good guys. Good guys. Now these fuckin'
business guys, that's why I say sometimes you're better off.
Say I'm doin' this, you make 'em three million a year; even
if it was my racket or my thing, whatever it was, and the
other two million, split it up. Now down the line while I'm
making this three million higher up I talk to this guy, I talk
to that guy. A guy that I meet, he's earning two million
anyway, so he's gotta come in. Everything's fine as long as
everybody's happy. Now the next move—the agents get on
us. They start to follow me . . ." Scopo hesitated, bliss-
fully unaware of the irony that not only was he under surveillance but that his conversation was also being recorded.
". . . and they piece together and bingo I'm indicted! The
other part of the Family, they're not gonna indict them. All
the weight is on me."

"Yeah," agreed his "friend."

"Now I get indicted and they're afraid. The only guy
they got to worry about is me. If I open my mouth, they're
dead. So to kill the case—bango!"

"Really?"

"Yeah," sighed Scopo who knew the rules of the mob as
well as the Club. "Here I am all my life makin' them make
money. I'm takin' the fuckin' chances in the street. I'm

willing to go to jail, never gonna open my mouth, but they're not sure of that, see?"

"I don't blame them not bein' sure. Everybody and his brother-in-law is . . ."

"That's it," continued Scopo with an air of resignation. "Now what happens? So we meet, the five guys that they mentioned in the fuckin' paper, I'll stake my fuckin' life on it, that they would never have opened their mouths. There was one guy named, uh . . ." For a moment Scopo had forgotten his name. "Roy Di Meo."

"Didn't the guy or the guys that, uh, that got picked up, aren't they made guys?"

"Shit," swore Scopo. "Jimmy, when I tell you the guy had cast-iron balls. Where they says he was the street enforcer. His name's Roy Di Meo. I'm tellin' you he had balls. This guy used to be with the Gallos. At that time we were havin' a war, alright? With the Gallos. And Roy, Roy was on the Gallos side. Alright? Then when it was all squared away and peace was made, he was really supposed to come with us. Instead, he went to another Family and they straightened him out. Once that was straightened out, that alleviated us and deleted us from hurtin' him. We weren't gonna hurt him anyway."

"Hmmm," said his friend.

"But now we had the insurance that he wouldn't . . . So what happened? The Gambinos had the guy killed. Not over our problem, but their own problem. He was the one that created the problem where the cars were goin' over . . ."

"Yeah."

"And I mean he was a tough guy, alright? Bein' he got picked up, they figure, 'Maybe this guy, under pressure, he'll rat.' That's bullshit. But not to take the chance, not knowin' whether he would or not, they went and killed him. It's just like what I'm doin' now. Say this thing kinda blows up, I'll be one of the first guys to get arrested."

"Why?"

"We talked about this Club shit . . ."

"Why?"

"Because my name's mentioned wherever there's . . ."

"Really?"

"Sure," admitted Scopo. "Now when that happens, if they got, no matter how much faith they got in you, there's always that little bit. They say, 'Oh, geez, maybe he'll open his fuckin' mouth.' And then you don't see the guy no more! Then, then Vinny Di Napoli got locked up for, uh, five years. Teddy Maritis. Everyone knew him."

"Right."

"When was the last time you saw Teddy Maritis?"

"Oh, I don't know."

"So there's the answer," reflected Scopo, looking out of the windshield. Scopo just figured the best thing to do was to keep making money. He couldn't see any agents in the car park today. Maybe he wasn't going to get "pinched."

In the meantime there were still buildings going up all over New York City. It was business as usual.

One building contractor, Jim Costigan, was in the middle of bidding for a variety of construction projects in Manhattan. Costigan worked for XLO, one of the large concrete companies that mediated their deals through Scopo. Costigan suggested they sort out one of the contracts directly with Castellano.

"Let me say another thing," said Scopo. "If I went direct to Paul without no Club members, without resortin' to this company, to that company and said, 'Paul . . . we're having a few disagreements over the status of this job, over this . . .' There's no question that I could get the job. But I'll owe him my life."

"Yeah," sighed Costigan.

"He'll ask me for a hundred different favors for that one favor."

"I know," said Costigan.

Owing favors to the head of the Gambino Family was something Scopo was keen to avoid. The grasping nature and greed of Paul Castellano was viewed with increasing distaste by his fellow members of the Commission. Despite the distractions of the court case, he seemed determined to chase every last cent that was owed to him. It was making him distinctly unpopular with the other New York Families. As the surveillance team from the New York State Organized Crime Task Force trailed Sal Avellino and the head of the Lucchese Family in their Jaguar XJ6 they picked up a conversation about an argument concerning the leader of the Manhattan Carpenters' Union, John Cody, another mob-connected union official at the heart of the construction business.

"He says, like with the Carpenters, and he says that Cody was Paul's . . ."

"Cody's?" asked Tony Corallo.

"He says . . ."

"That the Carpenters was his?"

"Something like that, uh, he was talkin' to Tom in private and I didn't pay, you know, they didn't want me to hear, so I didn't listen."

"Cody, huh?"

"So he said that Cody and Duffy at the end of the year used to send him a bone, he says. 'They used to send me a bone every year, about 200,000 a year. That's a bone,' he says. 'A bone. They used to send me a bone.' "

"Who used to send him?" asked Corallo.

"Cody and Duffy," answered Avellino. "Carl, they said, he says, 'They used to send me a bone every year and the bone was 200,000.' "

"He's full of shit," exclaimed the irascible old Godfather. "He's full of shit that comes out of his fuckin' ears. You couldna got 200,000 off Cody for as long as the . . . Listen, this guy only knows about this here when Carl died . . ."

"Well, I'm tellin' you what he said."

Corallo didn't like to think of Paul Castellano getting that much money and as far he was concerned Carl, Carlo Gambino, hadn't been getting it either. "And Carl never got 200,000. They used to give him a fuckin' pretzel."

"Well, he said, 'They gave me a bone. I used to get about 200,000.' "

"Yeah!" smirked a disbelieving Corallo.

"And I took a gulp when he said a bone, 200,000. I said, 'Holy Christ, that's a bone?' You know. See, so when we went out, I said to Tom, 'Tom, did you hear what he said?' Tom says, 'He's full of shit, he only made it 200,000 because now he wants, he's gonna make a claim, hey, "I was gettin' a lot of money over here, and now you only, you wanna cut me down?'' ' "

Exactly as Tony "Ducks" Corallo suspected. "Now who's cuttin' him down?" he asked.

"Something to do with Petey Vario."

"What's it got to do with Petey Vario? We're talking about the Carpenters."

"Petey Vario picks something up with the Carpenters," explained Avellino.

"Yeah, he picked up on one job."

"He says that Cody is makin' a beef and complainin' about that because that was theirs."

"Let him go complain to Fat Tony," said the head of the Lucchese Family dismissively.

"He said this was theirs," repeated Avellino.

"This is the Carpenters. Let him go complain to Fat Tony. Listen to me please," said Corallo, getting annoyed.

"I'm listenin' to ya. I'm only tellin' . . ." said his driver.

"He's got to go complain to Fat Tony. What the fuck has he got to do with Carpenters?" Corallo was annoyed that The Pope should be trespassing on other Family territory. "He's got no right shaking the Carpenters down. I've got to tell him straight talk. I'll sit there and tell him when he complains, this guy. I'll tell him! I'll tell him, 'You cocksucker, I'll give you a fuckin' . . .'" Tony Ducks was either momentarily lost for words or the Jaguar had slipped out of range of the trailing surveillance cars. "I got to listen to him bullshit, 'a bone.' Two hundred thousand dollars. Twenty-five thousand dollar shakedown. Fuck him. And he said to tell Tommy to get another one. Imagine that, he didn't get enough. I don't understand this for the fucking hell of me—he didn't get enough. Imagine that, he didn't get enough money? Huh? Twenty-five thousand dollars, he even tried to the last minute to get the other $10,000 off him. If I would have seen that guy, I'd kill him. I'd kill him. You kill the cocksucker."

It's unclear exactly who Tony "Ducks" Corallo was aiming to kill. But there was no doubt that Paul Castellano's greed had put him in a murderous mood.

A few weeks later the underboss of the Lucchese Family, Salvatore Santoro, "Tom Mix," was complaining about Ralph Scopo. There had been a meeting with Gerry Langella, acting boss of the Colombo Family, and Neil Dellacroce, representing the Gambinos, where it transpired that they were going to create problems on a building site, despite the fact that the contractors had already paid their dues to receive protection.

"Seen that fuckin' Gerry Lang," muttered Santoro, referring derisively to the acting boss of the Colombo Family. "He's supposed to give a guy problems and they were takin' 25,000 a month from the guy for unions! And this Ralphie Scopo he came out with it like innocently, you know. And Neil picked it up, told me, go to the meeting because I had told Paul and I had told Fat Tony, 'Hey, how the fuck these people gonna give him a problem? He's takin' 25,000 a month for unions. They can't give him a problem.' "

"Uh hummmmm," replied Avellino working out that the insurance premium came to $300,000 a year. You could buy pretty good labor relations with that sort of cash.

"This is an outlaw," said Santoro contemptuously. "He's takin' all kinds of jobs, he's bidding all kinds of jobs. Lo and behold, yesterday we talk and talk and talk and nobody's talking about it! I wanna mind my business because I don't wanna be the bad guy. But you know, it's irritating. So I tell Ralphie Scopo. I says, 'Hey! You made a statement that you take 25,000 a month off this guy for the unions. How the fuck are you gonna give him problems if you're takin' 25,000 a month off him? Oh, wait a minute, wait a minute.' Nobody picked it up, nobody, so I forget about it. I didn't even mention it again, then when everybody went away, I grabbed Paul. 'What the fuck you doing, Paul? I told you, you didn't even press the issue about the 25,000 for the union. Well, what is it?' 'Oh, Tom, you know, eh, eh, you know . . .' [*said Castellano*] 'Hey you want to forget about it, it's okay with me.' I says, 'I know what you've been trying to do . . . that's what we're here for. Now we're talking about giving the guy a problem, how the fuck could they give him a problem?' "

Santoro thought Castellano was losing his grip. Salvatore Santoro was an old school Mafioso. There was nothing wrong with extortion. He'd done it all his life, but what was the point if you didn't keep your side of the bargain? What was the point of paying protection money if you didn't get protection? Whether it was a small-time grocer in Little Italy or a multimillion-dollar construction project on Wall Street, the principle was the same.

The underboss lamented the lack of "honor" in the mob nowadays. Still he was looking forward to retirement. He had enough money, he had no particular ambition to take over from Corallo. All he had to do was avoid getting into trouble. "Half of the fuckin' things that go on. I don't wanna wind up by goin' dyin' in the fucking can," complained the Lucchese underboss to Avellino.

"I agree with you, Tom, it's ridiculous after all the work to get to this stage . . ."

"After all my fuckin' work for nothin' . . ."

Although neither of them was under indictment at the time, they were all too aware that driving around town, fixing deals, sorting out loans, shaking down the unions or arranging a Commission meeting meant that at any time they might be followed, arrested or caught. It was always a risk but still they carried on.

"Then you say even at 70 years old, 'I got to jeopardize myself.'" Worried that his underboss might think that he was implying that he had lost his nerve, Avellino continued: "Not that you are afraid but . . ."

"No, no, no, no," said Santoro, muttering under his breath.

"It's just not supposed to be, you know what I'm saying. Something that you can't . . . Right, but you're not supposed to be looking for it."

"Yeah," agreed Santoro.

"In other words, this is actually you're inviting it."

"Right, right."

"And you know, ah, the odds, every time there's another meeting, there's another thing, the odds get smaller and smaller that someday one of these things is gonna pop!"

"That's right. That's right," agreed Tom Mix.

"To be truthful with you I don't need nothing. I got my own."

"Right."

"You know I got an income, forget about it. You know I don't need nothing, be bothered with nothin'. If you weren't such a dedicated person to 'This Thing,' you would turn around and say, 'You know what? I'm retiring. Leave me alone.'"

"Yeah," said Santoro, who felt that exactly. "I feel before I'm gonna start, saying, 'I'm sick, I can't go, I'm sick. I stay home.'" It seemed as difficult for an underboss of the New York Mafia to take a day off work as for anyone else.

"I'm sick," repeated Avellino.

"That's the end of it," said Santoro.

"And that's it."

Tom Mix sometimes wished it was as simple as that. But he was a man with heavy responsibilities—sorting out problems, deputizing for Corallo at Commission meetings. "Now a guy comes with problems," explained the underboss, "a guy comes with problems, I can't tell him, 'Hey! Don't bother me!'"

"Uh, uh," said Avellino, looking over the steering wheel, "you're too dedicated."

Part of Santoro's job was to supervise payments coming from the unions and construction, making sure that the Lucchese Family got their fair share. Tom Mix was a frequent visitor to Fat Tony's Palma Boys Social Club on 115th Street. "There's Tom," said one of Fat Tony's cronies as the Lucchese underboss entered the dingy, half-lit club.

Fat Tony looked up from his table and chortled. "Jesus Christ Almighty, what happened? I thought you got mad at me for Christ's sake! Hey, hey, Tom. How are you? How you feel, Tom?"

"Alright," grunted Santoro.

"You're all mad at me!" laughed the jovial head of the Genovese Family.

Santoro wanted to sort out some long-standing disputes between the Gambino Family and the other Families. Salerno listened as he ran through some of the problems that needed fixing. "We gotta have a meeting—we been afraid of meeting lately but . . ."

"Looks like we got to get together," added his consigliere, "Christie Tick" Furnari.

"We gotta do what's fast today. 'Cause this, what's his name's kid, Allie Boy, Michael . . . and Paul. I shouldn't say Paul, Ralphie. They were there ten years ago. With Ferraro Quadrozza, before Paul even knew what concrete was. And they were running Long Island the way they wanted to run it and they used to make big deals with Cody."

Another problem was that Fat Tony was owed some money by Castellano. He asked the Lucchese underboss if he knew what was happening.

"No we never got that money straightened out," replied Santoro.

"I didn't get it yet," pressed Fat Tony.

"No, no, no, no, no, no, no, no, no, I told Paul," said Santoro. "They say he's paid. They keep sayin' . . ."

"And when we see him again, we'll tell him again. I'll tell him," said Salerno. "He tells Louie he's not paying. He's supposed to be paid for the Taft."

"Well, what's that got to do with the money?" asked Santoro. It appears that "Louie" owed money to Paul which was due from a building project at the Taft which could then be used to pay the debt to Fat Tony—money owing from another construction project involving the Certified Concrete Company.

"He says he ain't got it," explained Salerno to the Lucchese underboss. "He said when he gets his ten million, another million for the Taft which this kid said he's got it now. For the first of January. We should get it. We're gonna get our 500."

Castellano owed the Genovese Family $500,000. But it seemed everyone was waiting for someone else to make a payment somewhere along the line in order to pass the money along. One of Fat Tony's soldiers knew the details of the Taft construction project. "Louie's splittin' 300,000 for the Taft. That ain't got nothin' to do with Certified. He owes Paul 300,000 for the Taft."

"Yeah, Paul says he can't get the money yet. He says when he gets the money, when he totals the Taft, he's gonna give him 500," said Fat Tony.

"Why don't he wait for the 300 he's got from the Big Apple. He kept the 300 from the Big Apple," suggested Santoro.

"I didn't even know that myself!" exclaimed a surprised Salerno.

"I know you didn't," said Santoro. "But with the point I'm tryin' to make, if you gotta wait for money, you listenin' to me? I got 300 from the Big Apple comin' to me, clean you up. Now I gotta take the 300 and then tell you I didn't collect the rest of the month. What kind of, I don't understand it. Am I explaining myself?"

Not very well—although no one said it. What was very clear was that there were huge sums of money involved due to the Commission and that Castellano was increasingly unpopular for the way that he seemed to be hanging on to more than his fair share.

Even when the tapes revealed some complex inter-Family dispute that no one could understand there were often chilling references to the hidden power of the Commission. One morning at the Palma Boys Social Club, Santoro was talking about one of the mob-run unions and elections. Santoro reminisced about a past union boss. "Only God knows how much fuckin' money he took when he had Manhattan. He had Manhattan and that's where everything is. And not only had Manhattan there, if there was a good job in Staten Island, he'd go to Staten Island. He'd put his fuckin' men there."

On another occasion the FBI bug recorded Fat Tony Salerno listening patiently in his role as a senior Commission member discussing problems within the strife-torn Colombo Family. Carmine Persico, Jr., known as "Junior" or "The Snake," was in trouble with the Feds and about to go on trial. His weakness and unpopularity with another faction of the Family was leading to an internal power struggle. Internal rivalries had been exacerbated by The Snake's frequently enforced absence due to a series of arrests and jail sentences over the previous decade. Now it seemed as if the balance of power was slipping away from him.

"Well we got to try and stop these guys before they . . ."

"Yeah," said Salerno.

"What are we going to do with these guys? Just last Saturday they were out looking . . ."

"Is that right?" exclaimed one of the wiseguys in the Palma Boys Social Club. "They were walking around with machine guns, these guys? Suppose we walk around with machine guns . . . ?"

"How the hell we're gonna do this?" grunted Fat Tony, realizing that the situation could get out of hand. He thought for a moment. "I'll send word to Junior to straighten this fucking thing out."

"That's fine, that'll be real good," said the Colombo capo who had come for Salerno's advice. ". . . and he can do it. He can do it. After a later date when things cool down a little bit, then come and sit down with him."

"These are different times now," concluded Salerno philosophically.

"Yeah—I know. I understand you got your own problems."

"They're all checking on me," continued Salerno mournfully. "You wouldn't believe it! I'll get hold of Junior, straighten this fuckin' thing out. The Commission wants it straightened out."

Fat Tony Salerno could still throw his considerable weight around. No out-of-town wiseguy could challenge him. "Tell him the Commission from New York. Tell him he's dealing with the big boys now. This is from the Commission!"

There was no higher authority. One of the problems that the elder statesmen like Corallo and Salerno faced was that the younger generation no longer held the Commission in the awe and respect that they felt they deserved. Apart from the fact that the younger generation of Mafiosi no longer held the institution in such high regard, both men were aging "Godfathers" in their seventies and approaching retirement age. Inevitably, their authority was diminished. Fat Tony Salerno looked as if he belonged in an old folks' home, hobbling around the streets with the aid of a walking stick. Tony "Ducks" Corallo was in slightly better health but had already suffered one heart attack. With Paul Castellano suffering from diabetes and Neil Dellacroce dying of cancer, the hierarchy of the New York Mafia was not in good shape.

Tony "Ducks" Corallo made it clear that he was getting too old to be forever "running around town" to sort out problems with the Families. FBI agents listened with amusement as the two old age pensioners of organized crime admitted that they were getting too old for the job. Corallo made a rare visit to the Palma Boys Social Club to commiserate with Fat Tony. He warned him that if they didn't sort out some pressing problems they would forever be "running downtown."

"No, I'll retire," quipped Fat Tony, half-serious, "I don't need that!"

"I know you'll retire, I know you'll retire!" soothed Corallo.

"Fuck that shit, I won't take orders from the guy!"

"The rest of the guys you got around here that you like, that you made," continued Corallo, trying to reassure his fellow Commission member by reminding him of all the faithful soldiers that Salerno had himself personally approved for membership of the Genovese Family.

"They'll always be here," mused Salerno. "Listen, Tony, if it wasn't for me, there wouldn't be no mob left. I made all the guys. And everybody's a good guy."

"I know, I know," said Corallo.

Salerno went on to openly acknowledge the growing generation gap. The circumstances were unclear but whatever the problem was it appeared to be something that in the past could have been easily dealt with. "I can't talk to no one. I used to do anything I wanted with the guy. All of a sudden. Since this fuckin' shit with this kid there, when this kid did that fuckin' job there, see?"

"Tony," said Corallo, trying to humor his old friend. "One thing, get rid of them, shoot them, kill them, but then you know, you can't go on. It's disgusting. Well here's to your health and fuck everything!"

The aging leaders of the Mafia were wistfully looking forward to a retirement that they all feared they might never make. Although they too had no direct knowledge of the bugs that were recording their hopes and fears as they talked, they had seen which way the wind was blowing with the advent of Giuliani and the renewed sense of mission within the law enforcement community. The heads of two of New York City's most powerful Mafia Families seemed to be resigned to their fate.

"I'm gonna get pinched," confessed Fat Tony.

"I'm gonna get pinched too," predicted the head of the Lucchese Family, 12 weeks in advance of the actual event.

Inevitably, news, gossip and rumor had circulated back and forth between mobsters, lawyers and law enforcement agents to the effect that something big was brewing. Salerno and Corallo didn't know exactly what, but they only had to have noted what had been happening to Paul Castellano to get an inkling of what might be in store for them.

"Big Paul . . ." said Salerno.

"Yeah," agreed Corallo.

They both knew that The Pope was in serious trouble, not just over the auto-theft case but there were rumors that they were going to hit him with another indictment. Hence the prophecy of the two Tonys that they would be pinched as well. Castellano had kept both Tonys up-to-date with the legal moves against him and had realistically assessed his chances of survival.

The hidden microphone in the Palma Boys Social Club revealed that Castellano was equally sanguine about his own prospects. In this conversation a Genovese soldier had asked Salerno about his plans for the day. "So where do you gotta go today?" he inquired.

"Today I gotta go to a meeting with Paulie. He thinks he's going away for a long time."

"Eh?"

"Paulie's going away for a long time. He's finished."

On February 25, 1985, the leaders of the American

Mafia, the Commission, were arrested in a blaze of publicity amidst the sound of motor-driven cameras and shouted questions from excited correspondents from the U.S. television networks. True to style, Giuliani orchestrated the arrests for maximum coverage.

"Go fuck yourself," muttered Fat Tony, cigar clenched between his mouth and his Homburg rammed down on top of his head, to one TV reporter who got too close to the head of the Genovese Family. Paul Castellano suffered the indignity of a second arrest in less than a year and the prospect of yet another lengthy and costly court case.

At least this time the arresting agents were the FBI's Andy Kurins and Joseph O'Brien, who deliberately treated their old adversary with the respect they felt he deserved. On the drive to the courthouse the elderly Godfather almost collapsed when they told him that they had put a bug inside his house. His embarrassment was acute, as much because in addition to eavesdropping on vital conversations about the Gambino Family, he realized the agents must have found out about a sordid affair he had been having with his Colombian maid.

Corallo was apoplectic with rage when he discovered that his Jaguar had been bugged.

As for Fat Tony Salerno, the agents decided not to tell him about the bug in his social club. It might still prove useful.

The pooling of evidence from the tapes of Ralph Scopo, the Jaguar and Castellano's house had provided Giuliani's office with sufficient evidence to go before a Grand Jury and return a 42-page indictment complete with a back-page Mafia chart showing the heads of the five New York Families. At the bottom of the Family trees, a drawing of a bundle of dollar bills represented "Extortion," a cloth cap, "Labor Racketeering," and the outline of a body, "Murder." It was a comic strip graphic version of the enormity of the Commission's power and it served its purpose in detailing the outline of the Government's case against the Mafia's own ruling hierarchy.

The indictment represented the U.S.A. versus Anthony Salerno, a/k/a "Fat Tony," Paul Castellano, a/k/a "Paulie,"

"Mr. Paul," "Big Paul," Aniello Dellacroce, a/k/a "Neil," "O'Neil," Gennaro Langella, a/k/a "Gerry Lang," Anthony Corallo, a/k/a "Tony Ducks," Salvatore Santoro, a/k/a "Tom Mix," Christopher Furnari, a/k/a "Christie Tick," Philip Rastelli, a/k/a "Rusty," and Ralph Scopo. For the first time in its history, the Commission of the American Mafia was charged as a "Criminal Enterprise." There were 15 counts of racketeering which ranged from "conspiracy to extort payoffs from certain concrete companies" to "count number eleven," the "murder of Carmine Galante."

Shortly after the arrests the decision to leave the bug in Fat Tony's Palma Boys Social Club paid dividends. It picked up the following conversation between Salerno and one of his soldiers.

"He [*Giuiliani*] had 'em put a bug in Tony's car?" asked an incredulous Salerno.

"In Avellino's car."

"Avellino's car," repeated Salerno.

"It was his office that put the bug. They got 770 hours, 770 90-minute tapes."

"They put a bug in Paul's house," added Fat Tony. "Unbelievable!"

"Seven hundred and seventy hours! They're unbelievable, you know how they do it? You gotta remember, they send ConEdison in. They send the telephone company in. What does it take? Two minutes, somebody's not looking. Even if you're looking you can't tell what they're doing!"

The expertise of the FBI "plumbers" had certainly fooled the Commission. It was a devastating blow against the Mafia. "The worst day ever" for organized crime, quipped Giuliani at the press conference. He hardly needed to add it was the best day ever for law enforcement.

But it was.

It was also an unique opportunity for certain other individuals who had long nursed similar ambitions to alter the status quo—not in the interests of putting an end to organized crime but rather with a view to opening a new chapter in the history of the American Mafia. John Gotti had long felt a sense of destiny: the time had now come to fulfill it.

15

THE FINAL ACT

THE HUNDREDS OF HOURS OF TAPES WERE ABOUT TO CRE-
ate massive problems for the beleaguered leadership
of the New York Mafia. There was hardly any top
Mafia figure who did not at some point figure prominently
in the FBI sound archives. The mere knowledge of the existence of the tapes was immensely demoralizing for those
arrested. Whereas in the past there had always been a fighting chance of beating the rap in a trial, it was much more
difficult for a mob lawyer to construct a meaningful defense when their own client's conversations were easily ac-
cessible to the jury. With so many hours to choose from the
prosecuting attorneys could afford to be highly selective in
their choice of tapes to be admitted in court. The defense
lawyers were reduced to raising obscure points of law and
challenging the meaning of particular words and phrases.
Combined with the application of RICO, Castellano and his
fellow Commission members didn't stand a chance.

Although Castellano's lawyer had been confident that
they could gain an acquittal on the auto-theft case, the
Commission trial, scheduled to begin almost a year later,
would be in a different league. Now Castellano would
spend lengthy and tedious days in court fighting the car-
theft case and his spare time helping his lawyer prepare the

defense for the Commission trial. As Fat Tony Salerno had astutely observed, Paulie was finished.

Inevitably, Castellano was distracted from his daytime job, namely running America's largest organized crime Family. That distraction provided John Gotti with the perfect opportunity to start canvassing support for his move against the head of his own Family. Like a hunter circling his prey, Gotti could sense that his victim was weakening. It was time to put him out of his misery.

First, he needed the approval of the remaining Commission members. Getting rid of Castellano would be easy; succeeding him and staying alive was more difficult. To do that required the prior approval of the other mob bosses. Discreet overtures were made to the heads of the Lucchese, Colombo and Bonanno Families. Gotti was helped by the fact that there was little love lost between Paul Castellano and the other heads of Families.

His main problem was the Genovese Family who had traditionally been close to the Gambinos. Gotti gambled that he could make his move without the backing of Salerno. Once the Commission trial was over there would be a new power structure and it was the next generation that Gotti had to convince. As for the others, Castellano's own greed had alienated them sufficiently for Gotti to emerge as a popular hero. In their eyes Castellano had let the side down. He had also brought the high office of "boss of bosses" into disrepute by allowing the FBI to bug his house.

Last but not least there was the Gambino Family itself. There were still those who were loyal to the Godfather but they too could be brought round, especially as Castellano had caused further embarrassment by leaving his elderly wife, Nina, and running off with their Colombian maid. Then there was the issue of narcotics. Many of the up-and-coming Gambino wiseguys couldn't comprehend the edict against drugs. Some of them liked to use cocaine themselves, others were secretly making millions out of drugs. How much easier it would all be if they didn't have to worry about The Pope's disapproval and an automatic death sentence should they be caught.

Gotti's plans came to fruition when his protector and mentor, Neil Dellacroce, finally succumbed to cancer on December 2, 1985. The Gambino underboss who had acted as peacekeeper between the warring factions of the Gambino Family had gone to meet his maker. Now there was no one to mediate between Castellano and Gotti, his younger brother Eugene and Angelo Ruggiero, whose narcotics case had led to the argument about the tapes from the bug in Ruggiero's house, there was a very real possibility that the Gotti crew would soon become history.

For John Gotti, the final straw came when Paul Castellano failed to pay his last respects at Dellacroce's funeral. The significance of the gesture was not lost on John Gotti. At a meeting shortly after the funeral, Castellano took Gotti to one side and casually remarked in a conspiratorial whisper: "You know, there was a rumor that Neil was a rat."

Gotti couldn't believe it. He looked aghast at the man for whom he now felt utter contempt and loathing. "What? Let 'em go fuck themselves! Whoever said that, I'll throw him off a fuckin' building!"

If Gotti had any doubts before as to what had to be done, now he had none. In preparing the ground it was crucial for Gotti to secure the future loyalty of those forming part of Castellano's inner circle. There was no chance of getting through to the vain and hot-tempered Tommy Bilotti who worshiped his boss. Instead Gotti suborned Frankie De Cicco, who had succeeded Dellacroce as underboss of the Gambino Family. De Cicco was a trusted confidant of "the old man" and because he was a potential rival to Bilotti, who was convinced that he would take over the Family if his boss ended up in jail, Gotti had an opportunity to play the one off against the other. De Cicco calculated that if Gotti was successful he stood to gain and that if he failed Gotti would be dead, so either way he couldn't lose.

On the night of December 14, 1985, John Gotti summoned his closest friend Sammy "The Bull" Gravano to a meeting. It was a counsel of war. Gravano was a vicious thug with an eighth-grade education and a reputation on the street almost as fearsome as Gotti's. Sammy the Bull was a multiple murderer. Although only five foot eight inches tall, he was a street hood with a face to match. He was also an obsessive bodybuilder who, in addition to pumping iron, popped mouthfuls of steroids. Gravano had a round, pitted face which one agent compared to a bag full of nails.

Rarely separated from Gotti, Gravano was an upwardly mobile gangster. As a high earner for the Gambino Family, Gravano oversaw a multitude of mob-controlled construction companies. He had several companies himself, including a drywall firm in Brooklyn. It was there that they had agreed to hold their secret meeting.

Surrounding Gotti and Gravano at the table were six other men that nobody in their right mind would willingly have met on a dark night—let alone in broad daylight. In a conspiratorial huddle, Gotti addressed the assembled team and informed them that they were being chosen to carry out a very important hit. The plan was to meet the following night in a small park one mile from midtown Manhattan to finalize details.

Next night, equipped with walkie-talkies and handguns and clad, somewhat incongruously, in white trench coats and black Russian fur hats, the gunmen were dispatched to 46th Street and 3rd Avenue. Frank De Cicco had already arranged a meeting between himself, Gambino, Tommy Bilotti and Paul Castellano for the evening of December 16 to discuss future plans for the Gambino Family. The meeting place was one of Manhattan's finest steak houses, Spark's Restaurant on 46th Street between 2nd and 3rd Avenues. Now four of Gotti's hit men staked out the restaurant while the rest took up positions as backup men in case anything went wrong.

That very same night, the heads of the FBI and the State Organized Crime Task Force and several United States Attorneys were invited to attend a law seminar at the New York University. The guest speaker was Robert Blakey, the law professor who had drafted the RICO statute.

Before setting off for the restaurant, Castellano stopped off at the offices of his lawyer, James La Rossa, to plan the next week's proceedings in his court case. "It was shortly before Christmas and he brought some gifts up for the secretaries and while he was here we discussed the case shortly. He was here about an hour and a half and then left," recalls La Rossa.

On the streets of Manhattan, shoppers were crowding the sidewalks. Office workers were taking advantage of the stores' late night openings and picking up presents for girlfriends, wives, mothers, fathers and children. Laden with gifts, New Yorkers struggled into the subway and onto buses or stood forlornly on street corners vainly trying to hail a yellow cab. No one paid much attention to the dark-suited man in a wig driving a black Lincoln Continental and negotiating the traffic along 3rd Avenue.

As usual when chauffeuring the Godfather, Bilotti was driving ultra-carefully, keeping a watchful eye out for police patrols and surveillance vehicles. He stopped as the traffic light on the corner of 3rd Avenue and 46th Street turned to red. Staring straight ahead, Bilotti failed to notice the occupants of another Lincoln next to them. In the driver's seat was a well-dressed man with dark-gray hair swept back off his forehead. The passenger, with short, crinkly dark hair and a pitted face, immediately identified both Castellano and Bilotti.

"They're right next to us," whispered the dark-haired man—picking up a metallic object from the dashboard of the Lincoln. Sammy "The Bull" Gravano pressed the button on his walkie-talkie and spoke into the handset: "They're at the light."

As the light turned green, Castellano's black Lincoln cruised along the corner into 46th Street. Bilotti was relieved to spot a parking place right outside the restaurant. The Lincoln pulled over to park and Bilotti turned the keys in the ignition and opened his door. Paul Castellano emerged from the passenger's side onto the sidewalk to walk the few yards into the restaurant entrance.

A tall man wearing a long, white trench coat and a black fur hat came up to him and without saying a word fired six shots into Castellano's head and another bullet into the old man's chest. Tommy Bilotti didn't even have time to close his car door. Squatting by the side window he heard the shots ring out in quick succession and watched in horror as his beloved boss began to collapse into a crumpled heap on the curbside.

Tommy Bilotti never saw the gunman stalking him from behind. Had he looked round he might have noticed that the hit man was wearing an identical trench coat and hat. The gunman fired four bullets at point-blank range into the back of Bilotti's head. Another four shots were fired into his back and chest. Bilotti tumbled backwards into the road, ending up sprawled diagonally away from the driver's side of the black Lincoln. Rivulets of blood began to seep slowly into the gutter.

Four men wearing white trench coats and black hats walked swiftly down to the end of 46th Street where they began to start running. As they turned the corner Gotti cruised down 46th Street, slowing to a crawl as he passed the bleeding corpse of Tommy Bilotti. Gravano studied the body for a few seconds before looking up: "He's gone."

Gotti accelerated to the end of the road and turned right into 2nd Avenue. The black Lincoln with its tinted windows now concealing the two most powerful Mafia gangsters in America vanished into Manhattan's early evening rush hour.

Back at Spark's, Frankie De Cicco came out of the restaurant with fellow Gambino captain Jimmy "Brown" Failla. Looking at the two corpses on the street, they both realized immediately what had happened. "Jesus Christ!" exclaimed Failla in a state of shock. "I could have been in that car with them!"

De Cicco was quick to reassure him. "You would have been alright," said the underboss.

They almost collided with an equally startled Tommy Gambino. Quickly taking him by the arm, De Cicco ushered him back down the street. "Your uncle just got shot," he explained. "Just go back to your car and leave."

In a New York University seminar room, law professor Robert Blakey had just finished his short lecture on the application of the Racketeering Influence and Corrupt Organization (RICO) statute. Amongst his attentive audience now standing up and drinking cups of coffee were New York City's most senior law enforcement officials. The assembled forces of law and order were hoping to use RICO to devastating effect in the forthcoming trial of the Mafia's ruling Commission.

Tom Sheer, head of the FBI's New York office, was remarking on the success that they had already achieved by using RICO. Their discussions were cut short by the sound of someone's beeper going off. And then another. Soon the whole room was alive with the sound of several beepers ringing simultaneously. The agents and attorneys rushed for the telephones. It didn't take them long to discover that the main target of the law they had just been discussing had come to a premature end.

"Our beepers went off," recalls Tom Sheer. "We went to the phone immediately and contacted the FBI office and found that Paul Castellano had been shot. They gave us the location, we responded and found the New York City Police Department on the scene. They had roped off the area. Mr. Castellano was dead—slumped against his car—and his driver and lieutenant, Tommy Bilotti, was lying sprawled on the street on his back. Both were dead as a result of multiple gunshot wounds."

Castellano and Bilotti had been murdered just after five o'clock in the afternoon. Fifteen minutes later 46th Street was swarming with police and ambulances. When Sheer arrived in an FBI car there was still the sound of sirens screaming and the sight of red and blue emergency vehicle lights reflecting off the surrounding walls. "It was hectic. A tremendous amount of activity, but it was pretty well-organized right from the beginning."

As Tom Sheer gazed down at the corpse he noticed that part of Castellano's head had been shot away. The FBI man reflected on how quickly the power that had been concentrated within this one man had vanished: just like the blood that was flowing from his head into the gutter. A fitting end to a life devoted to organized crime, thought Sheer as he looked down at the two corpses.

There was something strangely pathetic about Castellano's posture in death. His left hand was still clutching the expensive leather gloves which he wore to protect his hands from the cold. The startled look on his blood-spattered face testified to the shock he must have felt in the split second before he realized that his life was over. The flared nostrils and upturned head made his beaklike nose appear larger in death than in life. A pair of monogrammed Pierre Cardin silk socks were revealed by trousers that had been hiked up as the boss of bosses had fallen awkwardly against the door sill of his car. A pair of gold-framed spectacles had tumbled from his face and lay unbroken on his right-hand side underneath the car. The impression was of a frail and elderly human being. All in all it was a pathetic sight.

Yet in death Paul Castellano seemed to regain some of the dignity that he had lost in life. Death had bestowed upon him the appearance he had striven to cultivate all his life. Lying on his back on the 46th Street sidewalk, Paul Castellano could easily have been mistaken for a wealthy and successful businessman who had suffered the misfortune to fall victim to the random violence that plagued the innocent citizens of New York City. And in a way he had.

To the head of the FBI it was poetic justice. "His administration stopped that night on the street. He ceased to exist that night. We didn't know what would follow. We didn't know who would take over. We didn't know whether that would be the beginning of a war. We didn't know what would happen next. But it was significant that night and it remains significant to this day."

For John Gotti, it was a "piece of work" which was the crowning achievement of his life in organized crime. He didn't set out at the beginning with any sort of vow to murder his way to the top, yet that was how things had developed. He knew that after Castellano's absence at Dellacroce's funeral, his own might not be too far off. Castellano had been overheard bad-mouthing Gotti and muttering about "wrecking" John Gotti's crew. At best that would have destroyed his power base, at worst, resulted in his own death plus that of his brother and close friend Angelo Ruggiero. The Mafia logic was simple, kill or be killed.

Forty-eight hours after Manhattan's most sensational Mafia execution, a sober crowd of Gambino captains assembled in Caesar's East Restaurant on 58th Street. At the head of the table was Joe N. Gallo, the old-school consigliere. Sitting on either side of him were John Gotti and Sammy Gravano. In the immediate aftermath of the execution Gallo had become the "acting boss." Addressing the assembled company, Gallo confessed that he didn't know who was responsible for the murder of their head of Family but that they were "investigating" it!

Of course Gallo knew full well who was behind the killings. He didn't have to look any further than the men who were sitting next to him. His primary concern was to stabilize the situation. There were still those loyal to Castellano who out of fear or loyalty might try to avenge their boss's murder. Gallo issued an order that no one was to go around carrying guns or to overreact to recent events. Gallo ended his speech by saying that no one had anything to be afraid of. It would be business as usual.

Gotti realized that he couldn't afford at this stage to take the credit for the hit. There would have to be a cooling-off period before an election could be held allowing Gotti to take over the reins of power.

One week later in a lower Manhattan basement building the Gambino Family met to choose their new boss. Frankie De Cicco stood up to nominate John Gotti as their new leader. As they went round the table, each Gambino captain made his choice. "Everybody nominated John. John was the boss," recalled Gravano.

The decision was unanimous. John Gotti became the new head of the Gambino Family and the most powerful Mafioso in America. Emissaries were dispatched to the other New York Families to announce the change of leadership. The changing of the guard met with popular approval. One Mafioso came up to Gotti some months later and said, "Let me tell you, John, I never was so proud, so happy in my whole life. I was talking with a few skippers from another Family and since youse are here this is the first they could remember in years that the Families ain't arguing."

It was just the sort of testimony that he liked to hear.

One of John Gotti's first acts as boss was to promote his loyal sidekick, Sammy "The Bull" Gravano. Frankie De Cicco was also rewarded. Angelo Ruggiero and Eugene Gotti could relax in the knowledge that their head of Family would no longer be trying to kill them, although they still had the serious charges of drug trafficking to contend with.

Now John Gotti could run the Gambino Family in his own inimitable style. He would promote his loyal friends and ruthlessly eliminate those he couldn't trust. The Pope was dead. But just as the murder of Carmine Galante had unforeseen repercussions for those who had killed him, so too would the ghost of Paul Castellano return to haunt those who had destroyed his life to inherit his kingdom.

— 16 —

LONG LIVE THE KING!

THE FIRST CASUALTY OF GOTTI'S REIGN OF TERROR WAS the man who had made it possible. On the morning of April 13, 1986, Gambino underboss Frankie De Cicco opened his car door and triggered a car bomb which killed him.

The murder has never been solved. Some thought it was the work of Tommy Bilotti's relatives while others suspected the hand of Gotti. A Mafioso who could betray one boss could betray another. Alternatively, De Cicco may have been a sacrifice to appease the Castellano loyalists.

Now the two most powerful figures under Gotti were Sammy "The Bull" Gravano, his consigliere, and newly appointed underboss, Frankie "Loc" Locascio. Gravano, already deeply entrenched in the construction industry, used his additional power to expand his interests. From 1986 to 1990 he built up a formidable variety of front companies designed to enrich himself and the Gambino Family at the expense of New York City's long-suffering inhabitants. At one point Gotti himself complained that even he didn't know how many companies they had. Worse, all sorts of deals and partnerships were being set up which often ended in disagreement and death. Success, it seemed, created its own problems, as Gotti unburdened himself to Frankie Locascio.

"Every fucking time I turn around there's a new company popping up. Rebars, building, consulting, concrete. And every time we got a partner that don't agree with us, we kill him. You go to the boss and your boss kills him. He kills 'em. He okays it. Says it's alright, good. Where are we going here, Frankie? Who the fuck are we? What do I get out of this here? Better not become a clown. Where am I going? What do I do with the rest of the borgata?" complained the Godfather. "You throw 'em in the fuckin' street? The rest of the borgata. What do I do with the borgata? Hah? Twenty-five capodecinas, 25 beef to me. Sammy tells me you and him took a walk about a concrete plant in New Jersey? I told him when do youse decide to tell me about it?"

"There's nothing for sure," replied Locascio, anxious to mollify his boss. "I just got the land and I . . ."

His underboss's excuse didn't cut much ice with Gotti who had a keen eye for detail and was particularly annoyed with Gravano. "Yeah, but I told him, 'Don't I have the right? Frankie's my acting underboss. Supposed to tell me first, then I'll tell you if it's okay to go ahead or not.' I told him now, 'Sammy . . . Don't you people listen here?' I mean where are we going here?"

Later when Sammy the Bull was present Gotti reinforced his view that he needed to know what was going on when it came to money. "Take what you gotta take, Sammy. Take 20 percent, if there's such a thing. There's six guys in the fuckin' city. Whether it's right or wrong. I would be a billionaire if I was looking to be a selfish boss. That's not me. Cosa Nostra—we are where we belong. We're in the positions we belong in, Frankie, and nobody could change that!"

One group of people were intent on "changing that." As soon as he became the new boss of bosses John Gotti was under surveillance by all the agencies who had been targeting Paul Castellano. Initially such overkill was counterproductive. Competing interests in the law enforcement field resulted in a series of unsuccessful court cases from which Gotti managed to walk free. It all served to hype up the Gotti legend. For the Government the worst failure was a case brought against Gotti by the U.S. Attorney's office of the Eastern District in early 1987.

The Assistant U.S. Attorney handling the case, Diane Giacalone, was determined to press ahead with the prosecution despite the misgivings of many of the agents involved. The trial was a disaster. Gotti's flamboyant lawyer, Bruce Cutler, made all the running, destroying a succession of small-time sleazeballs that the Government produced as cooperating witnesses against Gotti. Towards the end of the case, the atmosphere in the courtroom was almost festive.

Ed McDonald, former head of the Brooklyn Organized Crime Strike Force, watched in dismay as the jury returned a verdict of not guilty on all counts. McDonald and the FBI had strongly advised against bringing the case in the first place but in the end both were overruled by the internal politics of the U.S. Attorney's office.

"It was a misguided prosecution," McDonald admits. "It was a case that should never have been brought. The evidence was simply not sufficient to proceed against Gotti at that time and it was an unfortunate mistake on the part of the Government."

For many of the agents and prosecutors involved in the first unsuccessful RICO case it became a matter of life and death to secure a conviction against Gotti. "It's very important to the Government that he goes down because the Government itself has made John Gotti," admits McDonald. "They've played into this whole thing, you know, the media campaign involving John Gotti. They have helped create the image of John Gotti as 'Public Enemy Number One.' They have made no bones about the fact that they have targeted him, that they consider him to be the most significant organized crime figure in generations."

For John Gotti, his 1987 acquittal was a moment of triumph. Mobbed by newsmen, reporters and camera teams, Gotti sprinted down the courthouse steps punching the air in triumph. The smile said it all. Nothing could stop him now. John Gotti positively radiated invincibility.

Sure, he was followed day and night. So what? The case had also shown him the extraordinary art of electronic surveillance and the need to talk only in places where the FBI microphones could be discounted or better still to "walk-talk"—go out on the streets and whisper away from the prying ears of law enforcement. It meant an upping of the electronic surveillance stakes. As the wiseguys became more conscious of hidden microphones, so the pressure was on the FBI to find even more ingenious places to install them.

Unlike his predecessor, who preferred to hold court in his Staten Island home, John Gotti was a man on the move. Chauffeured around town in his black Mercedes, Gotti favored the traditional Gambino social clubs as venues for business and pleasure. His haunts were the Bergen Hunt and Fish Club in Brooklyn and the Ravenite in Little Italy's Mulberry Street. Rarely did Gotti take business home with him. That left the Bergen and the Ravenite as possible sites to be bugged. Although the Bergen had been Gotti's main haunt when Castellano was alive, he now favored the Ravenite, which had long been the official headquarters of the Gambino Family.

The FBI discovered that Gotti had rented a second-floor apartment above the Ravenite from an 80-year-old widow, whose husband had been a Mafioso. One night an FBI technical team broke in and managed to place a number of bugs. Microphones were installed both in the upstairs apartment and in the downstairs club. Virtually the whole of the Ravenite Club was now wired for sound.

Almost as soon as the bug started to relay the innermost thoughts of the Mafia's new chairman, the FBI were surprised to hear Gotti was already making careful plans to ensure the smooth running of the Family in case anything happened to him. Gotti was constantly stressing the need for secrecy and giving instructions to his closest friends about what they should do if he was not around. It was almost as if he was trying to avoid the same fate which had befallen Castellano.

"You can't discuss life with a million people," he warned Gravano. "There are certain things only you or him could make," said Gotti, referring to Frank Locascio, his underboss.

"This is the inner circle," boasted Sammy the Bull.

"That's the law," said Gotti. "If tomorrow I was to die and the Family voted a new boss and they voted, let's make a wishy-washy guy downstairs. Let's get a guy that's, ah, Pete Castellano, our new boss. He'd hate you two with a fuckin' passion."

"Absolutely," agreed Gravano.

"Because he ain't a man," explained the head of the Gambino Family. "You a tough, hey, you a tough guy. He'd hate ya! Ah, and anytime he could knock you, he's gonna knock you."

"Yeah," agreed Gravano. "He's jealous . . ."

"Hoping that something would happen to us," added Locascio.

"That's right," said Gotti.

John Gotti took his responsibilities very seriously and unlike Castellano he carefully cultivated the loyalty of the soldiers in the street and his senior management. After all, he knew only too well what could happen to a boss who became too detached from the Family. He was careful to keep close to his friends and keep his friends close to him. He openly professed his feelings for the members of his "inner circle."

"Today I go and have lunch," mused the Godfather in the presence of his right-hand man Frankie "Loc" Locascio. "I mixed up about four lunches at once you know. You know, Frankie, I don't like you . . ." Locascio might have felt trepidation at his boss's sudden outburst of honesty. But he knew what was coming next. ". . . I love you! I don't like Sammy. I love him. As far as this life, no one knows it better than me. If a guy offends me, I'll break him. That's the fuckin' end of it. But not for me. It's this 'thing of ours.' It's gotten to be a circus. I'm not gonna leave a circus when I go to jail, Frankie. I don't wanna be a phony. I ain't gonna talk about a guy behind his back. Louie was a fuckin' coffee boy. Know what a coffee boy was? A motherfuckin' coffee boy!"

"You told me once," demurred Locascio.

"Never did nothin'," continued Gotti, warming to his theme. Louie was Louie Di Bono, the Gambinos' main construction partner. "I'm tellin' you again. Never did nothin'! He's a billionaire now. Billionaire now! Owns buildings. Throws half a million into fuckin' factories and bars. And all the rest of them. Yeah, yeah, make the faces. But anyway, this is all well and good. I got guys around me aren't makin' five cents. This is my back!"

Curiously, there were occasions when Gotti professed not to be interested in money. He would espouse higher values like the preservation of the Cosa Nostra. In Gotti's book, greed was something that could get a man killed, especially when it was at his expense. The Dapper Don could afford to be generous. After lambasting Locascio and Gravano for not keeping him up-to-date with all the construction companies that were being formed, Gotti insinuated that it was not the money he cared about but the formalities that had to be observed. As boss he had to be kept informed of every deal and every brick in any construction project that came under the wing of the Gambino Family.

"I want you to own 500 plants. But I wanna know about it, Frank. I got beef, guys beefin' at me every fuckin' hour every day. Yesterday one of them fuckin' capodecinas, they sent for me for a glory fuckin' meeting on Sunday. And the people think that this is my fuckin' green eyes!"

Locascio grunted.

"Couple of our capodecinas. You think it's my green eyes? You think this is me doing this? This is not me, Frankie! What do I get outta this fuckin' shit?"

"Which building, er, is this?" asked his acting underboss.

"It's a big building. I don't know where. Six million, 20 million, whatever it is? But what, where are we going here, Frankie? Frankie, where the hell did all these new companies come from? Where did five new companies come from? Ah, I mean when Nasabeak died, you were nothing. Louie had Gem Steel. You told me that the guy talked behind my back. Now you got Gem Steel. The other thing, you told me 'Di B' cried behind my back. Now you got all that!"

Gotti was referring to the inheritance from the two partners whose murders he had authorized. "Di B"—Robert Di Bernardo and Louie Di Bono—both had been major players in the Gambino Family under Castellano. Gotti reminded him that he also controlled Bobby Sasso, the bagman for much of the cash pouring out of the concrete industry and into the illicit coffers of the Gambino Family.

"Hey, Frankie, are you in with me, Frank? I'll walk outta here and we'll terminate our friendship. Is that what our 'marriage' is? That's not the way it's gonna be, Frank. I give you my word, Frank. I love you guys. I don't fabricate no part of it."

Once he'd become assured in his new position as head of the Gambino Family, Gotti would often philosophize about the values of the mob that he aspired to and expected his devotees to follow. At times when he feared that his arrest was imminent he would become both emotional and obsessed with preserving the life and society that he had sworn to live and die for. John Gotti was nothing if not a true believer: a disciple of Cosa Nostra.

"This is the new game," he lectured Frank Locascio, his acting underboss. "We got tough guys, tough guys with us. They look at me like I'm fuckin' nuts. And you think that I was reapin' billions of dollars, Frankie. I don't want none! I don't want a fuckin' thing! And this guy, I mean, what's, I love you! Where are we going here? You know what's frightening to me, Frankie? I love him. I don't give a fuck, because I know I blast him a little bit and he'll slow it down. What happens when I go away, or I'm gone? When I'm dead, Frankie? Youse two guys are the fuckin' guys, I, nothin'! Fuck me! The whole Family gotta go and find out. Is this what we gonna invite? This is probably what happen? I'm sick, Frankie," complained Gotti with unconscious irony. "I've been sick over the whole weekend. You know what I mean?"

Although Gotti would occasionally bawl Gravano out he was closer to him than anyone else. When one of Gravano's children was in the hospital after a traffic accident, Gotti went to visit. He reminded the child of the loss of his own son and warned him to be careful. "I love the guy. I go up to the hospital, I see his kid. I find out he bought the fuckin' moped. Hah?"

"He did?" said Locascio.

"Yeah!" replied Gotti.

"Thank God that he's alright. You would've thought . . ."

"Good he's alright," agreed his boss, "but then you wanna kill him for what he done, right? I mean right or wrong? He's got to whack the kid down."

"You done good," said Locascio by way of flattery.

Gotti, who rarely displayed any of the more human emotions in public apart from greed, anger and violence, then made a rare reference to the tragedy that left both him and Mrs. Gotti devastated. "I told him, 'I had a son like you.' Make it a little tough for the guy. 'I go and visit him every Saturday, Sunday, 11 o'clock in the morning. That what you want your mom and dad to do? They'll do it. You'll have your fuckin' home in the cemetery.' I mean where are we going here? We're creating these fucking kids. You know Frankie? I'm not a jerk-off. If I see kids go, I should never, I hate them, Frankie. I hate them. Nobody had it worse than I had it in life. And I didn't need that shit. Take a couple of Scotches and go fuck yourself, know what I mean?"

In another conversation, Gotti returns to his oft-repeated demand that he must be kept informed about what's going on. "I wanna know everything that every one of these guys are in. What businesses they're in. I wanna know when they got in them, and how they got in them!"

"That's it," agreed Frank Locascio, his newly appointed underboss. "The key, that's the key . . ."

"I wanna know when and how they got in them," continued Gotti. "These are all businesses that nobody had a fuckin' year ago, Frank! On my back? I got a million good guys. My son didn't open no new companies up. My brothers didn't, my son-in-laws didn't. Nobody opened no new companies up. They took it upon themselves."

Apart from the worry about losing track of all the deals

that Sammy "The Bull" Gravano was doing, Gotti was also concerned that other members of the Gambino Family were getting involved in businesses that he neither knew about nor approved. He blamed Gravano for getting his brother implicated in the "Windows" case, the lucrative offshoot of the mob-controlled construction industry whereby the five New York Families were skimming off the New York City Housing Authority contracts for replacement windows. The FBI had cottoned on to the cozy little arrangement and Peter Gotti was facing a racketeering trial as a result.

". . . Sammy, he made my brother Pete get involved with that fuckin' asshole with the windows. Never made a dime. He's going to jail for it. Well, tell me something, that one of my Family got that they never had it before? I'll make ya fuck me in the ass. But that ain't what I'm getting at, Frankie. That's not the way this is run. And you should know better than that. You've been around long enough. This is not the way a fuckin' borgata is run. And I shouldn't break my fuckin' heart!"

"In reality, you put everything on him," said Locascio, attempting to calm him down.

"Yes."

"If it's anything to do with construction."

Part of the reason for Gotti's reappraisal of the situation within the Gambino Family was his growing fear that he would soon be arrested and put in jail. "For Christ sake, I love you more than I love myself, for fuckin' Christ sake!" said Gotti, pleading undying devotion to his underboss. "I'm worried about you going to jail. I don't give two fucks about myself going to jail. Don't I know they ain't gonna rest until they put me in jail? So I fight it tooth and nail to the fuckin' end. But at least if I know you two guys are out, we got a shot. Somebody got a shot, Frankie. Maybe our kids gotta, my kid's in trouble. Maybe some other jerk-off's kid's in trouble, they come to you. You guide them right, give them a little lecture. And maybe, we gotta think there's some resemblance of a Family. Where else can you lead them? I didn't give him no fuckin' gift, bring you no gift, Frankie. I didn't give you no gift, because you make good

meatballs? You deserve to be here! But that don't mean
you gotta fuckin' rob the Family.''

Gotti wasn't accusing his underboss but was referring to
Sammy. In many ways Sammy was Gotti's closest friend,
not least because they had planned and executed the hit on
Castellano together. It had forged a secret bond of trust
and loyalty between them which Gotti valued above any
normal relationship between a boss and his consigliere.

"Where are we going here?" said Gotti, asking his favorite rhetorical question. "What, are you create snakes
here? Monsters? But I gotta be honest, I gotta be me,
Frank. If you tell me you put an extra $50,000 in the enve-
lope, I don't want it. If you're gonna fuckin' break everybody's heart, I don't want no extra $50,000. Keep it. I got
no big fuckin' needs. I ain't got no big mansion needs, you
know what I mean?''

Gotti liked to present himself as a man of modest means
and simple tastes. An image somewhat belied by the expensive suits, the black Mercedes limo and the luxury country
house in Milford, Pennsylvania. His frequent complaints
probably had more to do with the mob tradition of pleading
poverty while steadily amassing wealth. Certainly, Gotti did
not display the business acumen of the man he had killed.

"I got no companies," he groused. "The only fuckin'
thing I did, I went partners with a company that I put into
business five years ago, Albie Trimming, when Paul was
alive. Won the permission from him to fuckin' do it. Got a
fuckin' tongue-lashing, it's on the tape. And I just now got
on the fuckin' payroll. I'm trying to keep my ass out of
fuckin' jail, no other fuckin' reason. And this fuckin'
Marine Construction that the guy got chastised for, for having me as a partner. The guy got chased out of the fuckin'
country. He used to get five jobs a year. Now he gets none.
Get the fuck outta here! The only thing I'm on paper—I get
40,000 a year from the plumbing. We get, ah, a thousand a
week from ah, ah . . .''

"You're down for a hundred a year," added Locascio.
(One hundred thousand dollars from Arc Plumbing, one of
Gotti's front companies.)

"Nah, that's it, Frankie," said Gotti. "Just now tax purposes 85,000. At Easter and I'll be like at a 125,000 or 135,000 is good for me, Frank."

"You don't spend more than that shows," said Locascio.

"You know why, why, Frankie? Even though I never touched it, my wife gets like 33,000. So now it reads another 33 on top of it. Hah?"

"Between you and your wife, it's another 33 on top."

"Yeah, but not only that, Frank. I don't, we don't, have no mortgage or anything. The only bills that we got is the fuckin' car payments. Four hundred, three hundred and change. Yeah, nothing, I got nothing!"

"That's nothing, yeah," sympathized Locascio.

Gotti's plea of poverty was another way of contrasting his own situation with that of Sammy Gravano. It wasn't just the money that the head of the Gambino Family was worried about. Gotti was worried that Gravano's activities might create rivalry within the Family.

His underboss pointed out that Gravano's consolidation of the empire had mostly already taken place. "Whatever happened, happened in the past," demurred Frankie Locascio.

"But not only that," continued Gotti unabated. "But there's no past with him and I, and you and I, Frankie. We're too close for that. We're too close. I coulda done this a stupid way and there's no future. This bothers me and you shouldn't wanna bother me. Correct it. If I had an end coming, which is gonna hurt you there, keep my end. Do it right. Don't you understand, make people love you? Doesn't he understand people gotta like you guys? I mean don't you understand that, Frankie? . . . And you don't have to let people fuck you in the ass for people to like ya. Eh, believe me, Frankie, people are scared. Don't you realize people hate it? But you don't believe me. So now that's no good because it breaks my fuckin' heart. Breaks my fuckin' heart. Who the fuck wants to be here? We got nothin' but troubles. I got cases coming up. I got nothing but fuckin' trouble. I don't feel good. I gotta fuckin' sit here with my closest two friends. Not even, even if I sit here with guys which are, a capodecina that's from New Jersey, you wanna pull his cover a little bit? You guys are, ah, youse are supposed to be pulling my covers! I gotta pull his fuckin' cover! And I tell him a million times, 'Sammy, slow it down. Pull it in a notch! You come up with 15 companies, for Christ sake! You got rebars. You got concrete pouring. You got Italian floors now. You got construction. You got drywall. You got asbestos. You got rugs. What the fuck next?' "

"How the fuck did he get windows?" asked Locascio, unaware of the full extent of his consigliere's involvement in the building trade.

Gravano's earnings were increasing at a phenomenal rate. Within 12 months his annual earnings grew from $70,000 to $700,000. Despite Gotti's complaints, Sammy was doing little more than carrying out his boss's instructions. "Construction you take care of," Gotti had instructed as he divided up the empire. "Anything with construction. When it comes to garbage: Jimmy Brown's."

The leaders of the Gambino Family, "The Administration," had to supervise an unwieldy business empire. Then there was the more mundane business of the Family itself. Human resource management. New recruits who were looking to be "made," and who then had to be allocated to a crew they would get on with. Then there were the captains and their problems. Above all there was the difficulty of trying to keep track of all the different deals that were going down and making sure that no one was ripping anyone else off.

On top of all that there were the court cases which seemed to be coming at him thick and fast ever since the hit on Castellano. Although Gotti had won an acquittal in the Eastern District case and on two subsequent assault charges, they had all been time-consuming distractions from the real business of running the Gambino Family. Spells in jail, meetings with lawyers and weeks in court became an occupational hazard.

Then there were constant rumors that the Feds were about to hit him with an indictment for the Castellano murder. It all meant keeping one step ahead of the game. Lawyers had to be paid, informers put on the payroll and cops bribed to give information. The greater Gotti's power became the more isolated he felt, which was why he invested so much faith and trust in his beloved triumvirate—The Administration. Frankie Loc and Sammy were the only two people he felt he could really trust. His other old friend, Angelo Ruggiero, had survived Castellano's edict to hand over the tapes in the heroin case only to later die of cancer. Neil was gone, also dead from cancer a fortnight before they murdered Paul; his younger brother, Eugene, charged along with Ruggiero in the drugs case, was in jail. It was tough at the top—and lonely too.

But Gotti was not merely intent on self-preservation, he was determined that "this thing of ours"—"Cosa Nostra"—would survive anything that might happen to him. The head of the Gambino Family was building for the future, for a new generation.

Yet rather like a politician with ideals Gotti soon became disillusioned by the way things seemed to be going once he was in office. Far from changing the status quo Gotti began to worry that they were reverting to the way things had been under Castellano.

"Heh, but Christ Almighty! Where the fuck are we going here? This is not, ah, yours for keeping. You're gonna die someday. Even if, God forbid, hopefully, it's when you're 95, in your sleep, a heart attack. But like Angelo, he's gone; you're dead! Gonna go to jail, or some fuckin' thing. Is this what we're working for? To leave a fuckin' mess behind?"

"Messes we don't need," concurred his underboss.

"For Christ sake!" expostulated Gotti.

"Just got over messes."

"Minchia! And you know I tell you the fuckin' truth, Frankie, I don't believe I'm lying. And more important, I don't believe in that fuckin' bulldozin'. That's what made me hate, really fuckin' hate Paul. You, ya, you couldn't get a fuckin' ham sandwich. Everyone is right. He sold the borgata out for fuckin' construction companies. And that's what we're doing. That's what we're doing right now. I don't know if you could see it, but that's what we're doing

right now. Three, four guys will wind up with every fuckin'
thing. And the rest of the borgata looks like fuckin' waste."

As in the era of Paul Castellano, the key to the construction business was the Gambino-run Teamsters Union, Local 282. Their President was Bobby Sasso, the point-man
for Robert Di Bernardo and Sammy Gravano. Sammy the
Bull's principal business partner was Louie Di Bono, a
Gambino soldier in Patsy Conte's crew, the wiseguy who
according to Gotti had made the transition from "coffee
boy to billionaire." Both Gotti and Gravano fell out with Di
Bono, ironically over the issue of not paying taxes on one of
the companies on the Gambino books.

"He was told to pay . . ." complained Gotti in a conversation with Gravano at the Ravenite.

"He was stubborn," agreed Sammy.

"This thing eight months ago," said Gotti whose patience was beginning to wear thin.

"He was a little stubborn," repeated Gravano.

"This motherfucker! Fuck him, Sammy! . . . I'm not
gonna let that kind of shit interfere with this, Cosa Nostra.
When a fuckin' punk like him was told, nine months ago,
'Resolve this fuckin' thing.' I don't care if you don't pay the
outfit. When a guy tells ya, the boss . . . What am I, just a
punk?"

Being with Gravano in the construction business was
getting to be dangerous. Robert Di Bernardo. Di B [*Dee
Bee*], who had survived under Castellano, was one of the
early victims of the Gotti Administration's management
reshuffle.

Gravano had visited Gotti in jail to seek permission for
the murder. On the evening of December 12, 1989, as
Gotti and Locascio discussed Gravano's business deals, his
mind wandered back to the killing of Di B.

"Di B, did he ever talk subversive to you?"

"Never," admitted Locascio.

"Never talked it to Angelo, and he never talked to Joe
Piney. I took Sammy's word that he talked about me behind my back."

As Gotti pondered that Di Bernardo might have been
murdered for no apparent reason his attention turned to

another Gambino soldier whom Gravano had complained about. "Louie, did he ever talk to any of you guys?"

"No."

"I took Sammy's word. Louie Di Bono. And I sat with this guy. I saw the papers and everything. He didn't rob nothin'. You know why he's dyin'? He's gonna die because he refused to come in when I called. He didn't do nothin' else wrong. He's gonna get killed because he disobeyed coming. But where are we going? What am I doing here, Frankie? Where are we going here? Where's my end of these companies? These other people wanna open companies. Gonna give me a sixth. Gonna give me 10,000 every two weeks, a month, whatever the fuck it comes to. Where's my fuckin' end of these things there that my name is all over the fuckin' lot?"

In the period before Christmas, the last he would spend as a free man, John Gotti was not feeling well. In addition to the normal anxieties suffered by a major-league Mafia boss—worrying about being ripped off by those around him or whether he might have been too hasty in ordering the executions of those below him—the head of the Gambino Family was suffering from a common or garden cold.

"I'm sick, Frankie, and I ain't got no right to be sick. I had 20 capodecinas with us Saturday. Ten or 12 were ours. Five or six from other Families. I excused myself. I told them, 'I gotta go and meet a girl.' I went to the hospital to see Sammy's son. I gotta get myself double sick. I come home, I got caught in that fuckin' traffic. The next morning, triple sick, we're at the cemetery. Then go make other guys happy . . . then go to the fuckin' wake. I, I'm not going to race, popping girls. I'm not doin' nothin' selfish here, know what I mean? But I'm not gonna go every fuckin' block and hear a beef. And I keep telling people it's my fault! 'I told him to do that. I told the guy to do this. I told the guy to do that.' What the fuck, am I nuts here? If I go to jail they'd be happy—'Minchia, we finally got rid of him.' Hah! They don't know they got no new cazzu [*prick*]. I wasn't even gonna say nothing, until he was here. Ya know, I wanted to have the two of youse together. But I'm getting myself sick, Frank."

"Gotta get it out," counseled Locascio. "You gotta get it out."

Frankie's words seemed to cheer Gotti up a bit. "We're gonna be alright. We get rid of these fuckin' lawyers and fuckin' rat tapes, we're gonna be okay. We're all gonna be okay."

But Locascio knew his boss was still smarting about the Sammy problem over construction. He had an idea. "If I could suggest something? Why don't you try and get somebody that is qualified in construction? Make him just to handle the administrative thing, you know?"

Gotti wasn't convinced that was the answer.

"I think that would take the greed away from . . ." continued Locascio.

"You know what, Frankie? That doesn't bother me. It doesn't even bother me if he had six, seven companies, himself. You know what I would tell him? Let me know when ya feel you're gonna choke. Keep that . . . you're gonna choke. But you're not doing that. You're creating a fuckin' army inside an army. You know what I'm saying, Frankie?"

"End up creating another faction?"

"That's right."

"Another faction."

"And you're not gonna do that! I'm not gonna allow that!"

"Shouldn't be," agreed his underboss.

"He wants it, he could have 50 fuckin' businesses! I don't care, Frankie. If you, but I'm your brother, Frankie. You know when I hear something good about a guy, I'll probably be in jail, because I get caught on tape bragging about it. If I hear good about you and we got no problems, I'm glad. Minchia! Ah, I got one less Jackie to worry about, alright? But you ain't gonna create a fuckin' faction. No. That shit. I saw that shit and I don't need that shit."

Gotti knew all about factions. It was what had precipitated the downfall of "Nasabeak." In Gotti's eyes, Castellano had just been too greedy, creating a faction within the Gambino Family of the haves and the have-nots. There had also been rumblings of discontent outside the Family because Castellano wanted to keep more than his fair share, particularly the profits from construction deals.

"No good . . ." agreed Locascio. "And that's what got him weak. That's what got him weak." And paved the way for his own execution was the unspoken but shared assumption.

Gotti realized the consequences of that sort of behavior and was determined to avoid history repeating itself. "Cohesion" was Gotti's buzzword—a state of mind that could only be achieved if everyone was equally happy with their share of the profits. Hence Gotti's uncharacteristic assertions that he didn't care about Gravano's moneymaking endeavors providing he knew about them. John Gotti had an almost Catholic faith in the spirit of Cosa Nostra and a proprietorial sense of pride in the Gambino Family itself.

The Godfather was also determined to maintain his position vis-à-vis the other Families. The Commission trial and the murder of Castellano represented a fundamental shift of power to a new generation and a Mafia structure less dependent on its tradition than it had been in the past. Gotti knew that image was all-important. He had seen both the Bonanno and Colombo Families weakened as a result of internal power struggles and wanted to make sure that nothing similar happened to the Gambinos.

"We're making fuckin' laughingstock. We be back like other Families. Laughingstock! I called the shot. They already got that in the Colombo crew. Now they're getting it in, ah, Vic and Gas. For what? The troops can feel it. But it shouldn't be here. We see each other three or four times a week. It's not like the guy's in Boston, and we're in fuckin' Providence. We see each other three or four times a week. There should be nothin' that we can't talk about quick! Over with, next problem! Ya know what I'm saying?"

Gotti was referring to Vic Orena, the chosen successor to head the Colombo Family. Although originally backed by Carmine "The Snake" Persico, the two had fallen out when The Snake, serving a hundred-year jail sentence, had decided that the Family tradition would be better served by the appointment of his son, Alphonse, who was due to be released from prison within the next two years. Orena was unhappy about relinquishing the reins of power and was backed by a new generation of young and fiercely loyal Mafiosi. The dispute would break out into open warfare in the Christmas of 1992 when shoot-outs between the two factions threatened to turn Brooklyn into Dodge City. "Gas" was Anthony Salvatore Casso, a rising power in the Lucchese Family who earned a lot of enemies through his habit of ordering the deaths of those he didn't like. Casso was a ruthless killer in his early fifties who had earned his nickname "Gaspipe" through his proficiency with a blow-torch to open safes. Early in 1993 Gaspipe was ignominiously arrested by an FBI SWAT team who discovered him naked in the shower in his New Jersey forest hideout. The FBI claimed they had traced one of his calls on a mobile phone—others suspected that he had been betrayed by his enemies within the Lucchese Family. It was all a far cry from the ordered regime of Tony "Ducks" Corallo.

John Gotti had learned all he needed to know from the mistakes of his predecessor. The key was to keep the Family happy and cut dissent off at the source, hence his concern about Sammy Gravano. His management style was to keep on top of the situation by holding regular meetings with "line management." If John Gotti hadn't been head of the Gambino Family his management style would have been eagerly adopted by the corporate gurus of American business.

"And Sammy I meet four or five days a week," he confided to Locascio, letting him in on the inner secrets of management success Mafia-style. "There's no need for this fuckin' nonsense. Any good leader stops these things. He won't let these things happen. Can't see that situation happen. Someone'll think you're a figurehead, some jerk-off, and that I ain't, know what I mean, Frankie? You know I didn't care, ah, Louie Di Bono, opened up a business for him. He hates Louie, Louie hates him. Why did they go together, Frankie? You know, he wanted permission to shoot Louie Di Bono? Louie Di Bono wanted permission to get him shot! Why did they go partners, Frankie? After

Nasabeak got sick. Well, if the two guys hate each other, why would you think they become partners?"

John Gotti had the answer to his own question. "Greed! Both sides. I mean unless you can come up with a fuckin' magical word. To me it was greed on both sides. He was looking to fuck him and he was gonna fuck him. We got another fuckin' situation. They sent me word in jail that 'You got ten percent.' Guy never had nothin' in his life; a fuckin' jerk like me! Best I ever did was go on a few hijackings. Never had nothing in my life. Ya know they grab everything. You're telling me, I got ten percent of a million-dollar business!"

"Million, million dollars worth of business!" echoed Locascio.

"Yeah," sighed Gotti. "Minchia!" In fact Gotti was getting at least $120,000 a year from Gravano's construction deals. "But I just gotta say what I feel, Frankie. He's my brother. And if I think he done some wrong, I'll slap him on the hand. He knows it. You know that. You know I'll pull him up a million times. But do you agree with me . . . ?"

"Definitely," Frankie agreed. "It was wrong. There's creating, there's creating and there's creating."

Harking back to Castellano, Gotti had two problems with Gravano. First, he seemed to be exhibiting the same symptoms of greed, and second, their close relationship entailed grooming Gravano for the leadership in case Gotti himself was put away. On both counts there was cause for concern as Gotti began to suspect that Sammy the Bull might get too greedy for his own good or too ambitious for the good of Gotti himself.

"I'm gonna go to jail and leave him in charge! So obviously I gotta love the guy. I gotta think he's capable. But not for things like this!"

Locascio repeated his suggestion that Gotti should appoint an intermediary to take care of some of the construction business. "I'm sure you know somebody that's capable as him when it comes to business."

"Yeah, I could," agreed the boss. "You know why I didn't, Frankie? I put it all in his lap for one reason,

Frankie. You're the underboss. You're my brother. Why I gotta see a paper from you? If you tell me there's 200,000, there's 200,000, Frankie. So, he used to bring me the paper. I told him, 'Sam, don't bring me no paper. I don't wanna see no paper.' 'Yeah but what happens if something happens to me? What if that happens to both of us?' 'Look, I don't wanna see no paper.' I haven't seen a paper in two years. Joe Piney used to show me paper. You know why I used to look at 'em? Frankie, and I love Joe Piney! He's a fuckin' idiot. He used to go like this . . . he didn't know what the fuck he was talking about. I know that. But I figured, I didn't know what I'm talking about. He didn't know what he was talking about. So he won't know that I don't know what I'm talking about!" Gotti laughed. "Fuck this! I swear to God, Frankie, I still didn't show it! 'What's this?' I used to go: 'Huh, hah.' "

They both began laughing again.

"So like with Sam . . . 'Whatever you say is there, that's what's there. Take what you gotta take. Sammy, if you were broke take 20 percent, if there's such a thing.' I would be a billionaire if I was looking to be a selfish boss. That's not me. If I was that other motherfucker [Castellano] everything goes on there and nothin' goes out. You know I'm taking care of the people. If you don't believe me, you take care of them. God fuckin' bless you! Gimme 50 percent, take the other 50 percent. Knock yourself out because I'll be getting way more than what I'm getting now. What? Bring in papers, we don't need no papers. We brothers, Frankie. We don't need none of these papers, and shit, nothin' like that. We don't need none of that. We're too close for that shit. Know what I mean? But Jesus fuckin' Christ! Ya see I got that kind of fuckin' trust and put that . . . Cosa Nostra. We're in the positions we belong in, Frankie, and nobody could change that. But this business thing. Ah, it's brothers! Please. And if you robbing people on my behalf, stop. When I say 'robbing,' I don't mean robbing. You know, ya taking work out of other people's mouths. You wanna rob people on my behalf, stop on my behalf. Like you said, Frankie, guy's gotta right to be in businesses."

Gotti was determined to protect his consigliere from his own worst vices, not only for his own good but for the fortune of the Family. It would be bad for him, bad for the Family. "Sammy is the consigliere. He could turn the whole fuckin' industry into a private playpen."

"You know what?" said his underboss, "I gotta say it. You're telling of all the businesses that he's got, you don't get nothin'?"

"Other than that I know of. Well, let me put it this way, Frankie. I was getting x-amount of monies the day I became the boss, when he had nothing to do with this. And Di B and the other guy, and I said, 'Sammy, ah, ya got one, a lump one, these fuckin' guys.' We grabbed a hundred thousand, 20,000 went to Di Bono. Twenty thousand went to Bobby Sasso, three ways, I got maybe 20,000 or 25,000. Now with the money that comes in, that's my business if I wanna distribute it, Frankie. Someday I'll show you what I take out, what I give out."

The following night Gotti met with Gravano and the conversation that was recorded showed little evidence of the promised recrimination. Instead, Gotti raised the problem of Louie Di Bono, the business partner with whom Gravano was in dispute about payments from various construction deals.

"He was told to pay . . ."

"He was stubborn," advised Sammy the Bull.

"This motherfucker!"

Whereas the night before Gotti was blaming Sammy for picking bad business partners, now he seemed merely enraged that Di Bono hadn't obeyed their instructions to come and see him. Irrespective of the rights and wrongs of the situation, Gotti could not allow the open flouting of his authority. It set a bad example.

"I'm not gonna let that kind of shit interfere with this Cosa Nostra. When a fuckin' punk like him was told, nine months ago, 'Resolve this fuckin' thing!' I don't care if you don't pay the outfit. When a guy tells ya, the boss . . ."

Once he had made his feelings clear about Di Bono, Gotti reminded Gravano that he had plans for him as well.

"When I go away, I'm tellin' everybody, you're gonna be with me. And I could see it . . . Our lives . . ."

"Right," said Gravano.

". . . are in your hands."

"I know your position," said Sammy.

"But I don't want, I don't wanna make another faction, that's what I'm making here."

Faction or no faction there were other threats to the Family. Louie Di Bono for one. He was a dead man—a sacrificial lamb on the altar of Gravano's greed.

The Di Bono problem was also a useful diversion from Gotti's obsession about his consigliere's single-handed takeover of the Gambino construction interests. Sammy The Bull could lay the blame at Di Bono's door. Gravano's story was that Di Bono was ripping them off and therefore he had to set up new companies in his name to safeguard the Family's interests. Louie Di Bono would have to pay the price for annoying his partner. For their own separate reasons both Gotti and Gravano just couldn't afford to let "Jelly-Belly" challenge The Administration. If he wouldn't pay the money, he would certainly pay the penalty. There was just one small problem. Louie Di Bono had disappeared.

Word went out on the street. Gambino soldiers, associates, loan sharks, numbers-runners, car thieves and mob-drivers were told to keep a look out for Di Bono. The Administration didn't even have to offer a reward. The gratitude of John Gotti and Sammy Gravano was something to die for.

But several weeks passed with no news of Di Bono's whereabouts. The longer it went on, the more frustrated Gotti felt. The original sin paled into insignificance. Now it was a question of flouting the ultimate authority of the boss who appeared powerless in the face of Di Bono's nonappearance. If it went on much longer there was a real danger that Gotti would lose face.

The head of the Gambinos valued his reputation. Family honor was at stake. No one was going to treat Gotti like a punk. Louie, nicknamed "Jelly-Belly" for his refusal to face the music, had "challenged the Administration," an act of subversion which compounded the original offense. Di Bono was adding insult to injury by failing to keep his appointment with death. Gotti was so infuriated that when a rumor reached him that Di Bono was at his home, Gotti seriously considered carrying out the contract himself on Di Bono's doorstep.

"I gotta hit him coming out of the fuckin' door. I don't give a fuck! Right coming out of the door!" The fact that he might be caught red-handed didn't bother him. "They blame everything else on us, anyway. They'll blame that one on us!"

Wiser counsel prevailed. Gotti gave the contract to Pasquale "Patsy" Conte, the Gambino captain suspected as one of the masterminds of the Pizza Connection. Conte had also been arrested for his alleged involvement in the shooting of Pietro Alfano but when it came to tracking down Di Bono he had no more luck than anyone else.

Realizing his boss's frustration, Gravano spotted an opportunity to further ingratiate himself and rid himself of an awkward partner. Sam the Bull volunteered to carry out the hit himself. Gotti was grateful for his consigliere's devotion to duty but he turned him down and enlisted his "chauffeur" and bodyguard, Bobby Boriello, to lead the hit team. Boriello was a hulking soldier of limited intelligence, but as well as being Gotti's driver, he was a tried and trusted killer. Boriello and a couple of other hoods were assigned to Patsy Conte's crew to execute the contract.

Di Bono's luck finally ran out when a mutual friend informed Gravano that his former partner was working downtown at the World Trade Center for a major construction company. He handed Gravano a business card with the company's name. In turn, Sammy the Bull handed the card over to John Gotti. The hit team could now start to lay the foundations for the plot to kill their quarry.

Then, on March 28, 1990, to the utter astonishment of the Gambino Family, who should turn up unannounced at the Ravenite but Louie Di Bono himself. Di Bono waltzed in full of smiles, backslapping his friends, shouting cheerful greetings and seemingly ignorant of the fact that they were all dying to kill him. If the intention was to catch his would-be killers off their guard then Di Bono certainly succeeded.

More likely, Di Bono had gambled on the chance of talking his way out of his problem. Word would have reached him that he was in serious trouble. Di Bono probably calculated that if he could talk his way through the tax problem he might gain a reprieve. What he couldn't know was that it wasn't just about money anymore. The determination to kill Di Bono was out of all proportion to any offense he might have caused. His killers probably didn't even know why he was to be hit. They certainly didn't care. The only certainty was that the failure to get rid of Di Bono had infuriated both Gotti and Gravano. Hence the urgency of expediting the contract.

Di Bono didn't even have enough credit left to live on borrowed time. The good humor and smiles that greeted his unexpected arrival were genuine. John Gotti and Sammy Gravano were delighted to see their victim walk straight into the arms of his executioners. Gotti, Gravano and Patsy Conte were all inside the Ravenite and despite their initial shock at their intended victim's sudden appearance they quickly regained their composure. At last, they could relax, secure in the knowledge that Louie Di Bono had just been elevated to the ranks of the living dead.

So excited were they by Di Bono's actual presence on the premises that for a short time they actively considered doing away with him on the spot. Louie Di Bono might well have been murdered then and there had it not been for the fact that there were a number of suspicious cars parked on Mulberry Street which Gotti figured were FBI surveillance vehicles. Nobody suspected the bugs inside the club but surveillance from the street was a different matter. Even that was not enough to prevent Gravano from coming up with an improvised plan. Sidling up to Gotti in the hallway of the Ravenite, Gravano whispered: "If you send for somebody with a gun and silencer, we'll turn up the music. You leave. Tell Louie to come back in half an hour and I'll kill the motherfucker right there in the club! We'll close the club, come back, two, three in the morning and take the body out!"

Gotti considered his consigliere's outrageous suggestion for a moment before laughing out loud at the audacity of the plan. Maybe it would be better to bide their time.

Meanwhile their hapless victim launched into a last-ditch attempt to ingratiate himself back into favor. Di Bono swore blind to John Gotti that he would "Never, NEVER!" lie to him and explained that he was dealing with "the tax situation." "I'm in really good shape!" enthused Di Bono cheerfully.

"Whatever you do, it's no problem," soothed his self-appointed executioner, anxious to reassure their victim. "I'll stop them from anything."

Di Bono's strategy was to try and buy time. He was hoping to distract his would-be killers from any hasty moves by holding out the prospect of a series of lucrative new deals that he had in the pipeline. "We'll get a piece of the deal and we get all this," explained Gravano's business partner. "It's supply and everything. We put our own people in there. Do the roof . . ."

"Yeah, but what do we get . . . ?" asked Gotti, playing along.

"We'll get a piece of the action from him," promised Di Bono. "I'll make him declare what we get! I want somebody sit with me, to listen to everything. I don't wanna go alone," confessed Di Bono.

"Don't worry about it," said Gotti before reminding him of an earlier deal which had fallen through. "I was gonna make a quarter million!" complained the head of the Gambino Family. "I don't make five cents! I got nothin' but fuckin' heartaches and aggravation!"

"Hey, John . . ." pleaded the terrified Di Bono. "I wanna tell you, like a brother, I told this guy when we were together driving, I said: 'You know, I'll tell you, Joe, I love John, he's a good man. He's honest, he's straight as an arrow. I owe him so much—to make money for this man that you have no idea!' "

Di Bono delved into his briefcase to retrieve some tax papers, hoping to convince Gotti of his honesty. In the dispute over the money, Di Bono maintained that he had paid the taxes. If he could prove it he thought he would be off the hook. Going through the figures on the documents, he started to add them up. "$129,000 State Department of Taxation. Another $55,000 . . . I'm paying all the bills . . . !"

Ironically, Di Bono had failed to recognize that for the Gambino Family it was no longer a question of taxes. It was a matter of honor. The final account was settled on October 4, 1990. A patrolling New York City policeman stumbled over a bullet-riddled corpse sprawled across a cold concrete floor in the basement parking lot at the World Trade Center. It had been Louie Di Bono's last place of work.

— 17 —

THE PINCH

THE OTHER SHARED PREOCCUPATION OF THE GAMBINO
Administration from late 1989 through to 1990 was
the imminent threat of a "pinch," the indictment
that they collectively feared might take them off the streets
and jeopardize the day-to-day running of the multimillion-
dollar empire.

The success of the Commission case had made the leaders of the New York Mafia increasingly cautious. The huge
publicity following the public execution of Paul Castellano
had led Gotti to expect an imminent indictment for the
murder. Although there had been frequent rumors dating
back to the immediate aftermath of the killings, the police
were biding their time. The intervening and unsuccessful
prosecutions of Gotti induced an atmosphere of caution
and patience amongst those investigating the new head of
the Gambino Family. It would be almost four years before
Gotti stood officially accused of masterminding the murder
of his former boss.

In the meantime the rumor index rose and fell, convincing Gotti that any moment might be his last. The Gambino
boss was unusually well-informed about the police and
FBI's progress. His sources were corrupt officials and policemen on the Gambino payroll. These public-spirited ser-

vants were in an invidious position. None of them relished the prospect of acting as the bearer of bad news—at the same time they had to earn their money by providing up-to-date and accurate information on any moves being planned against the Gambino Family. As far as Gotti was concerned their news was invariably unwelcome.

Rather than risk meeting Gotti openly at the Ravenite, the main conduit for this information was one or other of a close-knit group of Gambino Family lawyers.

Mob lawyers who got too close to their clients had long been frowned upon by their counterparts in the Government. Prosecuting attorneys like Giuliani took a dim view of their colleagues growing rich on the proceeds of organized crime. Many were just professional lawyers whose probity was unquestioned and who enjoyed normal relations with Government prosecutors outside the adversarial confines of the courtroom. Yet there was also a small number of mob lawyers who had struck up something rather more than a normal professional relationship with their clients. Some were seduced by the charm and the charisma of the Mafia boss they were defending, others greedily sold out for large sums of cash slipped under the table. One such attorney who crossed the line was Michael Coiro, lawyer, confidant and friend of the Gambino Family.

Coiro had handled Angelo Ruggiero's defense in the drug trafficking case until he found himself sitting on the wrong side of the courtroom. Michael Coiro had been served with an indictment for corruption, a criminal charge which carried a maximum penalty of ten years. Ironically, the tapes from Ruggiero's house which triggered the showdown between Nasabeak and Gotti's crew were also responsible for the premature end of Michael Coiro's legal career.

When the trial was still in progress, Coiro had made several visits to the Ravenite. Gotti's Mulberry Street headquarters were conveniently close to the Federal Courthouse in Foley Square. In a bizarre reversal of roles the mob lawyer dropped in to seek advice from John Gotti, unaware that even as he spoke he was being recorded by the FBI bugs at the Ravenite! "I'm saying I can't believe it!" exclaimed the incredulous lawyer, relaying the content of some of the tapes that had been played in court earlier that day. "I'm hearing this for the first time: 'Mike Coiro told me this. Mike Coiro told us to do that . . . Mike Coiro . . .' Fuck! Fuckin' never had these conversations!"

Gotti commiserated with the lawyer. Not least because he had always subscribed to the rule that it was a mistake to bring work home and foolish in the extreme to talk about it. Gotti reminded the lawyer that it was a rule that he had always scrupulously observed himself. "How many times were you in my house?" inquired Gotti.

"Twice!" replied Coiro.

"You wanna know something?" boasted the Godfather. "I don't even remember them two times!"

Mike Coiro was trained to remember precisely that sort of thing and also never to allow himself or his clients to let slip anything which might be incriminating. "I'll tell ya the two times. Your son Frankie's wake . . ."

John Gotti's mood darkened at the recollection of the tragic accident that had deprived him of the life of his favorite son. "Yeah . . ." said Gotti slowly. "Well, I was in another world."

The second occasion had arisen because Gotti was ill. The flu-ridden Godfather was convalescing in bed at his Howard Beach home and summoned Coiro to see him. At the time Coiro had briefly whispered a message in Gotti's ear and then left the house.

Mafia protocol tended to separate home life from work. Wives and girlfriends were rarely involved, hence the existence of social clubs like the Ravenite for the Gambinos and the Palma Boys for the Genovese, which could be used for official business, whispered conversations and important meetings. Inevitably, because being a mobster was a 24-hour-a-day job, some wiseguys tended to take their work home with them. It was more comfortable and most people felt safe in their own homes, rarely suspecting that a concealed microphone might be lurking somewhere among the household furniture.

It proved a fatal miscalculation for both Ruggiero and Castellano, all of which confirmed Gotti's preference for doing business at the Ravenite—a preference duly noted by the FBI. In Gotti's eyes Ruggiero had flouted a cardinal rule which had put Michael Coiro in the dock.

Gotti had been following the case with the customary close attention he paid when any members of the Family or close associates suffered the misfortune to end up in court. The Godfather now found himself offering advice to a lawyer. Indeed, Gotti was no fool when it came to court procedure, having spent several months attending his own court hearings and discussing courtroom tactics with his own legal advisers. The Godfather was in fact uniquely qualified to comfort the lawyer through an ordeal which had placed him in the position usually occupied by his clients.

"I knew you was guilty there," confided Gotti. "And I don't think you're going to go away before the appeal. So you got a fuckin' another year on the street, maybe. I think he's gonna give you ten years and maybe look for you to do about three or four."

"I'll do it, John," said Coiro obligingly. Coiro was particularly anxious to display an attitude of macho indifference to the prospect of a lengthy jail sentence. The lawyer didn't like to contemplate the fate that might befall him if The Administration doubted his resolve to go all the way when faced with a heavy sentence. "Do you wanna know something, John? Fuckin' witch!" said Coiro, attempting to flatter Gotti by crediting him with magical powers of clairvoyance.

"No, but the shame is I wasn't a fuckin' witch ten years ago! I told ya, ya gotta wind up, be happy when ya get ten, 20 years, going over that house. Didn't I tell ya? Ten fuckin' years I've been saying that. That cocksucker, and I hate to talk about people that are dying, and I gotta. You know he ain't a rat. He ain't a mutt. But I gotta call him a cocksucker. His goin' to his fuckin' house! A guy was telling me this morning: 'All your troubles come from two places,' he says, 'Willie Boy Johnson and Angelo's house.' Willie Boy Johnson and Angelo Ruggiero decided they wanted to be a big-shot operation. That's all our troubles. Not mine, all our troubles. That's where they got permission for Paul's house, the fuckin' Bergen Hunt and Fish

Club, Neil's house, down here. Every fuckin' thing! They got him on a million tapes with me in Bergen Hunt and Fish Club!''

It was probably just as well that the garrulous Ruggiero was dying of cancer; if not, it was entirely likely that Gotti would have hastened his demise anyway. The penetration of the secret world of the Gambino Family had all been made possible by the irrepressible Ruggiero's inability to keep his mouth shut. To obtain judicial authority for the installation of a bug or a telephone wiretap, investigators had to demonstrate "probable cause"—the likelihood that criminal offenses were being planned or committed on the premises they intended to bug. The tapes from Ruggiero's house about his planned drug deals provided evidence which enabled the FBI to seek further court-ordered wiretaps in a whole host of additional locations. Angelo Ruggiero had unwittingly given the FBI license to bug their way through the hierarchy of the Gambino Family—from the Bergen Hunt and Fish Club and Neil Dellacroce's house all the way to The White House, Paul Castellano's Staten Island mansion.

Gotti's friend was entirely correct about the source of all their troubles. Unfortunately it was too late to do anything about it now. The irony was that none of the Mafiosi, from the soldiers to the bosses, ever seem to have considered that the FBI could have placed bugs in the locations that they did. Gotti does not seem to have allowed for the possibility of the FBI miraculously sneaking several bugs into the Ravenite. It certainly never occurred to him that there was one in the second-floor apartment where they held their most important meetings. That was also where Gotti was holding his secret meetings with Michael Coiro.

"They never played none a those," murmured Gotti, referring to the tapes from the Bergen bug. "Did they play any of them?"

"None," confirmed the Gambino Family lawyer.

Gotti was reassured. " 'Cause you know why? You wouldn't a got me talking!" Gotti reminded Coiro that he had constantly urged Ruggiero to keep his "big mouth" shut and had even warned the lawyer at the time to keep his "nose clean." "I kept telling him, 'You're gonna get yourself in fuckin' trouble. Ya cocksucker, ya better not be doin' nothin' wrong.' And you, all you kept sayin' was, 'I wouldn't do nothing wrong, what am I doing? I'm just a lawyer. Let them play 'em fuckin' tapes, ya know?' And that's all we kept sayin'. This was day in and time in, time out."

In fact Gotti was no more guarded in the Bergen than he was in the Ravenite but his memory could be very selective with hindsight, particularly when it had to serve his reputation by convincing those around him that no mere hidden microphones could outwit the brilliant criminal mind of the reigning head of the Gambino Family. After all, he had run rings around the FBI and everyone else by beating the rap three times in court.

At the same time Gotti was resigned to the fact that there was bound to be a fourth attempt to bring him to justice. The Ruggiero tapes, combined with the investigation into the Castellano murder, meant that it was only a matter of time before a case was brought against him. In the eyes of the federal authorities John Gotti was a marked man. Apart from anything else he had enjoyed unprecedented publicity from the national press which had placed him at the top of the agenda for all the agencies engaged in the fight against organized crime. It was a sure bet that someone was going to make a move against him. It was merely a question of when. That was where his informants and lawyer friends came in.

"Mike, I've been told by a source that a pinch is coming down. It's gonna be a joint pinch. The State, it's for murder, conspiracy to murder. Feds, it's gonna be, ah, they got a new statute. In enhancing your position, to commit murder to enhance your position. It's a new statute. They tried it two or three times and it works. Let me tell ya what happens. This here, I get told by a girl last night . . ."

Coiro was sympathetic. Gotti had already spoken to another Gambino lawyer, Gerry Shargel, who confirmed that RICO enabled the FBI to bring a new charge relating to murder carried out in furtherance of an overall conspiracy. Under State law, it was notoriously difficult to successfully prosecute a murder case in New York. The law required an exceptionally high degree of proof before a conviction could be obtained, but RICO provided an alternative legal avenue for the prosecutors. It was a law that could be used against the Mafia when murders were committed in the interests of the Family. In the past, the difficulties of bringing murder cases under State law had tended to favor the murderous activities of Gotti and his fellow mobsters. Only a tiny percentage of mob murders were solved and prosecuted.

"This is what I hear," Gotti told Coiro. "I hear that they feel, I think I feel that way myself, it's easier to beat the State. How do you feel about that, Mike? I think it's easier to beat a murder beef by the State . . ."

"No doubt about it . . ." agreed the lawyer.

"RICO's . . . ?"

"No doubt about it," confirmed Coiro.

"RICO's they'll get, ah, you can't beat these," offered Gravano, who had just joined the meeting.

"Federal Court: you get the kitchen sink in," added Coiro.

Gotti wanted his corrupt lawyer to try and extract additional information from his own sources concerning any moves that "The Feds" might be planning against him. Gotti even had the presence of mind to apologize for making such difficult demands on his friend at a time when the lawyer had to deal with his own "pinch." "You know, Mike, again I feel lousy for pushing your sins aside, your heartaches aside . . ."

Coiro was quick to reassure his boss that it was no trouble. "John, that's done, it's over with. Forget about it. It's over . . ."

"I think he, John . . ." added Gravano, anxious to placate his boss, "I think he already knows how you feel."

"Well, you know . . ." said the caring Godfather.

"And we're men. You can't do nothing about that," said Gravano. The steroid-popping bodybuilder was making an ironic reference to the collective machismo of the Gambino Family which allowed them to brush off the prospect of a prison sentence as a minor inconvenience.

"Exactly, that's true," agreed Coiro.

"There's nothing you could do about it," Gravano pointed out. "Just like there's nothing he can do about us getting hurt and he even sympathizes, I guess. I think he can understand that."

"Because ya know why, Mike?" asked Gotti. "Listen to me. If you're away even for three years, everything'll be status quo. Whatever we got, we got!"

"But at least if this happens . . ." Gravano began in support before Gotti interrupted him.

"If I'm away, status quo. But if we're all away . . ."

"Then we're all in trouble!" joked Coiro with a nervous laugh.

"Listen!" said Gotti, getting serious. "Not only we're in trouble, so be it. A lotta things in here. People will be in trouble!"

"That's right . . ." said Coiro sobering up.

"And that we don't want. You know that's the way I feel, Mike."

"Right," agreed Mike. "Always! That's the way you always were and you always will."

Before Mike Coiro left the Ravenite that evening John Gotti begged him once more to find out whatever he could about ongoing investigations against him. Coiro promised to do whatever he had to the very next day.

Before he left, Gotti gave him some friendly advice. "I'm not trying to be a wiseguy. Don't have any fuckin' drinks in between then and seeing me."

"No!" cried a shocked Coiro. "Come on, John!"

"Cocksucker!" teased Gotti.

"Will you stop?" pleaded Coiro.

"I know, Mike. But you try to ease your pain with a drink."

"No!"

"I do. He does! We all do!" admitted the Godfather in a moment of rare honesty.

"Believe me, it's done tomorrow," said Mike Coiro, desperately seeking to convince his head of Family that his loyalty was beyond reproach.

"Sneak and meet me tomorrow night . . ." implored

the Gambino boss. "I'll meet ya in the fuckin' graveyard! I don't care where."

"You got it John. I'll go see him tomorrow."

"You wanna know something?" said Gravano when Coiro had left Mulberry Street. "This guy is one of the best lawyers I ever known!"

"Yeah . . ." agreed Gotti.

"If he stays strong . . ." continued Gravano, seeming at least for a moment to admit the possibility that Coiro might indeed deviate from the straight and narrow.

His boss was more trusting. "He is!" confirmed Gotti.

". . . gotta respect this guy!" said Gravano coming round.

"And he's gonna! Sam, put it in the fuckin' bank. You know what the shame is, you see the way you just saw this guy?"

"We got skippers who ain't like that," pointed out Sammy the Bull, lamenting the fact that "tough guys" weren't so tough anymore.

Gotti and Gravano were mightily impressed by the way Michael Coiro was handling himself. At a time when mobsters seemed all too eager to switch sides, Michael Coiro seemed to be setting a shining example.

Gotti was relieved, not least because there were few things that he found more distasteful than wiseguys who couldn't do their time properly. Gotti was sickened by the fact that all too many of his contemporaries were crumbling at the prospect of a lengthy prison sentence.

"Yeah . . ." complained Gotti, remembering some of his weaker cronies. "Tommy cryin'. This fuckin' guy Fat Georgie did 14 hours in jail, crying fuckin' bum! This guy here, I'll tell you, you listen to what I'm telling you. He'll stand up to the fuckin' . . ."

As far as Gotti was concerned Mike Coiro was a real "stand-up guy." There was no way he would disgrace the Family by breaking down in tears at the prospect of a little jail sentence. As for becoming a rat, that was completely unthinkable. Everybody else in the city might have rats scurrying around their feet, but not the Gambino Family.

They were a different breed. Gambino loyalists like Michael Coiro were utterly faithful to the Cosa Nostra.

"Look at the way he talks," said Gravano in support. "You know what I liked? He got found guilty and then he go over to the judge's chambers, he asks to come here. And he came!"

John Gotti was overflowing with admiration. If only they had more men of the caliber of Michael Coiro it would be they who would be serving the indictments on the law enforcement community and not the other way round. "And how about better than that when he says, 'I already know what I gotta do. Don't worry about me, I'm dead.' That's over, this and that, and means it!"

Another pressing legal problem confronting Gotti was a subpoena that had been served on Tommy Gambino. It was little more than a tactic designed to harass the Family, but it meant that Government attorneys could also subpoena other alleged members of the Family and cross-examine them. It was all part of a cat and mouse game played by the prosecuting attorneys. They would then grant the reluctant witness immunity from prosecution which in turn effectively removed their right to invoke the Fifth Amendment, their right to silence lest they incriminate themselves with their own words. If they then refused to answer questions they could be jailed for contempt of court.

"Now you tell Tommy to fight it!" Gotti instructed a go-between. "Break their fuckin' holes, like I know he could! And don't worry about us going to jail. Me number one! I like jail better than I like the streets! And do what I'm tellin' ya."

Like a football team manger, Gotti chivvied his men's morale, hyping them up against the common enemy. "We're all in this together," he told them, sounding like one of the "Three Musketeers." "We're all for one and one for all . . . We're here together. You deny everything. The only thing we tell the truth about is our name. And we tell it to the lawyer. We don't even tell it to these cocksuckers. We'll be alright. We'll be okay!"

It was war. Name, rank and number. The enemy was not

going to get anything else. Not if John Gotti had anything to do with it.

As well as devising the legal strategies which only a foolish lawyer would disregard, Gotti also had the responsibility for arranging payments for the team of high-powered lawyers on the Family payroll.

Gotti set up a meeting with Tommy Gambino to discuss their legal arrangements. "What's wrong with $5,000 a week?" asked Gotti who resented the huge amounts of money that he was paying out. "What's $5,000 a week? You work four fuckin' hours, you know, or four days a week . . ."

"Yeah . . ." replied Gambino.

"$1,250 a day, ya know?"

It was nice work if you could get it and the FBI and the U.S. Attorney's office in the Eastern District of Manhattan had plenty more cases in the pipeline. It was one way of taxing the resources of the Gambino Family legal fund even if it did have the unfortunate side effect of enriching the lawyers who fed off the Family.

The Gambino Family's most successful lawyer to date was Bruce Cutler, a defense attorney who had earned the dubious distinction of securing three acquittals in a row for his notorious client. Cutler is a balding, bull-necked man in his mid-forties, with the appearance of an amateur wrestler, who became increasingly seduced by the aura of glamour and notoriety which began to rub off on to his well-padded shoulders through his association with John Gotti. As their relationship developed, the short, squat attorney even began to walk, talk and dress like his client. He began to favor razor-sharp, double-breasted suits, white raincoats and wide-brimmed fedora hats. Even his aggression in the courtroom seemed to echo a toned down version of the frequent fits of rage which Mr. Gotti would direct at hapless victims unfortunate enough to cross him in the Ravenite.

A new verb entered the legal vocabulary in the courtroom precincts where Bruce Cutler was operating. A witness cross-examined and torn to shreds by Cutler was deemed to have been "Brucified." Bruce's robust support of his client seemed to spring from something beyond the mere contractual relationship obliging him to offer the best defense that he could muster. Those who observed Cutler in court witnessed an outpouring of devotion and loyalty, often expressed in a stream of invective and insults aimed at prosecution witnesses. Cutler was clearly dedicated to maintaining his client in a state of perpetual liberty. It was an unnerving experience which startled even his fellow defense attorneys, to say nothing of the Government prosecutors who were equally dedicated to the proposition of putting John Gotti behind bars for the rest of his life.

"He's a super human being!" gushes Cutler. "He's a devoted father, grandfather and husband, a strong and courageous individual, with a tremendous amount of personal integrity."

In Cutler's eyes John Gotti can do no wrong. Although his hero is captured on tape threatening to cut someone's head off, Bruce's faith in his client's Family virtues is totally unshakable.

"We've had all of that," he says with a dismissive wave of his hand just before Gotti's last court appearance. "I don't mean to be cavalier about it but we've had conversations like that in all the other cases. We've had tapes like this before. Idle threats. Loss of temper. Er, puffing. Bravado. Machismo. We all do it! I do it every day! I'm threatening somebody every day over the phone, or I'm threatening and yelling at somebody every other day in my apartment who doesn't fix something right."

But threatening to "sever their motherfuckin' head off"?

"Oh sure," replied Bruce, totally unphased by his client's eccentric choice of phrase. "I mean what's the difference if you threaten to sever their head or threaten to throw someone out of the window? You don't mean it, you don't do it. I know the person whose head he's always severing and this is about the fifth time he's said it about this individual. And the individual is alive and well, of course. So these kinds of cursing and loss of temper are like a volcanic blowup and then John calms down. That's part of his nature. He says he doesn't mean it, but we've heard it before, there's nothing new about those kinds of things. Don't forget John Gotti's been overheard on tape more than anybody in this country since 1979 and I'm familiar with all the tapes. And I've heard hundreds of threats. And that's just what they are, they are just idle ruminations and threats that are never followed through because they are said half in jest and half in spontaneous temper with no follow-through whatsoever. If every loss of temper was a crime, I guess every friend I have would be in jail!"

Cutler's unshakable confidence in the innocence of John Gotti had served him well in the past but ultimately proved a somewhat misguided devotion. Although he had played a key role in Gotti's acquittal in three cases, Bruce Cutler would be denied his starring role in the fourth trial in January 1992.

Like Michael Coiro, Cutler and his fellow attorneys had been recorded on their frequent visits to the Ravenite Club and their conversations were sufficiently compromising for the prosecution to move a successful motion disqualifying Cutler from the trial and even threatening to call him as a prosecution witness. Cutler immediately denounced the move as an act of cowardice by the Government. He claimed they were motivated merely by jealousy and revenge because his successes had made them look stupid in the past.

"The Government rationale was that they had my voice on certain tapes where I was speaking to my client and they wanted to use those tapes as evidence in the trial. But the *real* reason was that we felt, on the defense team, and, of course, the clients felt, that it was an act of desperation and vindictiveness on the part of the Federal prosecutors who hate me, hate the way I have fought them, hate the way I have embarrassed them, hate the fact that I've told the truth and they went and moved heaven and earth to break up what they perceived as a team, and they felt that would be a setback to Mr. Gotti. But, it's not a setback to Mr. Gotti. It's a frustration for me, but it's not a setback for him. They know that Mr. Gotti and I have a symbiosis, they know that we've worked well together in the past and they feel this will somehow give them an advantage."

Cutler was confident right up to the weeks before the

trial, commenting on Gotti's frame of mind. "His days are spent in jail, vigorous exercise, that includes a great deal of reading and other things and the longer he stays in the better he looks. He's just able to muster that inner fortitude and strength and conquer."

Shortly before six-thirty in the evening, on February 27, 1990, Bruce Cutler had been in conclave with his beloved client at the Ravenite, reminding him of their past triumphs. "Johnny . . ." whispered the overweight lawyer, oozing with pride. "Everybody, all over the country is always asking me to send them the openings to your Federal case."

"Yeah . . ." muttered Gotti, sounding less than impressed. He found Cutler's fawning attitude faintly embarrassing and yet knew that they both needed each other. Gotti also knew that his jury-tampering efforts had been instrumental in securing at least one of his acquittals. Besides which Gotti prided himself on masterminding the legal strategies which had been so successful. At times he considered Cutler to be little more than an errand boy carrying out his instructions.

Still, even errand boys had their place. "What you gotta do . . ." Gotti began to instruct him, "is tell them that people that I know, that I'm friendly with, don't wanna make no admissions. I don't give a fuck what the tapes say . . . we got a new method of fighting. You know what I'm trying to say? There's no gang, or no mob. But this is our personal families and we're entitled to our personal family . . ."

"Conventionally, they lost," bragged Cutler somewhat prematurely.

Gotti wasn't convinced either. "But if they fight it the way I've been telling you fucking guys two, three years, you gotta attack them!"

Bruce Cutler's mere presence at the Ravenite on Mulberry Street was compromising. All the defense lawyers knew perfectly well in private that it was the Gambino headquarters where they masterminded their criminal enterprise. The seductive notion of being close to the center of power seems to have affected Cutler's judgment. But this was a man who had to be a master in the art of self-deception to maintain the extraordinary fiction that John Gotti was a respectable and much maligned businessman whose only failing was to suffer from the occasional loss of temper. In this state of massive self-delusion, the lawyer probably didn't realize that behind his back his "beloved friend," John Gotti, was mercilessly mocking his pretensions.

In conversation with Gravano, Gotti made it clear who was really pulling the legal strings. "I'm trying to think what's good for the overall picture, Sammy," murmured Gotti, speaking sotto voce in the apartment above the Ravenite—reserved for the innermost deliberations of the Gambino Family. "First thing is this. With these fuckin' lawyers on all these cases like even for a bail application, they gotta go in there, argue for your client within certain parameters. Then after that, keep your fuckin' mouth shut!" If there was one thing Gotti couldn't abide, it was one of their lawyers speaking out of turn when he had instructed them to keep quiet.

"Your Honor, those charges don't pertain to my client," mimicked Gotti, imitating one of their lawyers in court.

"Sit the fuck down, or I'll knock you down, you cocksucker," said Gotti, imitating the instructions he would then give the attorney. "Sit down or I'll knock you down, you motherfucker! Talk within certain parameters and we'll win, we'll win. We'll win, Sammy! We'll win these fuckin' cases. And we'll be out a year from now, laughing a little bit. Believe me!"

Despite his confidence in his own legal expertise, the Gambino boss knew that he still needed the services of Bruce Cutler and Gerry Shargel, the other highly paid Gambino defense lawyer. But the greater the need, the higher the bills they had to pay, a tiresome detail which Gotti loved to complain about. "You know these are rats, Sam . . ." Gotti explained to his consigliere. "And I gotta say, they all want their money up front. And then you get four guys that want $65,000, $75,000 apiece up front. You're talking about $300,000 in one month, you cocksucker!"

Gotti complained that he had to pay nearly $20,000 in printing costs alone for the preparation of legal briefs and documents plus $135,000 for an appeal. "Where does it end?" Gotti complained to Gravano. "Gambino crime Family? This is the Shargel, Cutler and whattya call it 'crime Family'! You wanna go steal! You and your fuckin' mother!"

"They wind up with the money . . ." agreed Gravano.

"The fuckin' you kiddin'? You know what I mean?"

"They're overpriced, overpaid and underperformed!" said Frankie Locascio by way of support.

As well as costing too much, The Administration detected the same affliction among their legal team as that which affected some of their weaker brethren within the Cosa Nostra. "You know why they can't win, Sammy? They got no fuckin' cohesion. They got no unity. It's like us!"

"And they ain't got the balls to do what they supposed to do," added Locascio darkly.

"Don't you know why they ain't got the balls, too?" said Gotti, picking up on the theme. "You don't wanna do it because, you cocksucker, you know and I know that they know that you're taking the money under the table. Every time you take a client, another one of us on, you're breaking the law."

In the paranoid world of John Gotti there lurked the suspicion that perhaps his lawyers might even have a vested interest in losing their cases so as to keep the fees rolling in for endless appeals. But maybe that was a little unfair; after all there were success fees for acquittal, and most of the defense lawyers knew that the route to real wealth lay in getting their clients off. That way the mobsters could get back out on the streets and start to earn serious money to pay for the future legal bills—and so it went on. Ultimately, the lawyers could earn more with their clients able to break the law, so there was some mutual interest.

Even so, Gotti felt they were probably getting ripped off. He was probably right. There was also a good reason for much of the fees having to go "under the table." In Gotti's position, tax evasion and false declaration of income were essential. For both sides there was a need to maintain the fiction of artificially low legal fees, the ones that were published anyway. If Cutler's official accounts recorded that Gotti had paid him $300,000 then questions might be asked as to where the money came from.

"They don't fuck with youse and youse don't go all out in court, you know that. If they wanna really break Bruce Cutler's balls, what did he get paid off me? He ain't defending me three years ago. I paid tax on $36,000. What could I have paid him? You follow what I'm saying? They didn't ask him, he didn't answer them. And then he sees them behind our back, 'Hello, Mrs. Giacalone!' [*Diane Giacalone was the Assistant U.S. attorney who led the first RICO case against Gotti which proved to be such a catastrophic failure for the Eastern District prosecutors.*]

"It's no good, Sam," said Gotti, continuing his grouse about his lawyers. "But worse than that is, you see me talk for ten minutes in the hall? What do we talk about? You see me talk for ten minutes in the hall? What do we talk about? Nothing! I say: 'Go find out information what's going, when the pinch is coming, you cocksucker!' We're making you an 'errand boy.' High-priced 'errand boy'! Bruce, worse yet! They got a routine now, the two lawyers. 'Muck' and 'Fuck,' I call them. When I see Bruce: 'Hi, Gerry loves you,' he says. 'He's in your corner hundred percent!' When I see Gerry: 'Hi, Bruce loves you! He's in your corner a hundred percent!' 'I know youse both love me!' . . . Dumb fucks, you know? . . . I'd like to kill all the lawyers!'"

It was fortunate that Bruce Cutler didn't take any of the tapes seriously. If he had done, he might just have questioned his unwavering hero worship of his client, but he didn't. At least not in public.

In the meantime, short of conducting their own defense, which one Mafia boss had done with disastrous results, there was little they could do about it, other than curse their highly paid attorneys behind their backs.

Lawyers or no lawyers, Gotti was gambling on the fact that if they all played their cards right they could keep the Family going and keep themselves out of jail. They might be living on borrowed time but Gotti was confident that his leadership would usher in a new dawn of harmony amongst the Families. Cosa Nostra under the dynamic leadership of John Gotti would be invincible.

"None of the Families are arguing with nobody," Gotti boasted to Gravano.

"No . . ."

"Everybody sedate . . ." boasted the "boss of bosses."

"That's true."

"You know, think about it. Greatest thing ever!"

"It would be so united," chimed Gravano, warming to the theme.

"We'd have somebody indicting the fuckin' agents and the fuckin' prosecutors!"

"We'd be so fuckin' close, forget about it!"

"Not only that. If there's a bad situation, hey, rules need a little changing or something . . ."

"Five minutes . . ." muttered Gravano.

"Send the five underbosses, or the consiglieres. Together, boom. This is my way, my thinking, because this 'thing,' in other words, the five Families, put together, bi, bah, bang," exclaimed Gotti, clapping his hands together to emphasize the point. "That's the law."

Whatever might be coming his way in the shape of indictments, Gotti was confident that he was laying the foundations for the Cosa Nostra's survival into the 21st century. A key component of his strategy was to ensure "cohesion" by upgrading the intake of new recruits into the Gambino Family. Gotti was going to have "made guys" that could do more than merely kill, and if he was temporarily out of action through the efforts of the FBI or anyone else, there was always Sammy the Bull to mind the store. He lectured Gravano with the blueprints for his master plan.

"Tomorrow, I wanna call all our skippers in. I'm gonna tell them, 'I'm the "Representante" till I say different. Soon as anything happens to me, I'm off the streets, Sammy is the acting boss. He's our consigliere.' So I'm asking you, how you feel? You wanna stay as consigliere? Or you want me to make you official underboss? Acting boss? How do you feel? What makes you feel better? Think about it. Think about it tonight."

"Acting boss," answered Gravano. "Really it's . . ."

"That's nothing! I'm gonna tell you why. Here's what I'm talking about . . ."

"Go ahead."

"The underboss should take charge of the Family. Ya know what I'm saying? You don't need a consigliere. We'll put somebody acting there. Know what I'm saying? You're official, Sammy, and that's where it's gonna stay . . . and I'm gonna make our skippers understand that. 'This is my wishes that if I'm in the fucking can, this Family is gonna be run by Sammy. I'm still the boss. If I get 50 years I know what I gotta do. But when I'm in the can, Sammy's in charge. Now, or you go in the can, God forbid!' "

"I could go away too!" complained Gravano, with greater prescience than he could have imagined.

"You see what I'm sayin', Sammy," continued Gotti, undeterred by his sidekick's pessimism. "We gotta fuckin' think and I know what I'm talkin' about. If I could just get this fuckin' probation I want, you'll get bail. Who gives a fuck! Nobody comes to see ya. They'll send some jerk to see ya. Just the fact you're out there. That you could sneak out in the middle of the night and hit a guy in the fucking head with a hatchet. You follow, understand, Sammy? All you're gonna do is, you're gonna have a good time, six months, then you're gonna be in the next cell to me. We ain't goin' nowhere the fuckin' hurry, Sammy!"

"If they ain't got me already down there," warned Sammy, injecting a note of realism into his boss's dreams.

"No, I agree with you. But, Sammy, if they ain't got us, they'll never get us! But we feel if they ain't preparing a coupla humdinger cases for you, I'll take it up the fuckin' ass, Sam."

"Well, I believe they are."

"And all . . ."

Gravano interrupted his boss again. "I believe they are. See last night over there, you know they followed me to my door?"

"I believe it . . ." said Gotti. "Let me tell you what . . ."

"To my door!" complained the aggrieved consigliere.

"You know why, Sammy?" said Gotti whose mood of optimism could even find solace in the fact that his anointed successor was under 24-hour surveillance. To Gotti it was a flattering vindication of the fact that law enforcement were taking his closest associates sufficiently seriously to devote such resources to keeping track of their movements. "They're not stupid. I telegraph my voice. I couldn't help it. And they know how I feel. And they know any fucking serious thing that I need done that I can't do, you'll do it. I'm not just talking about this. I'm talking about meeting with people. They're not stupid."

"It would be my pleasure to be . . ."

"I'm just thinking if I got a hundred years, Sammy, and you beat the case . . ."

"The door is open," replied the loyal Gravano.

"Yeah, come in!" joked Gotti in an inviting manner.

The door Gotti was edging open for Sammy Gravano led to a world of awesome power, limitless wealth, immense prestige and constant danger. For a street punk who five years ago had been a mere soldier in the Gambino Family it was a stunning climb to the peak of Mafia power. As well as heading the Family, Gravano would become the most powerful Mafioso in America.

"It's not a toy," Gotti proclaimed, waxing philosophical about the essence of power within the Cosa Nostra. The Godfather was speaking softly in the apartment on January 17, 1990, surrounded by the men in whose company he felt sufficiently comfortable to be able to communicate his innermost thoughts about the organization that he served with an almost religious devotion. His faithful acolytes, Gravano and Locascio, were all ears.

"I'm not in the mood for toys or games or kidding, no time. I'm not in the mood for clans. I'm not in the mood for gangs. I'm not in the mood for none of that stuff there. And this is gonna be a Cosa Nostra till I die. Be it an hour from now or be it tonight or a hundred years from now when I'm in jail. It's gonna be a Cosa Nostra! This ain't gonna be any bunch of your friends are gonna be 'friends of ours.' It's gonna be the way I say it's gonna be and a Cosa Nostra. A Cosa Nostra!"

Gotti warmed to his theme about the type of recruit who would be a "stand-up" guy in the Cosa Nostra: not someone who was just doing you a favor, but a wiseguy who was worthy of the organization, a patriot to the cause which had no country but which offered a sense of belonging that no nation could ever rival.

"You might, because a guy's nice to you and I'm not controlling the way you are, the guy that gives you a basket, makes you a good guy. It makes him a motherfucker to me! Don't make him a good guy. It makes him a good guy when he's one of us and he proves he's right for us. And I'm the best judge of that, I think right now. So you got a reason, Frank, say it. 'I love you,' say it. Ah, this thing here. I'm not so sure the five guys that I'm putting in are the first five guys that should be going. But we'll do it. I'm doing it because I want this thing to be proper, eh, we got some guys that deserve it. And they'll be here forever! They won't be havin' the secret fuckin' parties when people won't be around. That we don't want and that we don't need. That's for sure! I wanna see an effort. I gotta see an effort for starting now a Cosa Nostra! I don't need a guy who come tell me, 'I feel sorry about trouble.' I ain't got no trouble. I ain't got no trouble. I'm gonna be alright. They got the fuckin' trouble. And I don't mean the cops. I mean the people who can make this a joke. You know what I mean? That's not a fucking joke. See, even some guy, some of the people downstairs now, even I know who's fuckin' stomach is rotten. And I know whose stomach ain't rotten. You think I could smell it? The way a dog senses when a guy has got fear in him, you know what I mean?"

During his six-year reign as head of the Gambino Family, Gotti smelled quite a few "rotting stomachs." Anyone suspected of being a rat or crossing him or Gravano in a business deal was whacked.

On December 12, 1990 John Gotti, Sammy "The Bull" Gravano and Frankie Locascio were arrested. All applications for bail were refused. Gotti's carefully laid plans for the succession to pass to Sammy the Bull came to naught.

Worse was to follow. On November 24, 1991, Sammy

Gravano fired his lawyer and, to the stunned disbelief of both the law enforcement community and the Cosa Nostra, began talking to the FBI. Ironically, one of the reasons for his betrayal was the Ravenite tapes themselves. When Gravano heard Gotti insulting him behind his back, he knew he'd been betrayed by his boss.

It was the most devastating betrayal in the history of the American Mafia. Sammy the Bull, the tough guy's tough guy, had become a rat.

John Gotti was shattered. Combined with the loss of his fawning but successful defense lawyer, Bruce Cutler, John Gotti was now totally isolated by the two people on whom he had pinned his survival. The prosecution held all the trump cards. Realization that all his most intimate conversations in the Ravenite had been recorded for posterity was bad enough, but even that paled into insignificance when compared to the Judas-like actions of his beloved Sammy. In addition to the hours of incriminating tapes culled from the Ravenite, the prosecuting attorneys would have a live witness capable of corroborating the recordings and providing the prosecution with the most detailed insight ever obtained into the inner workings of the Cosa Nostra.

It was an act of epic betrayal which sent shock waves through the underworld empire which Gotti and Gravano had once bestrode like giants. Even hardened agents and FBI officials were puzzled by the enormity of the treachery which on a personal level probably outweighed the significance of the information that would be provided, substantial though it was. It was the act itself which was imbued with a historic sense of importance, combining as it did the elements of a Greek tragedy with black comedy.

From the witness box Gravano's testimony provided a blow-by-blow account of the planning and execution of Paul Castellano. Gotti's defense team, minus the ebullient Cutler, stood little chance and at the end of a ten-week trial, the FBI and the prosecutors of the Eastern District of New York finally achieved their goal. The jury returned a unanimous verdict of guilty.

On June 23, 1992, John Gotti was sentenced to 100 years in jail.

The Mafia tapes had spooled to an end. So effective had they been that even if Gotti himself had confessed it is doubtful whether he could have supplied such a damning self-indictment as had been achieved by the successful bugs that had been secretly installed in the Ravenite Social Club and the second-floor apartment.

John Gotti's conviction combined with the earlier success of the prosecution of the Commission and the Pizza Connection were historic victories for the American Government. The American Mafia had effectively choked themselves to death with their own words.

But what the tapes really achieved was altogether more abstract yet more important. They recorded the reality of the Cosa Nostra in the 20th century and in the process provided a legal instrument to prosecute the perpetrators of the crimes which the tapes documented.

Apart from destroying Gotti, the behavior of Gravano dealt a serious blow to the image of the American Mafia as an organization bonded together by acts of unspeakable cruelty and loyalty. Worse still, the image of the Cosa Nostra as a secret society welded together by strength, fear and honor was degraded beyond redemption. It was the image that Gotti had lived for and to destroy that was far worse a punishment for the swaggering gangster than anything a federal judge could hope to throw at the "boss of bosses."

Ironically it appeared that the reason for Gravano's act of treachery was the prospect of serving the rest of his natural life in jail. John Gotti had been known to order executions of underlings whom he thought might be tempted to rat because of their fear of a prison sentence. But never in his wildest nightmares had he considered that the man he had once trusted above all others in the Gambino Family, the Mafioso whom he had personally chosen as his anointed successor to ensure the survival of the Family into the 21st century, would turn his back and betray the sacred oath of Omerta. Yet that is exactly what Gravano did. It was a severe blow to both the New York Mafia and John Gotti—a blow from which he would never recover.

18

EPILOGUE: WINNERS AND LOSERS

AN EXPANSE OF IMMACULATELY KEPT GRASS INTERSECTED by a newly surfaced road and a low-key security checkpoint marks the gateway to America's most notorious federal prison. Marion, Illinois, is nearly three hours' drive from St. Louis, Missouri, and even further from Chicago. It is, appropriately, in the middle of nowhere.

The penitentiary houses the most dangerous and notorious prisoners in the country. Its inmates include John Walker, the naval spy; Ed Wilson, the renegade CIA arms dealer; Gaetano Badalamenti, the former head of the Sicilian Mafia; and Nicky Scarfo, the psychotic boss of the Bruno Family from Philadelphia. According to a document prepared by the prison's information department: "The facility houses adult male offenders committed from all parts of the country who have demonstrated a need for high security confinement. Offenders at Marion have compiled serious records of institutional misconduct, have been involved in violent or escape-related behavior, or have lengthy and complex sentences, which indicates they require an unusually high level of security."

Inmates arrive at Marion as the prison of last resort. The same document reveals that the guiding principles of the high security operation are: "Priority of Safety and Deterrence . . . Limited direct physical contact between Staff and Inmates [with the exception of pre-transfer units]. When direct Staff-Inmate contact is required, Inmates in restraint. Elimination of direct contact with outside visitors through the physical design of the visiting room."

Despite the massive security precautions John Gotti was still able to run the Gambino Family from inside the prison. The Mafia boss, who once boasted that he liked jail better than the streets, is confined to a small concrete cell for 23 hours a day. The two-thousand-dollar suits have been exchanged for a drab prison uniform and the menus of Manhattan's best Italian restaurants have been replaced by the unwholesome diet of federal penitentiary food.

Gotti is permitted five visits a month of up to seven hours per visit. According to prison regulations: "A maximum of three visitors per inmate are allowed to visit at any given time. Visiting hours are from 8:00 A.M. to 3:00 P.M., Thursday through Sunday and Federal Holidays." In keeping with the prison's stated goals no physical contact is allowed during visits. The prisoner and his visitors are separated by thick, wire-meshed glass and separately enclosed in spartan wooden booths. They can only communicate via a black telephone. Facing to their front, on the prisoner's right-hand side stands a raised booth, with a commanding view of the row of booths used for visiting days. Here the prison guard can sit and monitor the conversations over the telephones.

The certainty with which law enforcement officials insist that Gotti is still the head of the Family suggest that his discussions are amongst those which are both monitored and recorded. It is even possible that these 1993 conversations could form the basis of further charges in 1994 against Gotti and his henchmen. According to Bruce Mouw, head of the FBI Gambino Squad: "John Gotti is still running the Family from prison in Marion, Illinois. John Gotti has an older brother named Peter who's a captain in the Family. He also has a son, John A. Gotti, who's a captain in the Family. John and Peter Gotti both visit Marion. Through these visits he's able to convey messages to them and different instructions. These two go back to New York, relay instructions and that's how he's able to exercise control over the Family."

It is testimony to Gotti's strength and determination that he is able to control the Gambino Family despite his current predicament. When he declared, "This is gonna be a Cosa Nostra 'til I die, be it an hour from now or a hundred years from now . . ." inside the Ravenite he clearly meant it.

Yet even Gotti's power cannot last forever. By the end of 1993 his control was beginning to slip. Loyalists prepared to support his continuing reign as head of the Family were increasingly isolated as the legal avenues for the release and reincarnation of John Gotti began to be closed off. On October 8, 1993, their hopes were dashed when the three-judge panel of the United States Court of Appeals for the Second Circuit in Manhattan unanimously rejected Gotti's request for a new trial.

Although it has been traditional for mob bosses to hand over the reins of power once it seems certain that they will not get out of prison, Gotti remains convinced that further appeals could still reverse his conviction. Gotti's optimism is buoyed up by the indefatigable Bruce Cutler. Barred from defending him at his 1992 trial, Cutler is still advising his most famous client. On a recent visit to the prison, Cutler claimed Gotti was in fighting spirits and more confident than ever of eventual victory. He said that Gotti's optimism and enthusiasm were so overwhelming that he could have flown back to New York without an aircraft!

Even after the failure of the October 1993 Appeal, Cutler remains unbowed. He has vowed to take the fight all the way up to the United States Supreme Court. "This is just the beginning of the appellate process and the fight to vindicate him," says Cutler. Ironically, his own exclusion from the 1992 trial was one of the key arguments that was lost on appeal. Charles J. Ogletree, Jr., a Harvard law professor, argued that the lawyer's exclusion meant that Gotti had been denied a fair trial. In their submission to the Appeal

Court, the Government countered: "Gotti and Locascio claim that the court abused its discretion in disqualifying attorneys Bruce Cutler and George Santangelo from participating in the trial. These claims should be rejected. As the record amply demonstrates, both Cutler and Santangelo were members of the Gambino Family's corps of house counsel. As such they were witnesses to the existence of the RICO enterprise and also to particular events probative of specific crimes charged in the indictment. Given the admissible evidence of their relationships with the Gambino Family, neither attorney could possibly contest the existence of that enterprise without placing his own credibility in issue or becoming an unsworn witness. Cutler, in addition, had represented a Government witness and was also himself implicated in some of the very crimes with which Gotti was charged. Because their presence threatened to undermine the fairness of the proceedings, the district court properly disqualified both attorneys."

Ironically, it was Gotti's own words, heard on the Ravenite tapes, which revealed the relationship between the Godfather and his lawyers. On one tape (January 4, 1990), Gotti complains about giving his lawyers $300,000 in one month to defend him and another $300,000 in one year to defend his associates. Gotti adds that the lawyers were taking money "under the table" and opined that "every time you take a client, another of us on, you're breaking the law."

The prosecution had a wealth of evidence to substantiate their claim that Bruce Cutler was the "house counsel" to the Gambino Family. Their appeal submission highlighted one of Gotti's most damning asides: "Indeed, Gotti complained that the lawyers were getting so much of the Family's money that the enterprise should be called, rather than the 'Gambino Family,' the 'Shargel, Cutler and whattaya call it crime Family.' "

The legal (to say nothing of the moral) significance of being "house counsel" lay precisely in the nature of the RICO legislation itself, the necessity to prove in court the existence of the "Continuing Criminal Enterprise." As John Gleeson argued to devastating effect in the Appeal on the section supporting their disqualification of Santangelo: "On January 21, 1992, the court announced its decision to disqualify Santangelo and to deny as frivolous the motion to disqualify the prosecutor. In disqualifying Santangelo, the court noted two bases for its decision. First mutually corroborative evidence from both Gravano and the Ravenite tapes supported the inference that Santangelo was 'answerable to Gotti,' a term semantically equivalent to 'house counsel.' Such evidence was 'immediately probative of one of the elements' of the RICO charges, namely, the existence of the Gambino Family enterprise."

In their judgment the Appeal Court found that Cutler had "allegedly entangled himself to an extraordinary degree in the activities of the Gambino crime Family." It was game, set and match to the prosecution.

Despite Bruce Cutler's optimism it is extremely unlikely that John Gotti will ever be freed. Even if he wins a new trial, there can be scarce hope for acquittal. The best Gotti can hope is that he will serve his life sentence in surroundings slightly more congenial than Marion and that he can parlay his leadership of the Family into the appointment of a new boss who will remain loyal to him.

The Government's victory in the Appeal was the climax in a series of successful prosecutions and convictions over the last decade. With many more in the pipeline, the law enforcement community can justifiably claim to be winning the war against the Mafia. But opinion is sharply divided between those who foresee the mob being reduced in power and size back to the level of a street gang and those who take a more long-term view.

Colonel Justin Dintino, the head of the New Jersey State Police, is a veteran crime fighter with a healthy skepticism towards those who predict the imminent demise of the mob. "They are saying that five years from now the Mafia will no longer exist—they'll be reduced to a street gang. They were saying that ten years ago and you will hear other people say that we will eliminate La Cosa Nostra—both of them are wrong on both counts. We've had organized crime in this country since 1931 and we're going to continue to have organized crime and we will not eliminate it until the public stops utilizing the services that provide gambling, narcotics and loan-sharking. Do you think that the public is going to give up those services? I don't. Somebody's going to be there to provide it."

Undoubtedly the Gambino and Lucchese Families have taken some heavy hits in recent cases. Many in the Gambino Family curse the day when John Gotti was born, let alone the date of his usurping the role of overall boss. His high profile triggered a crackdown by the FBI on the Gambinos and a greater urgency in the assault against the other Mafia Families. The relentless prosecutions had the desired effect of persuading those who had nothing left to lose that it was in their interests to become Government witnesses. The last decade has seen an unprecedented number of high-ranking members agreeing to cooperate, their evidence in turn initiating new prosecutions, some of which have then resulted in more defendants agreeing to cooperate.

In the case of Sammy Gravano, the evidence he is still providing has enabled the prosecutors to gain a much higher level of convictions. Not only has he been able to ensure the conviction of The Administration that he was part of, he has also been able to put a premature end to the aspirations of the new "Administration." The FBI are now in possession of a wealth of intelligence that they can use against the next level down in the Gambino Family. As Sammy the Bull was in day-to-day charge of running the Family, his knowledge is priceless. In theory his evidence would be enough to put the entire membership of the Family behind bars. However the courts require a great deal of evidence in addition to that provided by a witness even if he was the former underboss of the Family. Gravano's defection has sent shockwaves through the Gambino Family.

In practical terms, communications within the Family have been made extremely difficult. If Gotti insists on maintaining control for too long, it could precipitate a war. His son, John A. Gotti, "Junior," a hulking capo with a lightweight mind and a heavyweight physique, is bitterly resented by a powerful faction of the Family. Old-time survivors of the Castellano era bitterly resent taking orders from the young thug.

Gotti's high profile in the press was a major factor in contributing to his downfall. It also played a part in exaggerating the significance of his demise. Greg O'Connell, an Assistant U.S. Attorney in the Eastern District of New York, whose office brought Gotti down, believes that putting Gotti behind bars may not be quite such a significant a victory as many have claimed. "The elimination of Gotti didn't really put much of a dent in organized crime generally, just as the elimination of any other crime figure wouldn't put that great a dent because they are all replaceable. Gotti will be replaced. The Gambino crime Family is going to go on. It will be hurt now more than the others because of the cooperation we have from its underboss, Sammy Gravano, just as the Lucchese crime Family is being hurt with the assistance of Alphonse D'Arco and Peter Chiodo and the way the Colombo crime Family has likewise been taking very major prosecution hits over the last two years. The Genovese crime Family on the other hand hasn't. We convicted the underboss Benny 'Eggs' Mangano but that's just one person. We hope to convict Gigante which would have a very major impact on that Family because it would disturb its entire structure. However, the bottom line is that each one of these high-ranking members will be replaced by someone else and the only way that we'll be able to eliminate this problem is by keeping steady pressure with continuing prosecutions and keeping the same amount of pressure as we have over the last two years until finally they have a quality control problem where they no longer have members with talent to run the crime Family."

By all accounts Tommy Gambino was one of the most talented members of the Gambino Family. Son of its founder Carlo Gambino, Tommy Gambino is a multimillionaire who singlehandedly made millions of dollars for the Family. By successfully targeting Tommy Gambino the Government has now drastically reduced the Family's influence in the garment district.

Civil RICO cases are being pursued against Tommy

Gambino's companies and against the unions allied to the construction business in New York City. Both were major sources of power, influence and income for the Gambino Family for the last 30 years. Their removal amounts to a significant loss of revenue for the coffers of organized crime.

Today, Tommy Gambino has been forced to relinquish control of Consolidated and Dynamic, two of his trucking companies which were bringing in $12 million a year. So pervasive was his influence and the malign power of his reputation that companies in the garment business were paying tribute to the Gambino Family, whether they used his trucks or not. Salesmen, Gambino enforcers, would visit companies and work out how many garments they were making and charge a "tax" as a result. Not all of Tommy Gambino's companies in the garment trade have been affected. Indeed the corporate interests of the Family are likely to survive the fate of the son and heir of the founding father.

So far success in removing Mafia influence from the garment industry has not been matched in other sectors, notably their control of garbage disposal—the carting industry. If it has taken more than 30 years to tackle the influence of one Mafia Family over the garment district, it is likely to take much longer to remove their control of waste disposal, particularly as it involves the interests of several Families.

Organized crime has dominated the industry for more than a decade. In the early 1980s the Lucchese Family even set up a trade association to represent the industry they themselves controlled and extorted. If Mafia strategists had studied *Das Kapital* by Karl Marx and synthesized the essence of economic power into an organized system which allowed them to reap the profits by exploiting the strengths and weaknesses of both sides of the labor and capital equation, it is unlikely that they would have come up with a better industry upon which they could practice their philosophy.

Organized crime is not that organized but once it institutionalizes the corruption it generates, it becomes much harder to root it out. New York City authorities recently took over some of the Mafia-dominated cement companies; the strategy has not been successful and mob influence has begun to creep back. Companies run by the authorities have once again been infiltrated by the mob.

If the jury is still out on the success of law enforcement in disentangling the tentacles of organized crime from many of America's legitimate businesses, the Government can at least highlight cases where they have regained control of a union and, using civil RICO laws, reinstated democracy and reduced Mafia influence. A prime example is Local 54, the Bartenders Union in Atlantic City, and Local 282 in New York City, the construction union. Both unions have been given Government-appointed administrators who have successfully rooted out the organized crime connections.

As with the criminal application of RICO, the civil version of the law also requires a heavy commitment of resources to maintain the pressure. There have been many examples, particularly with the Teamsters, where the union has been given a clean bill of health only for it to be discovered at a later date that the officials are either made members of the Mafia or deep inside their pockets.

As Mafia control over industries and unions begins to wane in the 1990s so too does their political influence. Owning the unions provided tremendous leverage at election time. It was a power wielded to great effect by the Bruno Family in Philadelphia and Atlantic City. "If we want to help somebody run for election," explains Nicky "The Crow" Caramandi, a soldier under Scarfo who specialized in extortion and embezzlement, "we could get union members to vote for them, we could let people know that we want to see this fella win. We have people in all walks of life, the highest to the lowest. I fixed many a case with judges, I dealt with Congressmen . . . I dealt with all different types of people."

Even allowing for a wiseguy's natural propensity to exaggerate, the Bruno Family under Scarfo did have extensive political influence. It is fairly well documented how they "ran" the Mayor of Atlantic City, Michael J. Mathews, in the early 1980s. The Mayor later received a 15-year sentence for bribery.

Philip Leonetti, former underboss of the Family, told me about their relationship with the politicians. "We backed Mayor Mathews to win the election. He came to Frank Gerace [*head of Local 54, the Bartenders Union*] and needed our help. Frank came to my uncle and my uncle said, 'Yeah, we'll help him.' He told me to go and introduce him to Kenny Shapiro who was a guy that was with us. He was a land buyer, builder, land, you know. He had a company called Seatex. He owned the property where Trump built his casinos—he leased the land to Trump. He was in the know. He knew Trump, he knew a few people. He helped Mike Mathews become Mayor of Atlantic City. Naturally, I told Mike: 'Don't listen to nobody but us, you know, don't talk to anybody. You're with us. You do what we tell you to do.' He was under the protection of our Family. He would listen to whatever our Family told him to do."

But if he didn't? I asked.

"He would get killed," replied Leonetti in a matter-of-fact tone.

Did he know that?

"Yes."

An unexpected bonus in the May 1982 Mayoral race was that another friend of Leonetti's was also angling for the office. "I had a friend of mine, he was also a councilman and he wanted to be the Chief of Police. He was also running for Mayor at the time Mike Mathews was running for Mayor. Now, he would have took a lot of votes away from Mike Mathews so I went to him. First, I went to Mike Mathews and says, 'Look, Mike, you promise this guy to be the Chief of Police. When you become Mayor you make him the Chief of Police if he doesn't run.' And he said, 'Yeah.' So I went to Joe and I said: 'Look, Joe, drop out of the race and I guarantee you if Mike wins you'll become the Chief of Police.' And he said, 'Okay.' And Mike won, appointed Joe the Chief of Police and we had the Chief of Police and the Mayor of Atlantic City. We got all the unions to support Mike Mathews. We had everybody going for him, you know, the casinos, everybody, and he won."

Mathews made a pact with the devil and paid the price, although the Chief of Police quietly retired.

The Bruno Family were also able to use the unions to intimidate the casinos. Leonetti explains, "We could have stopped everything. We could have shut them down, you know . . . We've got our businesses in the casino. Everything was done legally, you know, whatever businesses, maintenance companies, we wanted, whatever contracts. They really couldn't say anything."

On one occasion when there was a problem between the union leader, Frank Gerace, and the Playboy Casino, the ultimate threat had to be invoked. "Frank Gerace, the President of Local 54, he dealt with the casinos, with the owners. He dealt with the contracts. One time in 1983, he was having a problem with the Playboy and they didn't want to sign a union contract. They tried to break the union. So I sent somebody to see the owner that I knew and told them if you don't sign it we'll be going to kill you. And he signed it."

As an underboss, Leonetti was privy to some of the innermost secrets of his own Family and those in New York. Because of his rank Leonetti would have to deputize for his uncle, Nicky Scarfo, if he was in jail or otherwise indisposed. That meant that his position had to be approved by the Commission in New York. The only concern was that he would be regarded as being too young. To be an underboss before one's 40th birthday was considered fast work! Scarfo took his nephew on a trip to New York to meet their contact on the Commission, Bobby Manna, the consigliere of the Genovese Family. "He [*Scarfo*] wanted to make sure the Commission approved me being the underboss. He asked Bobby Manna if it was okay. If he thought I was too young to be the underboss. And Bobby asked him, 'Does he know what's going on with La Cosa Nostra?' And he said, 'Oh, he knows just as much as I do, Bob.' He said, 'Well then he's not too young. As long as he knows what's going on.' So that's when he made me the underboss and that's the first time he introduced me to Bobby Manna, just in case something happened to my uncle I would go see Bobby on my own."

In the spring of 1986 Leonetti also accompanied his uncle on trips to New York to see members of the Gambino Family. "Sammy Gravano came down to see me and my uncle and said: 'Look, John wants to meet you as the new boss of our Family. He's a great guy, Nick, you know, you've got to come down.' So we made an appointment and we went to go down and see him and we met him in Staten Island. He was there with a ton of guys. There were guys outside—all over the place! Joe Farinelli, one of the guys that lives in Trenton, that belonged to their Family, drove us down. And it was really something to meet him because we'd seen him in the papers and all, you know, he's like a big public figure and he was a nice guy. He was a handsome man. He was more handsome than what we've seen on TV. He's a good-looking guy. He was like my uncle, that type of personality, a killer, you know. Old-school and didn't take no shit. That type of person. He was nice."

From all accounts Gotti was indeed a "gangster's gangster" and Leonetti was as starstruck as the rest of the population in the face of the massive publicity that Gotti was beginning to receive after the murder of Paul Castellano. Ironically, Gotti confided to the young underboss that he too was regarded with suspicion because of his relative youth.

"He was telling me that people in his Family resent him a little bit because they feel like he's too young to be boss, you know. Sammy came over, he said: 'Look, John, look at Philip, he's a young guy and he's the underboss!' And then John started telling me, 'Yeah, Philip, a lot of people in my Family resent me because I'm so young, you know.' But I said, 'Yeah, John, but . . .' I said, 'Look at Lucky Luciano and Albert Anastasia and Meyer Lansky. All them guys— they were all bosses and they were young guys. They started everything in their twenties. I mean as long as you know what this thing's about, the La Cosa Nostra, that's all that counts. That's all that matters.' And they said, 'Yeah, you're right.' And I was telling him about Ange [*Angelo Bruno, the former boss of the Philadelphia Family who was murdered on March 21, 1980*], the type of guy he was and that's when he told me Paul was the same type of guy. You ask him to go into business, he goes behind your back and try and take it from you afterwards. He would never give you the OK for nothing, you know."

Interestingly, the Gambino Family had enjoyed a close historical relationship with their Philadelphia cousins. Angelo Bruno had been close to Carlo Gambino, and both were wedded to the same traditions of low-profile racketeering. When Bruno was murdered, the New York Commission had demanded that his killers be brought to justice. Only the Commission could sanction the murder of a boss and in this case they had not. (Although the killers claimed they thought that New York had given the go-ahead.) Bruno's killers were duly executed and the Commission was satisfied that justice had been dispensed. One problem remained in the shape of John Stanfa, a surly Sicilian who was Bruno's driver on the night of the killing. Stanfa was suspected of setting his boss up and was also earmarked for execution but high-level Mafiosi interceded on his behalf and he was sentenced to be exiled back to the old country. In fact he never returned there and has now risen to become the new boss of the Philadelphia Family, or what's left of it.

At the time of Leonetti's meeting with John Gotti, the sentence of exile was still standing. Gotti huddled over a table with Scarfo and brought it up. "John asked my uncle if he could do him a favor with this John Stanfa because he was due out of jail soon. He told my uncle, 'Nick, I know you had an agreement with Paul about John Stanfa, sending him back to Italy and you weren't going to kill him, but is it OK if we keep John Stanfa in this country and everything would be OK?' My uncle said, 'Yeah, John, whatever you want.' He [*Gotti*] said, 'Of course, there are a lot of guys in my Family, Nick, that are related to this guy and they keep bothering me to ask you if it's OK if he stays in this country.' And my uncle said, 'Look, John, if you want it, no problem. As long as he reports to whoever he's supposed to report and does the right thing, he can stay in this country. Nobody will bother him.'" And nobody did! Except the FBI and Scarfo loyalists who, after Nicky Scarfo was convicted on November 19, 1988, fought against him to prevent him taking over the Family. In September 1993, Stanfa's son was shot in the face and seriously wounded in Philadelphia. It is believed that the gunmen were after his father and got the wrong man.

At the time of the meeting with Gotti, Stanfa was in prison and presented no threat to Scarfo or Leonetti. Besides they had a favor they wanted to ask in return. There was a group of distant relatives of Carlo Gambino who were living in New Jersey in an area which the Philadelphia Family regarded as their territory. Also they had been spotted in Atlantic City and were regarded by Scarfo as troublemakers. One of them had even pulled a gun on one of Scarfo's soldiers in one of the bars in their area—a sure sign of disrespect. "We were hoping we could kill them. So we told John about it," recalls Leonetti, "and he said, 'Look, Nick, I promise you they're going to be out of there and I'm going to tell you, if they don't listen, I'll kill them myself!' He said, 'You don't have to kill them, I'll kill them myself!' "

Although Philip Leonetti may have been starstruck at the time of his meeting with John Gotti, by the time he decided to cooperate with the FBI, the glamour had worn off. He remembered key conversations with Gotti, which were quickly relayed to Bruce Mouw, head of the Gambino FBI squad in the Queens office.

Leonetti began to cooperate in June 1989, a time when the FBI was still struggling to make a case against the Teflon Don. News that one of the Mafia's highest-ranking defectors could testify to Gotti admitting to the killing of Paul Castellano was a vital breakthrough. Gotti explained the problem with the Ruggiero tapes and that they were refusing to hand them over to Castellano. "So eventually there was a hit put out on John. John told us this. Paul wanted to kill him and he found out about it and he moved first. He knocked Paul out of the box and he took over. He said he got the okay from the Commission. When we first walked in before we even sat down, Sammy introduced us to John. He introduced my uncle as the boss of the Family and John as the boss of their Family. He introduced me to him and he told my uncle, he said, 'Look, Nick,' he says, 'before we even get started I want you to know we did everything the right way, you know. I killed Paul with the okay of the Commission and I did it all, I followed the rules on everything.' My uncle said, 'I know that, John,' but we still double-checked it afterwards."

(A curious footnote to Gotti's assertion that he had a "license to kill" from the Commission comes from a recent case in New Jersey where Bobby Manna was convicted of conspiracy to murder Gotti. Wiretap evidence resulted in several members of the Genovese Family being indicted and Manna was found guilty. Yet Leonetti swears that Manna confirmed what Gotti had told them, i.e. that he had sought and received permission from the Commission. Although it is only speculation, it may be that this is what occurred. Gotti knew at the time of his plot to kill Paul Castellano that he had to tread very carefully. The Pope was sufficiently unpopular for Gotti to be able to confidently sound out some of the Families to get the go-ahead. The Genovese Family was his biggest problem as they were closest to Castellano. Gotti may have taken soundings, yet stopped short of formally seeking permission for fear of exposing himself to counterassassination. It is known that Vincent "The Chin" Gigante loathed Gotti. The Chin's carefully cultivated low profile, and his successful act of appearing mad to fend off law enforcement, were totally at odds with Gotti's high-profile celebrity status. There were also disputes between the two families over unions. This was sufficient justification for Gigante to have ordered the hit. Gotti's "failure" to get official permission was probably no more than an excuse for the contract.)

By the time Gotti came to trial, the FBI had a new witness to testify against the Teflon Don. Sammy "The Bull" Gravano's testimony was devastating to Gotti at the trial but Leonetti's pretrial evidence had been instrumental for the FBI in building their case against Gotti. Indeed, Gotti is said to be currently plotting ways to kill Leonetti from his prison cell in Marion. By coincidence, Scarfo is in the same prison and although they are not allowed to meet, rumor has it that the two Mafia bosses have found ways to get together. High on their agenda is the treachery of Scarfo's nephew and underboss, Philip Leonetti. Gotti blames him for his downfall.

"He feels that I'm the cause of all his problems because before Sammy cooperated I was the only guy that was going to testify against him. In Sammy's situation, he also had a death penalty murder case that me and him were involved with from Philadelphia and maybe he's blaming me for Sammy cooperating and then Sammy testifying against him. He feels like I was the root of all his problems. I went to a Grand Jury and I told them everything I knew about John and the meetings we had, him saying that he killed Paul Castellano . . . saying he got the okay from the Commission, and I would testify about the Family, him being the boss, the structure of his Family, the things, the favors that my uncle asked of him, some bookmaking involvement. The Gambino problems and everything that our meetings were about. That's what I would have testified about."

Since his Grand Jury appearance Leonetti has testified at a number of major Mafia trials and is regarded as one of the best witnesses ever to have taken the stand. He politely answers the defense attorneys' questions and refuses to be goaded by their attempts to portray him as a cold-blooded killer. At a recent New Jersey trial in Tom's River, some Lucchese members were being tried for murder. Leonetti appeared looking immaculate and assured in a suit and tie. A defense lawyer immediately tried to rattle the witness and win over the jury by asking Leonetti which hand he had used to shoot a gun. Leonetti obligingly held up his right hand. "This hand, sir," he replied politely. The lawyer proceeded to ask Leonetti whether it was the same hand that he had used to swear an oath on the Bible before giving evidence. Once again Leonetti calmly agreed. Even Leonetti's calm admission to multiple murder seemed to have little impact.

The defense lawyer then unveiled a list of names and dates. Louis di Marco, 1976, Pepe Leva, 1977, Judge Helfant, 1978, Dominick de Vito, 1982, Robert Riccobene, 1983, Sal Tamburino, 1983, Pasquale Spirito, 1983, Sal Testa, 1983. As Leonetti was taken through the list the underboss admitted his role in the various murders, some where he had pulled the trigger and others where he had merely planned. Like many Mafiosi Leonetti has little remorse over the murders; to the wiseguys, it is business. Leonetti claims they were all "bad guys" and most of them deserved to die. Besides he had already pleaded guilty to ten murders. (The one exception was Sal Testa, a close friend. Leonetti was unable to prevent his murder—a situation which troubled him greatly.)

It wasn't remorse that led Philip Leonetti to secretly telephone the FBI from his prison cell, it was fear for his son. On November 1, 1988, in the middle of the RICO trial, Nicodemo Scarfo's youngest son, Mark, aged 17, had walked into his father's office on Georgia Avenue, Atlantic City. It was the headquarters of Scarf Inc., the construction company that Leonetti and Scarfo had run together. It had been the location for the planning of countless murders, extortions and acts of violence. As if haunted by the malevolent spirit of the place, Mark Scarfo tried to hang himself. His body was discovered by his mother and he was rushed to the hospital. The teenager was still alive but went into a coma. The federal trial was adjourned and his father was escorted in irons to visit his son in the hospital.

Scarfo's response is unknown but Philip Leonetti remembers his reaction. "I was sick. My uncle was upset about it, he started to blame me afterwards: it's my fault, my mother's fault, that my mother always hollered at him. And I was worried about my son. I said, 'What the hell's going on? I mean these kids are killing themselves.' Here's a kid, he left a note that his father gave him too much of a hard time about his hair . . . You see Mark wanted to work, he wanted to be a normal kid. He wanted to play sports in school, but his father said if you play sports in school, you're a jerk-off. I played sports in school, in high school. He didn't want him to work for anybody. He thought that was like lowering yourself. The kid wants work, you know, what's the big deal about that? But he was on this kid like he was already a member of La Cosa Nostra. He didn't want him to grow his hair long . . . he gave him a hard time about that. Whatever he could give this kid a hard time about he gave him a hard time. The kid couldn't take it no more. He goes in my office and he hangs himself.

"They caught him in time but I don't know if they should have kept him alive because he's in a coma now. He was a good-looking kid, he was a natural athlete and he's comatose. It's a terrible thing. A 17-year-old kid and he signed 'Your Jerk-Off Brother Mark' because they always called him names. It's a shame what they did to this kid. He destroyed a young life and I was worried about my son because that was his best friend.

"My kid, when this happened, he went like into shock; he couldn't believe it. My kid's going to school, he's doing very bad in school. I got a teacher in his Civics class teaching him about organized crime in high school: '. . . the boss: Nicky Scarfo, the underboss: Philip Leonetti: the underboss . . .' His name's Philip Leonetti. I mean the kid don't have a shot. I say, 'What am I doing here?' So I swore to myself if I win this case, I'm leaving. We're going to head out, me, my mother and my son and go—because my uncle still won't be able to leave. Not only was he indicted on another murder, he already had 14 years. And I had figured out we're going to move but I got convicted!

"And before I was sentenced, I don't know how I did it, I got enough strength, I called the FBI. Because it was hard, I was thinking about it, thinking about it, thinking about it, I didn't know what to do. I finally called them before I was sentenced and I got Jim Maher on the phone. I said, 'Hello, Mr. Maher?' He said, 'Yes.' I said, 'Do you know who this is?' He said, 'No.' I said, 'I thought you were a voice expert. You recognize all these voices on tape in court.' He said, 'Who is this?' I said, 'This is Philip Leonetti.' I say, 'Would you like to speak to me?' He says, 'I have to notify your attorney before I talk to you, Phil. By law we have to do that.' I say, 'Well, if you do that then everybody's going to know that I'm going to cooperate. I can't take a chance like that.' He said, 'Well, let's wait 'til after your sentence and then I won't have to notify him.' I said, 'OK.' So after I was sentenced I went right there and I said: 'Look, I'm concerned about myself and I'm concerned about my son, I want my family out of this area and I want my son to have a shot in life. I mean 'cos right now he has no shot. What could you do? What could you do for me that way?' "

Jim Maher, part of Squad One, the FBI team in Philadelphia who had been on the trail of the Scarfo Family for years, was elated. Although he realized that Leonetti couldn't testify against his uncle, as Scarfo was already convicted and serving a life sentence, Leonetti's knowledge as underboss was priceless—to say nothing of the coup of actually turning an underboss. It would be the first time such a high-ranking mobster had agreed to cooperate. True, the elderly boss of the Cleveland Mafia, Angelo Lonardo, had done a deal, but his testimony had not been that startling—besides Cleveland was relatively provincial within Mafia circles. Lonardo himself had quickly become senile, proving to be of limited use to prosecutors. Leonetti was of a different stature; a modern mobster with the good looks of a film star, and the ruthless intellect of a cold-blooded killer —a Mafioso who had risen through the ranks: from soldier to capo to underboss. Throughout the 1980s he had been the right-hand man to the most notorious gangster that Philadelphia ever had the misfortune to experience. His position made him privy to the innermost secrets of the Mafia in Atlantic City, Philadelphia and New Jersey, the major centers of Mafia power in America. Last but not least, the nephew of Nicodemo Scarfo was the underboss of a Family with close links to the two most powerful Families in New York—the Genovese and the Gambinos.

Jim Maher told Leonetti what they could offer. "Look, we'll move your family. I can't promise you anything because we don't know what we can do for you, but we'll move your family, your son, to a different area."

"All right," replied Leonetti. "Not right now, I haven't even talked to my family yet. I don't know how they're going to accept this or what's going to happen."

Leonetti's family was right behind him. His mother, Nicky Scarfo's sister, urged him "Do it! Do it! Do it!" The family was relocated and Leonetti moved to a new prison where he would eventually meet up with his former friend

Sammy "The Bull" Gravano who agreed to cooperate with the FBI in November 1991.

Leonetti agreed to tell everything he knew to the FBI. "I agreed to testify for them truthfully about any criminal activity I knew about myself and other people. You know, whatever I knew, but the main thing they emphasized to me, but I emphasized it more to them, I told them I'm never going to lie about anything and naturally they won't want it that way. They wanted only the truth about everything and that's what I gave them. Whatever I knew."

Leonetti's reward for testifying against La Cosa Nostra in a series of trials was a recommendation for leniency endorsed by prosecutors and the FBI alike. His sentence was reduced to five years and today Philip Leonetti is a free man. He has a new identity and a new life although both his identity and his whereabouts are known only to a handful of people at the FBI. Even his personal attorney is unable to contact him. The security precautions are serious— not least because the two most feared Mafiosi in America would give their collective right arms to kill him. "Yes, there are people looking to kill me," admits Leonetti. "My uncle won't rest until he kills me or my mother or anybody in my family. I know how he is. He won't die until he can do something. That's the type of person he is. Everybody would be looking to kill me. When I think of between my uncle and John Gotti and other Families who I testified against, I think they would like to make a statement so other people won't cooperate by nailing me or a guy like Sammy Gravano. I think that would be something they live for, something that would keep them going in prison—if they could get somebody like me or Sammy. I testified against a lot of Families. There are people all over the country looking to kill me and I'm very careful and I'm going to make the best of it—the best I can do."

In the war against the Mafia, the defections of Philip Leonetti and Sammy Gravano represent significant victories for the FBI. They have been followed by significant defections from within the ranks of the Lucchese Family which have contributed to major prosecutions in New York in 1993. So far no bosses have agreed to cooperate, but on present form it is only a matter of time.

The FBI and other law enforcement agencies have won some significant battles in the war against the Mafia in the last decade. Some would even go so far as to say that the war has been won, while the realists warn that victory is by no means assured and that La Cosa Nostra may be as powerful as ever.

It is unlikely that the political influence of today's Mafia is as extensive as it was in the past. As prosecutors target individual unions and dismantle their links with specific industries, such as the garment center in New York, and the Bartenders Union in Atlantic City, they simultaneously reduce a source of wealth and an ability to corrupt both businessmen and politicians.

As to the cumulative effect of the Government's assault on the Mafia, there can be no doubt that there have been more major cases and successful convictions against major Mafia figures in America during the last decade than at any other time in the country's history. Clearly that constitutes a considerable triumph for the forces of law and order. The war is not over and there are many more difficult wars to fight—not least against the wholesale crime and violence which has become an all too familiar feature of the modern American city. It could be argued that America's nightmare is not organized crime but disorganized crime which requires a whole different set of skills and agencies to tackle.

Perhaps the most valuable indication of the achievements of the last decade comes from those who have been players in the battle. There are also some interesting perspectives from former members of La Cosa Nostra whose experience inside the Mafia makes them uniquely qualified to judge its strength from the outside. Many have a vested interest in making the judgment that they do. Prosecutors and FBI agents tend to color their opinions to reflect successful cases which they have been part of; similarly, former Mafiosi are prone to exaggerate the part they may have personally played in the "downfall" of the American Mafia.

Philip Leonetti feels that ". . . it's falling apart. There's no more respect. There's no more honor—and it's because of the drugs in my opinion. I mean it's a bad business—things aren't the same as they used to be in the old days. I mean you have these young kids coming up, they show no respect for their elders."

Bruce Mouw, the head of the Gambino Squad in Queens, New York, certainly believes that there is a lot of work ahead: this from an FBI man who has been responsible for some of the major breakthroughs in the last decade, not least considering the fact that when he took on the responsibility for targeting the Mafia he discovered there was an embarrassing lack of material with which to work. As Bruce Mouw was forming his Gambino squad in 1979, he discovered that the "cupboard" was literally bare. There was virtually no intelligence on the Gambino Family. It meant starting from scratch to devise a strategy to launch an assault on the most powerful crime Family in New York. "We had to start from ground zero," Bruce Mouw recalls, "The FBI had not worked the Family as such for a number of years, so basically for the first year we had to do intelligence."

As a pipe-smoking former submariner, Bruce Mouw was uniquely qualified for the job. His naval experience on nuclear-powered, hunter-killer submarines tracking the Soviets required a mixture of stealth, cunning and patience, tactics which proved immensely valuable as he began to target a very different sort of enemy.

Bruce Mouw is the first to acknowledge that the FBI has made significant advances—not least as the result of the teamwork from his own squad. "I think the FBI has been very effective during the last 15 years. We've limited the hierarchy and eliminated some of the most important capos, like Tommy Gambino. We've taken away a lot of their labor unions. We indicted the hierarchy of Teamster Local 282, we've got a lot of Gambinos throughout this union and we've taken the International Longshoreman's Association away from them. Slowly, but surely, we are destroying their grip on the City of New York and a good indication of this is a lot of the money is not flowing in. A lot of people aren't paying off like they were a couple of years ago; they know John's in jail and nobody's around to replace him. So, month by month, their control of this city is slipping away. The Gambino Family has literally gone underground. They're afraid to meet because of electronic surveillance. There's very little communication in the crews, because they're always fearful of FBI wiretaps. And so right now they're in a state of disarray."

A high-ranking former Gambino associate, Dominic Montiglio, who acted as the liaison between Paul Castellano and his psychotic capo Roy Di Meo, agrees with Bruce Mouw's assessment. "I think the FBI has done a lot of damage to the Gambino Family, like it's done a lot of damage to all the Families. Now if you become a boss you're an immediate target with the RICO statutes. They have the ammunition to go after you but I don't think the people that were in my generation could run the Families like they used to be run. I don't think there's a Carlo Gambino out there any more, you know. The drugs are too rampant. I'm talking about the consumption of drugs. I just don't think that the people in the Mafia today are what they were 20 years ago. Yeah, I think they've done a hell of a job on them, you know, and they've weakened them in a sense with the other mobs. You've got the Chinese, the Jamaicans and they're only going to get stronger. The FBI has definitely put a crimp in their style, that's for sure."

Montiglio was the nephew of Nino Gaggi, a senior capo under Paul Castellano. He served in Vietnam in his early twenties and when he came back he started to work for his uncle, sometimes filling in as the overseer of the Di Meo crew. He himself acquired a heavy cocaine habit and when his uncle suspected him of running off with Gambino Family funds, Dominic feared he might be killed. The former Vietnam vet turned Mafioso decided to cut a deal with the FBI and appeared as the star witness in the 1984 auto-theft case. Today, Montiglio is in hiding with a new identity but he is under no illusions that if they could find him they would not kill him. He also believes that despite their success, the Gambino Family is still a formidable outfit. "It is a multibillion-dollar business," admits Montiglio, "and there is always somebody wanting to do that business, there is always somebody out there that's going to want to do it.

Could you put General Motors out of business? I mean, you put the Gambinos out of business you're talking everything that goes along with it, unions, etc. You just couldn't do it. I think what they've done today with it is they've thrown it into turmoil and they've made it real dangerous to want to be the boss, but there's always going to be somebody with those aspirations, you know, there's just too much money involved."

Bruce Mouw, the head of the Gambino Squad, still receives daily intelligence on the activities of the Gambino Family. A network of informers, new bugs, the continuing cooperation of Government witnesses, intelligence from defectors in other Families, all help to build up an accurate picture of the current strength of the Family. Mouw believes, "We will never in my lifetime put the Gambino Family out of business. Our mission is to try to neutralize it, where it's no longer effective or has any impact here on the people of New York . . . If we keep the pressure on we've a chance of really neutralizing this Family. If we go away and address other criminal problems here in New York, three or four years from now we'll have John Gotti II and Frank Locascio III and Gravano IV! It would be starting all over again. So, we have to keep the pressure on, eliminate the powerful captains who are out there and also slowly eliminate those unions they control."

Many in law enforcement predict that there could be a new wave of violence within the Mafia. John Gotti and Nicky Scarfo were representative of a new breed: the gangster Mafioso rather than the "racketeers," personified by their respective predecessors, Paul Castellano and Angelo Bruno. Frederick Martens, the Executive Director of the Pennsylvania Crime Commission, which has published some of the most authoritative reports on organized crime in the country, observes that the change in style could signal a shift in the balance of power within the Mafia hierarchy. "The mob boss of today isn't the mob boss of yesteryear. They're not as important to the operations of an organization as is middle management. If you look at an organization, most of the power is at the lower end today and in the middle. The bosses are merely symbolic figures.

They don't have the power they once had because bosses aren't the moneymakers they were years ago. Years ago you became a boss because you were a moneymaker; today, you could become a boss because you can pull a trigger. That's the fundamental difference."

Evidence of a new wave of violence was provided recently by members of the Lucchese Family. Under the leadership of Tony "Ducks" Corallo it was a smooth-running organization with relatively little violence. When Corallo's reign came to an end as a result of the Commission case in 1986, the leadership that followed was bloodthirsty by comparison. As in Philadelphia, it led to bloody infighting and acts of terrible revenge. Tom Boudanza, in charge of the FBI's Lucchese Squad, describes what happened. "I think the Commission case which wiped out the hierarchy of the Lucchese Family changed the attitude of the hierarchy of the Lucchese Family. Casso and Amuso were much more violent people, much more prone to violence. The members that came in after that were much more prone to violence and drug use. People who were made members were not brought along like in the old days. They were more prone to violence and this is being expressed in some of the murders that were committed. The one that really changed the code of the Mafia in America, the first time we'd ever seen this, was the shooting of Peter Chiodo's sister."

One of the unwritten codes has always been not to harm women and children; Chiodo, the high-ranking Lucchese capo, was suspected of cooperating when he pleaded guilty to a racketeering charge in the "Windows" case. Because he hadn't consulted the Lucchese hierarchy, they suspected he was cutting a deal with the FBI. They put out a contract on his life. In May 1991 Chiodo was shot at a gas station in Staten Island—more than a dozen bullets ripped into the gangster's body. Chiodo is an imposing six-foot-five, weighing over 400 pounds—a factor that may have saved his life. Recovering in the hospital, he began to cooperate with the FBI. Infuriated at their failure to kill him and realizing the immense danger he could inflict on the Family, Lucchese hit men were sent after Chiodo's relatives. Targeting

Chiodo was understandable within the Mafia code but going after his family was a departure from tradition. As well as his sister they also killed Chiodo's uncle and burned down the house of his 95-year-old grandmother. These were tactics similar to those of the Sicilian Mafia but previously unheard of in America.

The worry now is that there may be an end to restrictions of violence against agents and prosecutors. Boudanza fears that the war could intensify. "Over the years it was taboo amongst the American Mafia Families to touch prosecutors and FBI agents here in America, whereas in Italy that went out of the window a number of years ago. They've been killing police officers and judges over there for the last 20 years. I think that's going to be a new trend here. Shooting of police officers, shooting an agent or trying to kill a prosecutor will become part of the modus operandi of the crime Families. I think that the Lucchese Family will move on to that."

Ironically, this new wave of violence has directly benefited the FBI. One of the latest high-level defections has been Alphonse D'Arco. D'Arco was the leader of the New Jersey faction of the Lucchese Family. When Vic Amuso, the boss, and Anthony Casso, the underboss, became fugitives as a result of the 1990 "Windows" case indictment, Amuso and Casso passed all their instructions through D'Arco—effectively making him the "acting boss."

"D'Arco was like a lightning rod," explains the head of the FBI's Lucchese Squad. "All the instructions from Mr. Casso and Mr. Amuso passed through him to be carried out by the soldiers in the street. So I call him a lightning rod because it was like high-voltage current passing through him. He had knowledge of almost every criminal act being committed by the Lucchese Family. His information and testimony are invaluable and he came armed with this information to the FBI."

The reason that he defected in 1991 is because the paranoid Casso began to distrust him and started to spread the rumor that D'Arco was already an informer. D'Arco became suspicious when he was in a hotel room with another Lucchese soldier and noticed the outline of a gun against his shirt. After he returned from the men's room, the gun was no longer visible. D'Arco realized it was a setup and left immediately and began to cooperate with the FBI in September 1991, just a few months after Peter Chiodo.

Along with Philip Leonetti and Sammy Gravano, Al D'Arco has swelled the ranks of high-level mob defectors. He followed Philip Leonetti into the witness stand at the Tom's River murder and racketeering trial in the early summer of 1993. Their evidence has helped to convict five members of the New Jersey faction of the Lucchese Family for the murder of Vincent J. Craparotta, a Tom's River car salesman who had been beaten to death with golf clubs in 1984. Amongst those convicted in the autumn of 1993 was Anthony "Tumac" Accetturo, a 54-year-old Lucchese capo who succeeded D'Arco in leading the New Jersey faction of the Family. Within hours of his conviction, Accetturo contacted the New Jersey State police and offered to cooperate! The readiness of so many senior Mafiosi to cooperate is evidence that their code of silence, "Omerta," which was once a great source of power, no longer holds sway.

Despite all the defections within the ranks of the New York Families and in Philadelphia there are indications that the power of the Mafia may be undiminished in other parts of the country and even poised for a renaissance. Out on the West Coast, a former prosecutor with the Los Angeles Strike Force is skeptical about some of the optimistic claims that have emanated from prosecutors on the East Coast and the Department of Justice in Washington. Richard Stavin launched an investigation into Mafia links with Hollywood in the mid-1980s and discovered connections with the giant MCA corporation, the parent company of Universal Studios. Stavin's case and an earlier one developed by Marvin Rudnick, another Strike Force Attorney, were both eventually dropped. Rudnick had been investigating a multimillion-dollar record deal. His case involved mob figures from both the Gambino and the Genovese Families with connections to the music division of MCA. Although a prosecution and conviction was secured in New Jersey, principally against Morris Levy, a multimillionaire associate of the Genovese Family, Rudnick's investigation on the West Coast was stalled. Rudnick believes that his attempts to investigate MCA resulted in high-level obstruction orchestrated by the Justice Department in Washington.

When Richard Stavin pursued a separate case involving the head of MCA's Home Entertainments Division, he found that mounting obstacles were being put in his way as well. Stavin resigned and whilst he does not subscribe as strongly as Rudnick to the "cover-up" theory, he has no doubts that the evidence was strong enough to go to court. Today, Richard Stavin believes that there may be other instances of corporate involvement with the Mafia which have never been investigated.

"My investigation revealed that there is an organized presence in the entertainment industry; anyone who says anything to the contrary is naive and ill-informed. The Los Angeles faction of La Cosa Nostra was not a factor. The Families that are a factor are the Chicago Family, the Gambino Family, the Genovese Family, the Colombo Family and probably one or two other ancillary Families. They were a problem four years ago—they're still a problem today. What law enforcement has not been able to do, to a large degree because it's much more difficult, is to pierce the corporate veil and find organized crime in the underbelly of corporate America. Because they are there. So when we say we've got the Mafia on the run, they're on the run in the streets because you can see them in the streets. You can't see them behind closed doors. That's where they are."

In Atlantic City, Ron Chance, a highly experienced investigator from the Department of Labor's Racketeering Section, fears the worst as he surveys the familiar skyline of Atlantic City. Having stood by powerless as the casino building boom of the 1970s fueled the coffers of organized crime, Ron Chance predicts that it could happen all over again. "Today we're having a second boom in Atlantic City. Initially with the building of the casinos there was about three billion dollars in construction that was done. What we have happening now is there's a new convention center being built, that's two hundred and fifty million dollars. There is a new entrance to the city which is called the 'Corridor Project,' that's about five hundred million dollars. The casinos have all been given a break on the taxes that they owe to the State of New Jersey if they build additional hotel rooms that open before the Convention Center opens up. The State is building a new airport and rebuilding the entire northern section of the city—the State is spending six hundred and fifty million dollars. So we have somewhere between two and a half and three billion dollars that's being spent right here within the next three years. What we've seen so far is that the exact same thing is happening now that was happening before, that the mob sees three billion dollars out there and they want their share of it. Though they don't control the unions in Atlantic City the way they used to, they still control unions in New York. They can make their agreement in New York and they can bring their own people here from New York and the same exact thing will happen on these projects that happened on the last projects.''

Ron Chance knows only too well that the Mafia will succeed in getting a large piece of the action. The state authorities can vet some of the companies and limit the profit potential for organized crime; but they have not been that successful in the past and it is unlikely that they will be able to keep out more than a few of the more blatant mob front companies.

The best hope is that the decline of the American Mafia accelerates to such an extent that the New York Families are unable to provide the caliber of people with the necessary skills of ruthless cunning and criminal intelligence which in the past have served them so well across a wide spectrum of economic activity. Without the skilled personnel, the Philip Leonettis, Peter Chiodos, Sammy Gravanos and Alphonse D'Arcos of their world, it is doubtful whether they will retain the ability to capitalize on golden opportunities such as those presented by the building boom that will be transforming Atlantic City into the year 2000 and beyond.

INDEX

TIM SHAWCROSS is an award-winning producer and director who has made several television documentaries investigating the activities of both the Sicilian and American Mafia. His programs have been broadcast all over Europe and the United States and featured exclusive interviews with high-ranking Mafia figures from both Italy and America. His previous book, *Men of Honour: The Confessions of Tommaso Buscetta*, was an in-depth account of the Sicilian Mafia from the postwar years to the mid-1980s.

WHAT'S IN IT FOR ME?

by Joseph Stedino with Dary Matera

Working with the Phoenix District Attorney's office, Joseph Stedino posed as a mobster out to legalize gambling in Arizona by buying votes. Once the word was out, legislators and lobbyists came running. The successful sting led to twenty indictments and shed glaring light on how politics in Arizona—and across America—really works!

THE KENNEDY CONTRACT

by John H. Davis

In 1979, the House Select Committee on Assassinations concluded that President John F. Kennedy's assassination was most likely the result of a conspiracy, and that the Mafia had the motive, means and opportunity to execute JFK. Including new information from key witnesses and shocking details surrounding the cover-up, *The Kennedy Contract* blows the lid off the most fascinating murder case in U.S. history. John H. Davis is an expert on the Kennedy and Mafia dynasties.